Beneath the Banyan

Beneath the Banyan

Uchinā Damashī: The Hidden Strength of Okinawan Karate & Kobudō

Nathan Batson

Guardian Arts Press, Murchison, TX

Published by Guardian Arts Press

Murchison, Texas

Book Cover design and photography by BatCave Studios

ISBN: 979-8-9924113-1-7

Library of Congress Control Number: 2025920441

Printed in the United States of America

Guardian Arts Press

To my students whose questions turned notes into papers, and papers into this work, your curiosity transformed my own search for understanding into the studies gathered here.

Preface

This book is dedicated to my students, whose curiosity inspired its creation. My own research began as scattered notes; an attempt to better understand Okinawa's martial traditions and their origins. However, as I discussed these topics with my students, it was their curiosity that pushed me to refine those notes into essays for them, and eventually into the collection you hold in your hands today. Their desire for understanding not only mirrored my own; it challenged me to see more deeply, articulate my thoughts more clearly, and preserve the heritage of karate and kobudō with greater care. Without their persistence, this collection would have remained just a private notebook instead of the work it has become.

The chapters that follow are not intended as a training manual or a how-to guide for techniques. Instead, they serve as a record of inquiry, a series of studies exploring the history, philosophy, and cultural context of Okinawan martial arts. Some chapters examine the roots of specific kata, tracing how these forms evolved over generations of masters. Others investigate the influence of Chinese envoys, the impact of the Satsuma occupation, or the enduring symbolism of Okinawa's weapons and traditions. A few chapters, more personal in tone, reflect on how Okinawan values of humility, perseverance, and spirit (Uchina damashii) continue to shape practice today.

This collection is aimed at two audiences. First, it is for the dedicated practitioner who wishes to deepen their understanding of the art beyond its physical practice, recognizing the echoes of history and culture in its stances and movements. Second, it is for the historian or any interested reader who may never have stood barefoot on a dōjō floor but seeks to understand Okinawa's martial traditions within the broader narrative of the Ryūkyū Kingdom and its people.

Each chapter can be read independently, but together they weave a narrative that traces the foundations of Okinawa's empty-hand arts, explores the often-overlooked weapons of kobudō, and examines the broader cultural landscape in which these arts were forged. While every study is grounded in credible historical sources, oral traditions and contested accounts are also included, as they are part of the living heritage of Okinawan martial arts.

My hope is that this book serves not only as a reference but also as an invitation to question, compare, and continue seeking. Just as my students' questions shaped this work, may your own curiosities help carry Okinawa's traditions forward, ensuring they remain unseen yet unyielding, hidden yet alive, beneath the great banyan tree.

Acknowledgments

I am deeply grateful to my teachers, Kise Isao Hanshi and John Shipes Hanshi. Their guidance has been a consistent source of direction, reminding me that the true essence of karate and kobudō lies not just in physical practice but also in humility, perseverance, and the passing down of knowledge from one generation to the next.

I would also like to acknowledge the Okinawa Shorin-Ryu Matsumura Orthodox Karate and Kobudo Federation (OSMKKF). This federation has provided me with a sense of belonging within a living tradition, grounding my research and practice in authenticity and respect.

Much of what I have written here has been influenced by discussions rather than solitary study. The hours spent listening to and engaging with masters such as Kise Isao, his father Kise Fusei, John Shipes, Patrick McCarthy, and Hokama Tetsuhiro have offered insights that no archive could provide. In those informal moments, often in Okinawa itself, history came alive through the voices of those who have dedicated their lives to preserving it.

Lastly, I must thank my students at the Tyler Karate Academy. Many of them reviewed early drafts of these papers and provided feedback that sharpened my arguments and improved the clarity of my writing. More importantly, their questions and curiosity continuously inspire me to explore further. What began as a personal journey to understand has evolved into a book because my students sought more, and for that, I am profoundly grateful.

Introduction

The martial traditions of Okinawa are both local and global. Originating from a small island chain at the crossroads of East and Southeast Asia, these practices embody centuries of cultural exchange, political struggle, and the resilience of a people who have preserved their identity throughout changing historical tides. What we now recognize as karate and kobudō is not merely a collection of combat techniques; it is a repository of Ryukyuan spirit, known as Uchina Damashi, forged during times of hardship and maintained through dedicated practice.

This volume compiles a series of studies developed over many years, initially as personal research notes and later as formal explorations shared with my students. Their inquiries often prompted me to dive deeper, urging me to trace the origins of specific techniques or to explore how a kata's name reflects its cultural context. Over time, what began as a quest for clarity for my own curiosity evolved into a broader effort: to intertwine history, practice, and interpretation in a way that is accessible to both scholars and martial artists.

The essays in this book not only investigate kata, the formal patterns of Okinawan martial practice, but also their cultural origins and impacts. Some chapters focus on the origins of specific forms, unraveling the connections among oral tradition, legend, and historical documentation. Others examine wider themes of class, politics, and cultural identity, discussing how Okinawa's status as a tributary kingdom, a Satsuma vassal, and later a prefecture of Japan influenced the evolution of its martial traditions. Additionally, certain chapters consider the tools of kobudō, such as the bō, sai, tonfa, and kama, both as weapons and as symbols of Okinawan resilience.

This work is not intended as a technical manual. While applications and mechanics are discussed when relevant, the goal is not to instruct on fighting methods but to shed light on the history, significance, and evolution of these practices. The chapters draw from both Japanese and Western scholarship, archival materials, and firsthand conversations with teachers and historians in Okinawa and the United States. At times, interpretations may differ; this book embraces those contradictions, inviting the reader into the discussions that invigorate the field.

Readers will also find supporting materials designed to enhance the text's utility as a reference. A glossary clarifies terminology, while biographical sketches introduce many influential figures in these traditions. Sidebars offer cultural and thematic insights that connect the practice of kata to the broader tapestry of Okinawan history.

This book serves both as an invitation and a record: an invitation to perceive kata as more than mere movement, and a record of how martial practice embodies the essence of a people. Whether you approach these pages as a practitioner, historian, or simply someone intrigued by Okinawa's hidden strength, my hope is that you gain a deeper understanding of the spirit that continues to flow beneath the banyan tree.

Table of Contents

The Pen and the Fist 1

Under the Shadow of Satsuma 21

Unraveling the Myths of Ryukyu Kobudo 39

Ryukyu's Arsenal 51

Beyond the Surface 71

Traces of Steel in Ryukyu Wood 89

Tsuken Bo 107

The Evolving Lexicon of Okinawan Martial Arts.......................... 121

Beyond the Kata.. 133

More Than a Teacher 147

Unlocking Tuite.. 157

From Te to Tournament 175

The Enduring Heart.. 191

Glossary... 203

Biographies 211

References & Suggested Reading 261

About the Author.. 267

The Pen and the Fist
Warrior-Scholars of the Ryukyu Kingdom

Mind and Might in the Ryukyu Kingdom

In the annals of history, the figures of the scholar and the warrior are often presented as distinct, even opposing, archetypes; the intellectual wielding the pen, and the combatant mastering the sword. Yet, the unique narrative of the Ryukyu Kingdom reveals a compelling synthesis of these roles in the warrior-scholars of the Yukatchu. This paper explores the intriguing concept of high-ranking officials who were not only profoundly versed in classical scholarship and intricate civil administration but were also expected to possess formidable martial arts proficiency. This challenges the usual divide between mind and body, revealing a more unified model of leadership and power in East Asian society.

This study will focus specifically on the Yukatchu classes, the state ministers, and scholar-officials who formed the backbone of the Ryukyuan government. We will explore their intricate social hierarchy and the multifaceted responsibilities that bound intellectual acumen with physical capability. This analysis will weave together their documented historical contributions with the rich tapestry of folklore that often surrounds such figures, providing a holistic view of their lives and influence.

We'll show that these warrior-scholars were pivotal to the enduring stability and distinctive cultural development of the Ryukyu Kingdom. They served as the indispensable guardians of both its intellect and its defense, navigating a complex geopolitical landscape through diplomacy and subtle strength. In doing so, they profoundly shaped the very character and evolution of Okinawan martial traditions, leaving a legacy where the "Pen and the Fist" became a symbol of integrated power. To understand how the Yukatchu could fulfill such dual roles, we must first examine the unique structure of Ryukyuan society and the geopolitical constraints that shaped it.

Society, Sovereignty, and Symbolic Arms

The Ryukyu Kingdom, an archipelago nation that flourished between the 15th and 19th centuries, occupied a remarkably unique geopolitical position in East Asia. Strategically situated between the two powerful cultural and political giants, China and Japan, Ryukyu masterfully navigated a dual tributary status, sending regular envoys to both Beijing and Edo (later Tokyo). This intricate diplomatic dance shaped nearly every aspect of the kingdom's internal policy, fostering an environment of calculated neutrality and, perhaps counter-intuitively for a sovereign state, a pervasive emphasis on civil administration over overt militarism.

Crucially, Ryukyu's unique position was not merely tolerated but strategically utilized by Japan, particularly during the Tokugawa period (1603-1867). During this era, Japan implemented its strict foreign policy known as Sakoku[1] (鎖国, literally "closed country"), which severely restricted foreign influence and trade. However, the tributary agreement with the Ryukyu Kingdom provided a vital exception, allowing for the controlled flow of Chinese goods, culture, and information into Japan, effectively making Ryukyu a crucial, albeit indirect, trade conduit. A significant consequence of this delicate balance and the overarching strategy was a general prohibition on the possession of weapons by the common populace. Although a full weapons ban is an oversimplification, strict rules governed who could own or display weapons.

The nature of this prohibition, particularly after the 1609 Satsuma invasion, was primarily aimed at weapons of war, such as the katana (long sword), yari (spears), bows, and firearms, that could be used to raise or equip a military force and challenge Satsuma's authority; the goal being to prevent organized resistance. However, certain high-ranking Ryukyuan officials, including the Ueekata and the higher echelons of the Pechin class (who formed the administrative and judicial backbone of the kingdom under Satsuma), were, in fact, often permitted to wear a wakizashi[2] or a similar short sword openly. This wasn't about preparing them for battle, but about symbolizing their authority and status; the wakizashi served as a badge of their office and status, distinguishing them from commoners and reinforcing their role in maintaining order. It was a carefully controlled concession granted by Satsuma to maintain the local administrative structure. However, it is crucial to note that this allowance did not mean they could wear the full daisho[3] (the pair of katana and wakizashi) like a traditional Japanese samurai; the katana remained largely restricted. Swords and other traditional martial instruments were primarily reserved for the elite warrior-scholar class, the very administrators tasked with maintaining the kingdom's delicate balance.

Within this distinctive societal structure, a defined class system governed the Ryukyu Kingdom's upper echelons, each tier imbued with specific responsibilities that often intertwined civil duties with an unspoken expectation of martial preparedness:

- **Ueekata** (親方): Occupying the highest echelons of state ministry, the Ueekata served as the King's most trusted advisors and administrators. They held crucial positions within the central government, overseeing various departments and formulating policy. Given their proximity to power and their role in a potentially volatile geopolitical landscape, martial proficiency was not merely admired among the Ueekata; it was an unstated, yet critical, expectation for their executive and advisory roles.

- **Peichin** (親雲上): This title denoted a broad class forming the backbone of the Ryukyuan government and internal security apparatus. Though often grouped under a single designation, the Peichin rank comprised a tiered internal hierarchy, including:
  - **Satunushi Peichin** (里之子親雲上): A senior-level rank conferred upon those who had distinguished themselves in service. Satunushi Peichin were often court advisors, elite guards, or diplomats. Many of the most well-known historical figures in Okinawan martial arts, such as Sakugawa Kanga, held this designation. They embodied the peak of the warrior-scholar ethos within the administrative class. This rank also had a junior page-level counterpart (jige), a kind of apprenticeship that functioned as a stepping stone toward full status.
  - **Chikudun Peichin** (筑登之親雲上): A mid-ranking title often associated with accomplished scholar-officials, local magistrates, senior palace guards, or instructors. Chikudun Peichin were expected to demonstrate both administrative competence and martial ability, and many were responsible for managing specific domains or overseeing military training. As with the Satunushi rank, there existed a corresponding jige page rank beneath

Chikudun Peichin, intended as a training station for future advancement.

- o **Pekumi (or Pekumi Peichin)**: The entry-level rank, often tasked with basic administrative duties, palace service, or lower-level regional responsibilities. Members of this rank were typically in training for greater responsibility, and some served as junior attendants or aides to senior officials.

This sophisticated administrative framework underpinned the mandate for martial prowess among these classes. While there was no formal, explicit mandate requiring all Pechin or other high-ranking officials to study martial arts in a regulated manner, there was an overwhelming cultural expectation and practical necessity tied to their administrative and protective roles. Their position as the "warrior-scholar" class meant that martial training was an implicit and essential component of their upbringing and professional competence, typically passed down through private instruction and tradition. In a society where weapon ownership was restricted and overt military displays were minimized to avoid alarming powerful neighbors, the cultivation of personal martial ability became an expected, even compulsory, trait for the governing and administrative elite. It served not for conquest, but for personal defense, internal security, and perhaps most crucially, as a silent testament to the resilience and underlying strength of a kingdom that chose diplomacy and intellect as its primary shield. Thus, the pursuit of martial excellence was not divorced from civil service but inherently integrated into the very identity of Ryukyu's ruling and administrative classes. While the external structure of rank and responsibility defined their place, the internal world of education and values gave these officials their moral and intellectual foundation.

The Confucian Scholar: Administration and Ethics

While the previous section established the practical necessity of martial prowess for Ryukyu's elite, it is equally crucial to understand the profound intellectual and philosophical foundations that shaped their identity. The "scholar" in "warrior-scholar" was not a mere adjunct but a core component, deeply influenced by the prevailing intellectual currents of the region.

Confucian Ideals and Education

The Ryukyu Kingdom's close and enduring tributary relationship with China had a profound and lasting influence on its educational system and governing philosophy, marked by a strong and undeniable presence of Chinese Confucianism[4]. For the ruling and administrative classes, education was not merely about acquiring knowledge but about cultivating moral character, ethical governance, and the practical skills necessary for effective administration. Confucian ideals, emphasizing filial piety, loyalty, righteousness, propriety, and wisdom, permeated the curriculum. Literary and administrative skills were paramount; proficiency in classical Chinese texts, calligraphy, and bureaucratic procedures was a prerequisite for advancement within the kingdom's intricate civil service. This rigorous intellectual training instilled a deep respect for order, hierarchy, and the responsibilities of leadership, shaping the very mindset of those who governed.

Administrative Duties

A wide array of administrative duties essential for the stability and functioning of the kingdom consumed the daily lives of these high-ranking officials. The Ueekata, as top state ministers, were deeply involved in policy formulation, diplomatic relations, and the oversight of key governmental departments from the capital. Below them, the Peichin class, including ranks like Chikudun Peichin, Satunushi Peichin, and

Pekumi, performed the granular work of governance. They served as royal guards, palace attendants, local magistrates, tax administrators, and even diplomats on missions abroad. Their roles demanded not only intellectual acumen and literary skill but also a keen understanding of human nature, law, and the practicalities of maintaining social order across the kingdom's diverse islands and communities.

Philosophical Underpinnings

This scholarly background profoundly shaped their view of martial arts, not just as a ionphysical skill, but as a mental and ethical discipline. The emphasis on bunbu ryodo[5] (文武両道, "literary and martial arts in harmony") was not just a slogan but a lived ideal. For these elites, martial training was seen as a complementary path to intellectual development, fostering discipline, mental fortitude, and ethical conduct. Their understanding of strategy, derived from classical texts on warfare and governance, would have informed their tactical thinking in combative scenarios. Furthermore, the Confucian emphasis on righteousness and propriety likely instilled a sense of responsibility regarding the use of force, viewing martial skill as a tool for justice and protection rather than aggression. This fusion of the pen and the fist created a unique martial tradition where physical prowess was inseparable from intellectual rigor and moral integrity, reflecting the very essence of the Ryukyu Kingdom's governance. Yet mastery of texts and governance was only part of their identity; these officials were also trained for combat, not in battlefield warfare, but in a quiet, precise martial discipline suited to their civil roles.

The Hidden Blade: Training the Body for Service

Having explored the intellectual and administrative facets of the Ryukyuan warrior-scholar, we now turn to the physical discipline that completed their unique identity. In a kingdom where overt militarism was suppressed and weapon ownership tightly controlled, the cultivation of unarmed combat, known as "Te,"[6] became not merely a pastime but a vital component of their practical competence.

The Cultivation of "Te"

The unique circumstances of the Ryukyu Kingdom, particularly the nuanced weapon regulations imposed after the Satsuma invasion and the pervasive emphasis on civil administration, profoundly shaped the development and emphasis of unarmed combat within the ruling and administrative classes. For the Yukatchu, who were tasked with maintaining internal order, executing arrests, and protecting the royal family and key officials, overt displays of armed force were often counterproductive or forbidden. This necessitated the refinement of effective empty-hand techniques. Their martial prowess was not for grand battlefield engagements, but for close-quarter personal defense and the subtle enforcement of authority in a society that valued peace and diplomacy above all. Thus, the indigenous "Te" evolved to meet these specific, practical needs, becoming an indispensable skill for those who governed without the constant overt presence of traditional weaponry.

Training Methodologies

While detailed historical records on the precise training methodologies of these early warrior-scholars are scarce, we can infer the likely methods employed to develop the formidable physical attributes vital for their combative roles. Practical combat skill development would have necessitated various forms of partner drills, serving as the crucible for real-time application and tactile sensitivity. These would likely have included continuous-contact exercises such as Kakidī[7] (掛け手, hooking hands) and more free-form, continuous sparring formats like Kakedameshi[8] (掛け試し, testing hands). These interactive methods were crucial for developing tactile sensitivity, timing, and the ability to adapt to a live, unscripted opponent.

From these dynamic partner drills and the practical application of combative principles, solo kata (pre-arranged forms) likely developed as a sophisticated means of codifying and preserving techniques for individual practice. Serving as a repository of movements, principles, and body conditioning, kata allowed practitioners to hone their individual skill and internalize complex combative sequences in private, keeping their minds and bodies sharp even without a partner. This pedagogical evolution highlights kata not as abstract dances, but as living blueprints of effective combat. Furthermore, rigorous body conditioning would have been integral, utilizing simple, available tools and methods to strengthen physique, build resilience, and develop the powerful, connected body necessary for effective striking, grappling, and control. This private, often intense, training ensured that their martial abilities were practical and deeply ingrained.

Connection to Core Principles

The practical needs of the scholarly warriors directly fostered the development and internalization of core combative principles that defined Ryukyuan martial arts. The demands of close-quarter control, whether in a diplomatic incident or a law enforcement scenario, would have necessitated the cultivation of Muchimi[9] (むちみ, sticky body/ viscous power), a pervasive body quality enabling rootedness, absorption of force, and connected power. This, in turn, would lead to the refinement of Kakei[10] (かけい, continuous connection/tactile sensitivity), allowing them to "read" an opponent's intentions through subtle contact and maintain control. These principles were not abstract concepts but practical necessities for effective close-range engagement. This training naturally led to mastery of grappling (Tegumi[11]) and joint-locking (Tuidi[12]) techniques. These were not separate disciplines but natural extensions of their empty-hand combat, enabling them to neutralize threats effectively without relying on overt striking or weapons. Thus, their unique societal roles directly shaped a martial discipline deeply rooted in practical, integrated principles, forming the very essence of the Ryukyuan warrior-scholar's combative prowess. These principles and training practices weren't abstract; they were embodied by real individuals whose lives and legacies continue to shape the martial identity of Okinawa.

Historical Echoes: Figures of the Pen and the Fist

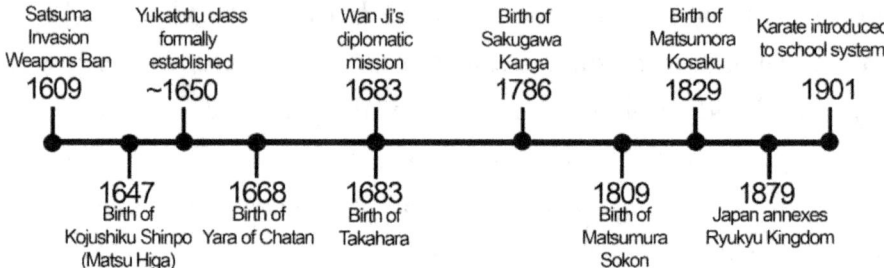

The abstract ideals of the Ryukyuan Yukatchu as warrior-scholar were not merely theoretical constructs; they were embodied by a lineage of remarkable individuals whose lives and legacies shaped the very fabric of Okinawan martial arts. These figures, often high-ranking officials and intellectuals, navigated the complex sociopolitical landscape of the Ryukyu Kingdom, their martial prowess becoming an extension of their administrative and philosophical duties. Their stories, a blend of verifiable history and compelling folklore, offer invaluable insights into the practical application of the "pen and the fist."

Kojushiku Shinpo / Matsu Higa (c. 1647–1721)

Known in oral tradition as Matsu Higa or by his formal name Kojushiku Shinpo, this early Ryukyuan martial figure is a foundational presence in the semi-legendary lineage of Okinawan bojutsu and weapon-based traditions. Though verifiable documentation is scarce, his name endures through kata such as Matsuhiga no Kon, Matsuhiga no Tonfa, and

Matsuhiga no Sai, practiced in multiple Ryukyu Kobudō systems today. These forms suggest his role as a proto-codifier of Kobudo principles.

Matsu Higa's martial development is said to have been profoundly shaped by interaction with Chinese emissaries, particularly Wang Ji (Wanshu), who led a well-documented mission to Ryukyu in 1683. Oral accounts maintain that Wang Ji recognized Higa's ability and passed on advanced Chuan Fa techniques that influenced early Okinawan Te. His prowess with the bo is central to accounts, including a widely circulated legend of a dramatic, hours-long duel with a Chinese master armed with an Iron Ruler, which, though unverifiable, symbolizes cultural fusion through martial artistry.

Chatan Yara (1668-1756)

Chatan Yara, a local official holding the rank of Ueekata, is celebrated in Okinawan martial arts for his exceptional martial prowess, particularly with weapons. Credited with disseminating te throughout Okinawa, Yara was a renowned weaponry master, displaying extraordinary skill with the bo, tonfa, and especially the sai. Famous tales of his strength and effectiveness in combat, often involving his adept use of weapons, highlight the practical integration of armed and unarmed techniques within the Ryukyuan martial tradition, a theme explored in greater detail in "Beyond the Surface: Reframing Karate as an Extension of Kobudo." His legendary status reinforces the idea that true martial mastery encompasses both empty-hand and weapon skills.

Takahara Peichin (1683-1766)

Among the earliest figures shrouded in the mists of Okinawan martial history is Takahara Peichin. While concrete historical documentation from his era is sparse, oral tradition remembers him as a scholar and a foundational martial arts figure, likely holding the rank of Pechin. His most enduring contribution lies in the articulation of the "principles of

Do," which emphasized compassion (ijo), dedication (katsu), and a deep understanding of techniques (fo). These principles, often seen as ethical guidelines for martial practice, beautifully blend scholarly philosophy with combative efficacy, illustrating an early manifestation of bunbu ryodo where the moral cultivation of the scholar was inseparable from the discipline of the warrior.

Sakugawa Kanga (1786-1867)

A pivotal figure in the lineage leading to modern Karate, Sakugawa Kanga, often referred to as Tode Sakugawa ("China Hand Sakugawa"), held the high-ranking official position of Satunushi Pechin. His extensive martial arts training included study under Chinese teachers, notably the military envoy Kusanku[13], from whom he inherited profound knowledge of Quanfa. Sakugawa's contributions were instrumental in synthesizing Chinese kenpo with the indigenous Okinawan te, and some postulate he even incorporated elements from Japanese kenjutsu. Tales of his formidable prowess and his role in transmitting specific techniques and concepts to subsequent generations, most notably Matsumura Sokon, underscore his role as a bridge between diverse martial traditions and a true embodiment of the integrated warrior-scholar ideal.

Matsumura Sokon (1809-1899)

Matsumura Sokon, a figure of immense historical significance, held the prestigious position of royal bodyguard to the last three kings of the Ryukyu Kingdom. By virtue of his crucial role and exceptional martial skill, he was widely acknowledged as a Bushi (武士), a term signifying a warrior or military man who embodied the highest standards of martial and ethical conduct. While not a formal title, "Bushi" was a recognized descriptor of his profound commitment to service and his mastery within the kingdom's gentry class. His scholarly background was as profound as his martial skill, evidenced by his mastery of classical Chinese texts and calligraphy. Numerous tales of his invincibility and unparalleled skill abound, cementing his legendary status.

Beyond folklore, Matsumura's actual contribution lies in his role in systematizing Shuri-te, laying much of the foundation for what would become modern Shorin-ryu. His "Advice to His Last Formal Student" stands as a testament to his warrior-scholar ethos, emphasizing not just physical technique but also moral character, strategic thinking, and the profound responsibilities that accompanied martial mastery.

Matsumora Kosaku (1829–1898)

Kosaku Matsumora, a Chikudun Peichin (a gentry rank indicating his status as a scholar-official), was a key figure in the Tomari-te lineage, known for his powerful techniques and for influencing later masters like Chotoku Kyan. He embodied the practical fighting spirit characteristic of the Tomari region. A widely recounted legend attributes to Matsumora Kosaku an encounter with a disrespectful Satsuma samurai on a beach (or similar public setting). In this tale, Matsumora, often depicted as unarmed or using only an everyday object (such as a wet towel, which he famously used to disarm a samurai in one variation of the legend, allegedly losing a thumb in the process), swiftly and decisively defeated or humiliated the armed samurai. This story, while possibly embellished, serves to highlight the perceived superiority and practicality of Okinawan Te even against the feared Japanese swordsmanship, solidifying Matsumora Kosaku's status as a folk hero and a testament to the effectiveness of unarmed combat within the warrior-scholar class.

These figures, through their historical roles and the enduring lore surrounding them, collectively illustrate the profound and practical fusion of intellectual and martial pursuits that defined the warrior-scholars of the Ryukyu Kingdom. Together, these historical figures illustrate how the Yukatchu's ethos became the bedrock for what would evolve into modern Okinawan Karate.

Legacy: The Yukatchu Influence on Okinawan Karate

The profound impact of the Ryukyuan gentry extended far beyond their individual accomplishments; their collective ethos and practices fundamentally shaped the blossoming Okinawan martial arts, leaving an indelible mark on its forms, principles, and very spirit. Their unique social status, practical duties, and intellectual pursuits converged to define the character of early Te.

Shaping Early "Te"

The Yukatchu's social status as the governing elite, coupled with their specific administrative and protective duties, directly influenced the evolution of early Te. Unlike martial arts developed solely for battlefield combat or peasant self-defense, the Te cultivated by this class was refined for close-quarter, often discreet, application within a civilian context. This led to an emphasis on control, precision, and the efficient neutralization of threats without necessarily resorting to lethal force, reflecting their role in maintaining civil order.

Likewise, their intellectual pursuits, steeped in Confucian philosophy, imbued the art with a strong ethical dimension, emphasizing discipline, respect, and the responsible use of power. This philosophical underpinning encouraged Te to be viewed not merely as a fighting method but as a path to self-cultivation and moral refinement. As a result, early Te combined practical needs, social duty, and scholarly influence in a way that made it both effective and refined.

Transmission and Preservation

In an era predating formal public instruction, the Yukatchu played a critical role in the transmission and preservation of Okinawan martial knowledge. Given the sensitive nature of combative skills in a weapon-restricted society and under Satsuma's watchful eye, martial arts were typically passed down through highly selective channels. Knowledge was often confined within families, from father to son, or through intimate master-disciple relationships that resembled familial bonds. This created what martial arts historian Patrick McCarthy refers to as an "ironclad ritual of secrecy," ensuring that the comprehensive understanding of Te, including its empty-hand techniques, body conditioning, and philosophical nuances, remained within a trusted circle. This clandestine mode of transmission, while limiting widespread dissemination, was instrumental in preserving the depth and integrity of the art's core principles, allowing them to evolve and mature over generations before their eventual introduction to the broader public.

The Transition to Modernity

The dissolution of the Ryukyu Kingdom in 1879 and its subsequent integration into the Japanese nation-state during the Meiji era marked a profound turning point for the Yukatchu class and their martial traditions. Stripped of their hereditary titles and administrative roles, the Ueekata and Pechin found their traditional way of life upended. This societal upheaval directly impacted the transmission of Te. While some masters, like Itosu Anko[14] (a former Pechin), actively sought to preserve the art by adapting it for public school instruction, this transition often necessitated simplification and the de-emphasis of combative elements deemed unsuitable for mass instruction or the new nationalistic ideals. The end of the kingdom thus represented both a challenge and an opportunity: it threatened the traditional, private mode of transmission but ultimately paved the way for Te to transform into modern Karate, eventually spreading globally, albeit with a character significantly altered from its warrior-scholar origins. Even as modernity reshaped Okinawan society and martial arts practice, the spirit of the warrior-scholar endured;

carried forward by those who sought to preserve both the art and its deeper meaning.

Rekindling the Warrior-Scholar Ideal

The narrative of the Ryukyu Kingdom's Yukatchu as warrior-scholars presents a compelling and distinct chapter in martial history, challenging conventional notions of power and proficiency. Our investigation has revealed that these high-ranking officials were not merely administrators who dabbled in combat, nor were they warriors who occasionally engaged in scholarship. Instead, they embodied a profound and deliberate fusion of intellectual rigor and martial might, a duality essential for the stability and unique cultural development of their island nation.

We have seen how Ryukyu's delicate geopolitical tightrope walk between China and Japan, coupled with nuanced regulations on weapons, necessitated the cultivation of a highly adaptable social elite. Within this context, their Confucian education instilled a deep philosophical foundation, guiding their administrative duties and shaping their approach to martial arts with an emphasis on ethical conduct and strategic thinking. This scholarly path seamlessly intertwined with their warrior's discipline, leading to the refinement of Te through practical needs. Training methodologies, from dynamic partner drills like Kakidī to the codification of solo kata, fostered the internalization of core principles such as Muchimi, Kakei, Tuidi, and Tegumi. The lives of notable figures like Takahara Peichin, Sakugawa Kanga, Matsumura Sokon, Chatan Yara, and Kosaku Matsumora stand as testaments to this integrated ideal, their historical contributions and enduring folklore painting a vivid picture of individuals who were simultaneously guardians of intellect and defense.

The legacy of these warrior-scholars profoundly shaped the character and development of Okinawan martial arts. Their social status, practical duties, and intellectual pursuits infused early Te with its distinctive emphasis on control, precision, and ethical application. Furthermore, their commitment to private, selective transmission, often shrouded in an "ironclad ritual of secrecy," ensured the preservation of the art's comprehensive principles for generations. While the dissolution of the Ryukyu Kingdom and the advent of modernity brought about significant changes, leading to the eventual public dissemination and specialization of Karate, the foundational contributions of these warrior-scholars remain deeply embedded. Their unique approach to martial arts, born from a necessity to thrive in a complex world, continues to influence the art's enduring spirit. The "Pen and the Fist" thus stands as an enduring symbol of their unique contribution to history and martial culture, a powerful reminder that true strength often lies in the harmonious integration of mind and might.

Notes

1.   Sakoku (鎖国): Japan's isolationist foreign policy during the Tokugawa period (1603–1868), under which most international contact and trade were strictly prohibited. Ryukyu's unique tributary relationship with China allowed it to act as an unofficial conduit for Chinese culture and goods into Japan.

2.   Wakizashi (脇差): A short sword typically worn as part of the traditional daishō by Japanese samurai. In Ryukyu, high-ranking officials such as Ueekata or senior Pechin were permitted to wear the wakizashi as a symbol of status, though not for active combat use.

3.   Daishō (大小): Literally meaning "big-little," this term refers to the pair of swords—katana and wakizashi—worn by samurai in feudal Japan. Ryukyuan officials under Satsuma were generally prohibited from wearing the full daishō, reflecting their subordinate status.

4.   Confucianism: A philosophical system rooted in the teachings of Confucius (Kong Fuzi), emphasizing moral virtue, filial piety, social harmony, and hierarchical order. Its influence deeply shaped Ryukyuan education, ethics, and civil governance.

5.   Bunbu Ryōdō (文武両道): A classical East Asian philosophical ideal meaning "the dual path of literary and martial arts." It emphasizes the importance of balancing intellectual cultivation with martial discipline, a concept foundational to the Ryukyuan warrior-scholar ethos.

6.   Te (手): Meaning "hand" in Japanese and Okinawan, Te refers to the indigenous unarmed combat traditions of Okinawa. It served as the foundational practice from which modern Karate later developed.

7.   Kakidī (掛け手): A traditional Okinawan two-person sensitivity drill often translated as "hooking hands." Used to develop tactile responsiveness, timing, and close-range combative control. It is a foundational exercise in many classical schools of Karate and Tuidi.

8.   Kakedameshi (掛け試し): A sparring method translated as "testing hands." It evolved from Kakidī and involves continuous, adaptive exchange of techniques in a semi-free format, emphasizing fluid control, counters, and real-time tactical decision-making.

9.   Muchimi (むちみ): A term meaning "sticky" or "heavy" body. It describes a quality of movement that is rooted, connected, and viscous, allowing practitioners to absorb, redirect, and generate force through whole-body integration.

10.   Kakei (かけい): A principle of continuous tactile connection between two practitioners. It enables one to sense, follow, and respond to an opponent's intentions through subtle physical contact—essential in close-quarter control and flow.

11.   Tegumi (手組): A traditional Okinawan grappling and wrestling art. Practiced especially among youths in Naha and Tomari, it emphasized throwing, joint manipulation, and close-quarters combat, and may represent one of the oldest combative practices in the Ryukyu Islands.

12.   Tuidi (取手): Translated as "seizing hand" or "grabbing hand," Tuidi refers to a system of joint-locking, controlling, and subduing techniques within traditional Okinawan martial arts. Often compared to Chinese Chin Na or Japanese Aiki-jutsu.

13.   Kusanku (公相君): A Chinese military official and martial arts expert who visited Okinawa as part of a diplomatic mission in the mid-18th century. He is widely credited with introducing Chinese Quanfa techniques that were later preserved in kata such as Kusanku or Kūsankū.

14.   Itosu Ankō (糸洲 安恒): A former Pechin and one of the most influential figures in modern Karate history. He adapted traditional Te for inclusion in Okinawan public schools in the early 20th century, introducing kata such as Pinan and formalizing Karate as a physical education discipline.

Under the Shadow of Satsuma
How Occupation Shaped Okinawan Martial Arts

A Kingdom Under Duress

The Ryukyu Kingdom, a vibrant island nation nestled strategically between the mighty empires of China and Japan, once maintained a delicate balance of diplomatic independence and flourishing trade. This equilibrium, however, was irrevocably shattered in 1609 with the swift and decisive invasion by Japan's Satsuma Domain. This event marked the beginning of over two and a half centuries of profound Japanese occupation, a period that would fundamentally reshape every facet of Okinawan society. While it is often understood that this era brought about restrictions on weaponry, the actual narrative of this long occupation reveals a far more intricate and compelling story of how political, economic, and social realities directly and indirectly influenced the unique evolution of Okinawan martial arts.

To truly understand the distinctive martial traditions of Okinawa, one must first journey through the era of Satsuma's prolonged rule. This historical exploration uncovers how the pervasive control exercised by the occupiers inadvertently fostered a distinct, pragmatic, and often clandestine martial culture.

We begin by setting the stage with the immediate aftermath of the 1609 invasion, detailing the political subjugation and the shrewd economic controls that systematically drained the kingdom's resources. From there, we delve into the popular notion of a universal "weapons ban," revealing its more nuanced reality and the psychological landscape it created, which in turn forced profound innovation in martial training. The narrative then shifts to the clandestine development of Te (empty-hand combat), highlighting its emphasis on practicality, intense body conditioning, and the ingenious use of kata as a form of encoded knowledge. Crucially, we also explore the emergence of Kobudo, the art of improvised weaponry, born from the necessity of transforming everyday tools into effective instruments of defense. Finally, we consider the broader social and cultural ramifications, demonstrating how these martial arts became a quiet assertion of Okinawan identity and reinforced the unique scholar-warrior ideal. This journey ultimately reveals that the shadow of Satsuma, rather than extinguishing Okinawan martial traditions, paradoxically forged an art that prioritized survival and quiet strength, leaving an indelible imprint on the global martial arts landscape.

Occupation and Oversight: Political and Economic Realities

The year 1609[1] marked an irreversible turning point for the Ryukyu Kingdom. A swift and decisive military subjugation by the Japanese Satsuma Domain established a new and harsh reality of foreign oversight, fundamentally altering its political landscape and ushering in over two and a half centuries of occupation. This was not a mere shift in diplomatic allegiance; it was a profound imposition of external control that would ripple through every aspect of Ryukyuan life.

The Invasion and Its Aftermath

Before the invasion, the Ryukyu Kingdom enjoyed a period of relative diplomatic independence and prosperity, skillfully navigating its position between the powerful states of China and Japan. However, this delicate balance was increasingly challenged by the ambitions of Japan's emerging unifiers. The pretext for the Satsuma invasion stemmed from Ryukyu's repeated non-compliance with demands from the Shimazu clan and Toyotomi Hideyoshi, including the kingdom's refusal to fully support Hideyoshi's planned invasions of Korea in the 1590s. King Sho Nei had not only deferred but had gone so far as to inform the Ming Court of Hideyoshi's intentions[2]. Later, the kingdom defied demands from the new Tokugawa shogunate[3] to formally recognize its authority and serve as an intermediary for re-establishing formal relations with the Ming. Citing these incidents and a broader narrative of Ryukyuan disrespect, the Shimazu house finally secured formal permission from Tokugawa Ieyasu in 1606 to launch a punitive mission[4].

The invasion itself, undertaken in 1609, was a swift military subjugation. After a few battles on smaller outlying islands, the samurai forces seized Shuri Castle, the heart of the kingdom.

King Sho Nei, along with a number of his chief officials, were taken captive and forcibly brought to Japan. There, they were compelled to meet with Tokugawa Ieyasu and his son, the reigning Shogun Tokugawa Hidetada, and were forced to submit to a series of humiliating demands and conditions. This established an undeniable new reality of Japanese oversight. Though the king was conditionally restored to his castle and kingdom in 1611, this signified an immediate and severe curtailment of Ryukyu's autonomy. The invasion brought not only political subjugation but also immediate human impact and disruption to daily life, as the populace grappled with the presence of an occupying force and the abrupt shift in their kingdom's destiny.

Dual Vassalage and Economic Control

Following the invasion, the Ryukyu Kingdom formally became a direct vassal state under the Shimazu clan, immediately subject to regular tribute and compulsory missions to Kagoshima, the capital of Satsuma. A land survey[5] conducted in 1610–1611 determined the kingdom's land productivity to be 89,086 koku, yet Ryukyu was permitted to retain only 50,000 koku. The 35% annual tax[6], known as shinobose mai, which was initially paid in commodities, was swiftly shifted to silver and then to rice by 1620, systematically draining the kingdom's agricultural wealth.

Crucially, Satsuma employed a shrewd and complex strategy by maintaining Ryukyu's existing tributary relationship with China. This dual vassalage allowed Japan to bypass its own strict Sakoku (closed country) policy, which severely restricted foreign trade[7]. Through Ryukyu, Japan gained immense profits from lucrative Chinese goods and invaluable intelligence on Chinese affairs that could not be obtained elsewhere. To meticulously preserve this diplomatic charade for Beijing, strict measures were imposed on Ryukyuans: they were forbidden from speaking Japanese, dressing in Japanese fashion, or otherwise revealing Japanese influence when interacting with Chinese envoys or if shipwrecked in China. Great efforts were made to conceal any signs of Japanese presence, maintaining a fiction that any remaining Japanese influences were due to trade with nearby islands, rather than mainland Japan. While Ryukyu became a vital source of sugar and Chinese luxury goods for Japan, it conversely grew heavily dependent on Satsuma for essential commodities like silver, copper, and tin, often using its sugar production as collateral for loans, thereby further draining the kingdom's resources and solidifying its economic subjugation.

Political Subjugation and Surveillance

The return of King Sho Nei to Shuri Castle in 1611 did not mark a restoration of true sovereignty. Instead, Ryukyu entered a new phase of indirect control, one characterized by symbolic subordination and strategic surveillance. Despite the king's restoration, Ryukyuan sovereignty remained severely limited. The kingdom was regarded by

Japan not as takoku ("other lands" within Japan's feudal order) but as ikoku[8] ("foreign lands"), a status shared with China, Korea, and European nations, underscoring its non-integrated position within the Japanese sphere. While Satsuma initially imposed more substantial and more direct interference in Ryukyu's governance, by the 1620s, it began to loosen its direct involvement, allowing Ryukyu increased autonomy[9] in domestic governance. This limited autonomy is exemplified by the significant reforms instituted by officials such as Sho Shoken (Sessei from 1666 to 1673) and Sai On (royal regent in the 1750s), who streamlined expenses, suppressed perceived "backward" cultural elements, and reformed the domestic economy. However, this flexibility operated strictly within a controlled framework, with Satsuma maintaining ultimate authority. The annual visit of the Ryukyuan crown prince to Kagoshima for formal rituals of subordination further cemented this political subjugation, serving as a constant reminder of Ryukyu's vassal status.

The Nuance of the "Weapons Ban" and Its True Impact

The popular narrative of a complete and absolute "weapons ban" in Ryukyu, often depicted as Satsuma confiscating all arms from every citizen, requires a more nuanced examination. While weapon restrictions were indeed a significant aspect of the occupation, their nature was more strategic and less universally applied than commonly understood.

Revisiting the Prohibition

Satsuma's primary concern was preventing armed resistance, not eliminating all tools of self-defense. The domain targeted battlefield weaponry such as katana, spears, bows, and especially firearms, that could enable organized rebellion. These were restricted from public use and manufacture. However, archaeological findings and historical documents suggest that weapons already in possession of elite families, particularly those of the Yukatchu class, were often allowed to remain in private hands under strict oversight. Some were even transported to Kagoshima for maintenance with official permission, underscoring that the enforcement was more tactical than absolute[10].

Privileges and Exceptions

Certain high-ranking Ryukyuan officials may have retained the right to carry wakizashi or other short blades, possibly as a mark of station rather than for combat. While no firm documentation conclusively proves this, the claim appears in a number of oral traditions and family records[11]. Whether symbolic or functional, these exceptions point to a calculated strategy of control: allowing the appearance of status while minimizing real threat.

A Climate of Caution

Regardless of the technicalities, the perceived danger of bearing arms or even training publicly in martial techniques created a pervasive atmosphere of caution. Surveillance was ever-present. Even a rumor of disloyalty could bring serious consequences. As a result, martial arts training, weapon development, and self-defense instruction were driven underground. The psychological impact of living under suspicion and threat necessitated a new approach to self-protection; one that favored secrecy, precision, and quiet resilience.

This environment laid the foundation for a pragmatic, internalized form of martial practice. Techniques became smaller, more efficient, and harder to detect. Improvisation and concealment became as important as strength or speed. In response to the nuanced realities of the "ban," Okinawan martial culture evolved, not through elimination, but through innovation.

Clandestine Training and the Preservation of Te

The clandestine nature of martial arts practice during the Satsuma occupation profoundly influenced the development, preservation, and transmission of Okinawan combat traditions. With overt instruction suppressed, practitioners were compelled to adopt discreet, often secretive methods of training, resulting in a culture of selective transmission and hidden knowledge.

Private Instruction and Secret Locations

Martial training moved behind closed doors, into private homes, courtyards, and remote outdoor locations, often under the cover of night. Instruction was typically restricted to trusted students, sometimes within the same family or tight-knit social circles. This model ensured not only the physical safety of the practitioners but also the preservation of their techniques and philosophies against misinterpretation or misuse.

This secrecy was not solely about avoiding detection; it became a defining feature of the art itself. Much of what is today considered traditional Okinawan karate was shaped during this time: a distilled, efficient system of combat that prioritized internal development, control, and effectiveness over spectacle or ritual.

Kata as a Vehicle for Preservation

One of the most significant innovations of this period was the deepening reliance on kata, not just as a method of training, but also as a mnemonic device and a coded record of combative knowledge. Through kata, practitioners encoded principles of timing, distancing, joint manipulation, vital point targeting, and leverage in a format that could be taught safely without openly displaying violence or resistance.

While the outer form of a kata might appear simple or dance-like, its bunkai remained secret and were passed down orally or through hands-on instruction. This ensured that only those with the proper context could understand their deeper intent. In this way, kata became a tool of resistance; a means to preserve and transmit martial knowledge openly.

Emphasis on Practical Application

Training during the occupation emphasized efficiency and realism. There was little room for ceremony or impractical flourish. The methods that survived were those that could be relied upon in real confrontation: close-quarters control, striking to vulnerable targets, off-balancing and takedowns, and counters against grabs or surprise attacks.

Physical conditioning also became essential, with an emphasis on toughening the body, improving reflexes, and developing internal attributes such as breath control, rooted posture, and explosive movement. This blend of physical and internal training made the Okinawan arts distinct from both Chinese and Japanese systems, which often emphasized formality or aesthetic performance.

In sum, the occupation did not merely suppress Ryukyuan martial traditions; it transformed and refined them. The necessity of secrecy gave rise to a discipline that was pragmatic, symbolic, and deeply tied to Okinawan identity. As we continue our exploration, we will next turn to the birth and evolution of Kobudo, the complementary weapons art that emerged from the same crucible of constraint and creativity.

The Evolution of Kobudo: Defense Reimagined

While the popular image of Okinawan martial arts often centers on empty-hand techniques, such as Karate, the historical reality reveals a parallel and equally rich tradition of weapon-based combat, known as Kobudo. Far from being a mere afterthought or peasant improvisation, Kobudo represents an adaptive evolution in martial strategy, forged under the constraints of occupation and surveillance. Born from the necessity to defend without access to conventional arms, it elevated agricultural tools, household implements, and utilitarian objects into precise and deadly instruments.

From Tool to Weapon: Improvisation and Necessity

Faced with restrictions on swords, spears, and other standard military implements, Ryukyuan martial artists began to refine and formalize the use of what had previously been ordinary tools. The bo, sai, tonfa, kama, eku, and nunchaku each found new purpose as functional weapons[12]. Contrary to the romanticized idea that farmers spontaneously weaponized tools in a secret rebellion, the reality is that most Kobudo practitioners came from the educated Yukatchu class[13]. They were officials, guards, and instructors who both needed and had the training to systematize practical combative applications.

The transformation of these tools into weapons was not haphazard. Over time, specific techniques, drills, and kata were developed to codify their use. These forms retained the principles of body mechanics, distancing, leverage, and timing found in empty-hand techniques, but adapted them to the weight, shape, and momentum of each weapon.

Stylistic Diversity and Regional Lineages

As Kobudo evolved, it branched into distinctive styles based on region, family, and individual innovation. Some traditions took root in specific villages, such as Tsuken Island; others were closely associated with individual masters or family lines. For instance, Tsuken Shitahaku is remembered for his contributions to bo techniques from the island of Tsuken. At the same time, legends surrounding Matsu Higa attribute the formation of early sai and tonfa methods to his legacy. Kata such as Shushi no kon, Chikin no sai, and Hamahiga no tonfa illustrate not only martial ingenuity but also regional identities and familial lineages[14].

Kobudo lineages were often closely guarded. Instruction was typically passed down privately, often from master to disciple through oral tradition. The retention of regional names within kata suggests pride in origin as well as the desire to honor the individuals who preserved and refined them.

Interplay with Chinese and Japanese Influence

The development of Kobudo also reflects Okinawa's unique position as a cultural crossroads. Chinese weapon arts influenced both empty-hand and weapons practice. Techniques for staff and truncheon use show similarities to Chinese gunshu and tiechi methods, possibly introduced through Chinese embassies or merchants[15]. Conversely, Satsuma's initial ban on swords meant that Japanese influence on weapons technique was more indirect. However, conceptual parallels, such as maai (combative distancing) and certain stances, can still be identified.

Pragmatism over Pageantry

Like its empty-hand counterpart, Kobudo emphasized function over flair. Kata were lean and efficient. Movements were structured to deliver maximum effect with minimal exposure. Strikes were direct, blocks doubled as counterattacks, and footwork emphasized stability and explosive power. The simplicity masked sophistication; every movement held layered intent, often concealed through deliberate ambiguity in form.

Symbolism and Cultural Identity

Practicing Kobudo became more than just a means of self-defense; it became a way of life. It was a cultural statement. By transforming fishing tools and farm equipment into symbols of resistance and refinement, Okinawan practitioners reclaimed agency in a society where overt martial displays were dangerous. Kobudo thus served not only as a method of defense but also as a quiet assertion of Okinawan resourcefulness, identity, and continuity.

Quiet Resistance and Cultural Identity

Okinawan martial arts, forged in the shadow of occupation, evolved not only as systems of self-defense but also as subtle instruments of cultural preservation and identity. Under Satsuma rule, overt rebellion was neither viable nor survivable. Yet, within the silent motions of kata, the encoded discipline of Tuidi, and the careful handing down of Kobudo forms, Okinawans found a way to resist, not through confrontation, but through continuity.

Martial Arts as Cultural Expression

Martial practice became a coded language. It was a way for Okinawans to remember who they were and where they came from at a time when much of their visible heritage was under pressure to conform or disappear. Techniques named after villages (e.g., Chatan Yara no sai, Tsuken no kon), figures (e.g., Matsumura no Passai), or events served as mnemonic markers of lineage and legacy. This preservation of identity through martial form is especially evident in the way kata were transmitted: not simply as physical routines, but as repositories of communal memory, often guarded within families or trusted social circles.

The Scholar-Warrior Ideal

Okinawa's Yukatchu class embodied a unique ideal, one that harmonized Confucian civil responsibility with martial capability. While their peers in China pursued the path of governance through learning, and the Japanese samurai class emphasized martial prowess, the Yukatchu blended both. For them, Bunbu Ryodo[16], the dual path of pen and sword, was more than a philosophical construct; it was a lived necessity. Under Satsuma rule, they were the civil servants, guards, diplomats, and educators charged with maintaining order and transmitting values. Their martial competence, though often hidden, was inseparable from their public duty.

This ethos produced figures such as Sakugawa Kanga, Matsumura Sokon, and Chomo Hanashiro, who were not only martial artists but also scholars, teachers, and cultural stewards. In them, we find the clearest expression of Okinawa's martial tradition, not as a cult of violence, but as a philosophy of stewardship, discipline, and quiet strength.

Ritual, Discipline, and Psychological Resilience

The strict forms, silent repetition, and reverence within Okinawan martial arts were more than methods of training. They cultivated psychological resilience. In a society that was watched, taxed, and subjugated, martial discipline became a sanctuary; a place where control could be practiced, strength developed, and heritage preserved. The kata performed in private courtyards, the weapons hidden in plain sight, and the lessons passed down in whispers were all acts of preservation under pressure.

Moreover, these practices instilled an internalized resistance; a mindset that valued self-mastery, preparedness, and loyalty to family and culture above performative rebellion. It is no accident that even today, Okinawan martial arts stress humility, control, and restraint. These were survival traits during occupation, but they have endured because they resonate with a more profound truth about martial culture: that real power is often quiet.

Echoes into the Present

The legacy of Satsuma's occupation can still be felt in the structure, tone, and transmission of Okinawan martial arts today. The traditions that emerged during those centuries, introspective, encoded, respectful, and efficient, stand in contrast to later iterations of Karate and Kobudo that appeared in Japanese or global contexts. While mainland systems often emphasized public display, rank, and competitive success, Okinawan styles retained a focus on personal development, practical effectiveness, and quiet refinement.

As the world continues to embrace Okinawan martial traditions, it is essential to recognize the historical crucible in which they were forged.

They are not relics, but resilient artifacts, born not from a desire for conquest, but from the need to endure, to remember, and to remain unbroken under shadow.

Forged in the Shadow, Enduring in the Light

The history of Okinawan martial arts cannot be fully understood without acknowledging the complex and often painful legacy of Satsuma's occupation. Far from being a mere backdrop, the socio-political realities of Ryukyu's vassalage actively shaped the evolution of its combative traditions. What emerged from this period was not just a set of techniques, but a philosophical framework; a martial culture that prized subtlety over spectacle, refinement over rebellion, and resilience over resistance.

By stripping away overt militarism and forcing martial training into the shadows, the occupation compelled Okinawan practitioners to develop systems that emphasized internal power, practical efficiency, and coded preservation. The resulting arts, Te, Tuidi, and Kobudo, represent not only the ingenuity of a subjugated people but also their unwavering commitment to cultural identity and survival.

Moreover, the fusion of scholarship and martial prowess within the Yukatchu class offers a powerful model of integrated virtue. In contrast to the often singular martial emphasis found elsewhere, Okinawa's warrior-scholars saw no contradiction in wielding both the pen and the fist[17]. They served as diplomats, guards, teachers, and civil administrators; individuals whose strength was not measured solely in combat, but in character.

Today, as Karate and kobudo continue to thrive on the global stage, it is crucial that we not forget the conditions under which they were born. These arts are not simply fighting systems; they are vessels of history, carriers of philosophy, and quiet testaments to a people's will to endure.

To study Okinawan martial arts, then, is to engage with a deeper narrative; one that honors the silent defiance of generations, the intellectual rigor of forgotten scholars, and the enduring spirit of a kingdom that refused to be erased. What was forged in shadow now endures in light, not merely as tradition, but as a living legacy.

Notes

1.   The Satsuma invasion of Ryukyu began in early 1609, with troops landing on Amami Ōshima before advancing southward. Shuri Castle fell in May 1609. King Shō Nei and key ministers were taken to Kagoshima, then Edo, where they were forced to submit to Tokugawa Hidetada.
George Kerr, Okinawa: The History of an Island People (Tokyo: Tuttle Publishing, 2000).

2.   Prior to the invasion, King Shō Nei declined requests to aid Hideyoshi's Korean campaigns and covertly informed the Ming court about Japan's intentions, placing Ryukyu in political jeopardy.
Gregory Smits, Visions of Ryukyu: Identity and Ideology in Early-Modern Thought and Politics (Honolulu: University of Hawai'i Press, 1999).

3.   Following Hideyoshi's death, the Tokugawa shogunate demanded that Ryukyu act as an intermediary in reestablishing relations with Ming China. Ryukyu's refusal further angered the Japanese leadership.
Kerr, Okinawa.

4.   In 1606, Shimazu Tadatsune formally received permission from Tokugawa Ieyasu to launch a punitive expedition against Ryukyu. This approval set the stage for the 1609 invasion.
Smits, Visions of Ryukyu.

5.   The 1610–1611 kokudaka survey assessed Ryukyu's productivity at 89,086 koku. However, the kingdom was allowed to retain only 50,000 koku, with the remainder appropriated by Satsuma.
Mamoru Akamine, The Ryukyu Kingdom: Cornerstone of East Asia (Honolulu: University of Hawai'i Press, 2017).

6.   The kingdom was required to remit 35% of its rice harvest (shinobose mai). Initially paid in goods, the tax shifted to silver and rice by 1620, deepening Ryukyu's dependency on imports.
Smits, Visions of Ryukyu.

7.   Satsuma preserved Ryukyu's Chinese tributary status to circumvent Sakoku, Japan's isolation policy. Ryukyuans were forbidden to appear "Japanized" when interacting with Chinese envoys.
Kerr, Okinawa.

8.   In the Tokugawa classification system, Ryukyu was designated ikoku ("foreign country"), as opposed to takoku ("other country") within Japan's feudal structure— underscoring its ambiguous legal status.
Akamine, The Ryukyu Kingdom.

9.   By the 1620s, direct Japanese involvement in domestic Ryukyuan affairs decreased. Reforms by officials such as Shō Shōken and Sai On modernized governance and curtailed expenses.
Kerr, Okinawa.

10.   Weapons bans targeted battlefield arms (e.g., swords, spears, guns). Elite families often retained traditional weapons under oversight. Some were even sent to Kagoshima for repairs with permission.
Tetsuo Yamakawa, The Hidden Roots of Okinawan Karate (Okinawa: privately published, 1995).

11.   Oral traditions and anecdotal records suggest high-ranking officials retained wakizashi as status symbols. No firm archival evidence confirms this, though the practice is widely cited in family lore.
Andreas Quast, Karate 1.0: Parameters of an Ancient Martial Art (Germany: Lulu Press, 2013).

12.   Many Kobudo weapons were derived from practical tools: bo from carrying poles, nunchaku from flails or bridles, tonfa from mill handles, eku from oars, kama from sickles, tekko from stirrups or horseshoes, and tinbe from shields made of turtle shell or metal.
Patrick McCarthy, The Bible of Karate: Bubishi (Boston: Tuttle Publishing, 1995).

13.   Despite popular myths of farmers repurposing tools, most Kobudo practitioners were from the Yukatchu class—civil administrators, bodyguards, and instructors with formal training.
Hokama Tetsuhiro, 100 Masters of Okinawan Karate (Okinawa: Ozato Print, 2002).

14.   Lineages developed around figures such as Tsuken Shitahaku and Matsu Higa. Classical kata—Shushi no kon, Chikin no sai, Hamahiga no tonfa—preserve regional and familial traditions.
Arakaki Kiyoshi, The Secrets of Okinawan Karate (Tokyo: YMAA, 2006).

15.   Chinese martial systems—particularly from Fujian—strongly influenced Okinawan weapons practice. Techniques for staff and truncheon (gunshu, tiechi) likely reached Ryukyu through embassies and trade.
Yamakawa, The Hidden Roots of Okinawan Karate.

16.   Bunbu Ryōdō (文武両道), the "dual path of literary and martial arts," was a Confucian ideal adopted by the Yukatchu, reflecting a balanced pursuit of scholarship and martial readiness.
Smits, Visions of Ryukyu.

17.   Prominent Yukatchu exemplars include Sakugawa Kanga, Matsumura Sōkon, and Chōmo Hanashiro—men who combined scholarship, administration, and martial training.
Joe Swift, The Karate-Do of Itosu Ankō (Osaka: Karate Culture Press, 2021).

Unraveling the Myths of Ryukyu Kobudo

Beyond the Battlefield and Ban Narratives

In the contemporary martial arts landscape, Ryukyu Kobudo stands as a distinctive and widely recognized discipline, celebrated for its unique array of traditional Okinawan weapon forms. Its imagery, of practitioners wielding staffs, tridents, and agricultural tools transformed into formidable instruments, captures the imagination, often accompanied by romanticized tales of secret training under oppressive regimes. Yet, beneath this widespread recognition lies a complex historical tapestry, interwoven with nuanced truths and popular misconceptions that warrant a more rigorous examination.

Unfortunately, the prevailing contemporary understanding of Kobudo frequently oversimplifies its true origins, misrepresents the nature of its traditional practice, and distorts the impact of historical weapons restrictions on its development. It is a misconception to view Kobudo solely as a direct descendant of battlefield techniques or as a singular product of an absolute ban on all weaponry. Instead, one should critically examine these facets, tracing Kobudo's evolution from its pragmatic adaptations of civilian tools and its discrete private transmission, shaped significantly by international martial influences, to its eventual transformation into the systematized forms practiced publicly today.

To achieve this, we must first unravel the diverse threads of Kobudo's origins, exploring its roots in everyday implements and critically re-evaluating the historical weapons bans alongside the profound impact of international exchange, particularly from Chinese martial arts.

Unraveling the Origins

The origins of Ryukyu Kobudo, the traditional weapon arts of Okinawa, are often shrouded in captivating narratives that, while culturally rich, frequently oversimplify a complex historical reality. A critical examination reveals a genesis rooted not solely in formal battlefield combat, but primarily in the pragmatic adaptation of everyday tools, profoundly shaped by Okinawa's unique geopolitical position and the influx of diverse martial traditions.

Beyond the "Battlefield Myth": Adapting Everyday Implements

The popular notion that Kobudo exclusively originated from formalized battlefield techniques of the Ryukyu Kingdom's warrior class requires careful scrutiny. While martial prowess was undoubtedly valued and cultivated, particularly among the Pechin[1] (gentry-warrior class), the specific implements now recognized as core Kobudo weapons, such as the bo (staff), sai (trident), tonfa (mill handle), kama (sickle), and nunchaku (flail), were, for the most part, pragmatic adaptations of essential civilian tools. These were implements crucial to the daily lives of farmers, fishermen, and tradesmen. The bo, for instance, served not only as a formidable cudgel or impact weapon for self-defense but also as a commonplace carrying pole for burdens, a walking stick, or even a rudimentary training stand for the yari (spear) in more formal martial practice. This multi-functional utility underscores their practical ubiquity and highlights that their martial application arose from inherent accessibility and utility, rather than solely from a dedicated military purpose. Such adaptations underscore a resourceful approach to self-preservation, where the inherent design and common availability of these tools made them ideal candidates for martial development in a society where conventional weaponry was often inaccessible to the broader populace.

Re-evaluating the "Weapons Ban"

Central to the mythos of Okinawan martial arts is the widely circulated, yet oversimplified, narrative of a comprehensive and indiscriminate weapons ban imposed on all Okinawans. A closer historical inspection reveals a more nuanced reality. The initial major "disarmament" often cited occurred under King Sho Shin (ruled 1477-1526). This was primarily a political maneuver to centralize power and quell internal strife among regional lords (Aji[2]). The directive focused on collecting and storing formal military weapons like swords and spears, thereby consolidating control and ending the era of internal warfare. This was not a blanket prohibition on commoners, who typically did not possess such weaponry anyway.

Following the Satsuma Invasion of 1609, stricter controls were indeed imposed by the Shimazu clan of Satsuma (now Kagoshima Prefecture, Japan). These restrictions primarily targeted firearms and longer swords (katana) to prevent any organized resistance. However, even under Satsuma's dominion, the Okinawan pechin (gentry-warrior class) were generally permitted to retain smaller blades, such as a wakizashi, as symbols of their status, albeit under strict oversight. Crucially, essential farming and domestic tools, which formed the basis of Kobudo weapons, were never universally or systematically banned; they were indispensable for daily livelihood. These specific, targeted restrictions and the broader political climate certainly contributed to the discreet, "behind-the-scenes" nature of martial arts training. However, it is a significant overstatement to assert that these bans were the sole or even primary impetus for the ingenious adaptation of everyday tools into formidable self-defense implements. The adaptation was a multifaceted phenomenon, born of necessity and influenced by existing martial knowledge.

The Impact of International Exchange

Okinawa's strategic position as a central point for trade and diplomacy positioned the Ryukyu Kingdom as a vibrant cultural and commercial crossroads between China, Japan, and Southeast Asia. This unique geopolitical role facilitated a profound and well-documented influence on the island's martial traditions. Chinese martial arts (quanfa), in particular, exerted a dominant impact on Okinawan fighting methods, both empty-hand and with weapons. Through constant diplomatic missions, visits from Chinese merchants, and the presence of Chinese martial arts practitioners, Okinawans were exposed to a wide array of Chinese weapon forms and combat principles.

It is highly plausible that Okinawan martial artists, exposed to these sophisticated Chinese weapon disciplines (even those designed for battlefield use), consciously sought readily available, discreet, and legal local implements that served as functional analogs to these foreign weapons. For instance, the common carrying pole or staff (bo) could effectively mimic the range and dynamics of various Chinese staves or even spears, allowing practitioners to train and apply similar principles. Similarly, a rice flail could serve as an effective analog for certain chain weapons utilized in Chinese martial arts, while the tonfa's design and movements resonate with techniques associated with Chinese mill handles or even specialized short weapons found in Thailand and Indonesia. This highlights a conscious and intelligent adaptation process, where the functional characteristics and combative principles of established Chinese weapon forms guided the transformation of indigenous tools into martial instruments. While the Southeast Asian martial traditions are also theorized to have exerted some influence due to active trade routes, direct evidence remains sparse compared to the pervasive and well-documented Chinese connections. These influences likely occurred through a combination of visiting martial artists, diplomatic exchanges, observation of foreign combat methods, and the general cultural diffusion facilitated by Okinawa's role as a bustling trade hub.

Secrecy, Family, and Specialization

Beyond the debates surrounding their origins and the true nature of weapons restrictions, the historical practice and transmission of Ryukyu Kobudo were shaped by distinct cultural norms and geopolitical realities. Far from the public, systematized training seen today, early weapon arts thrived in an environment characterized by discretion, familial lines, and a deep, often singular, mastery of specific implements.

Discretion and Transmission: The "Behind the Scenes" Era

Early Kobudo training was inherently private and discreet, a marked contrast to the openly public dojo culture that emerged in the 20th century. It is crucial to distinguish this from a conspiratorial, clandestine "secret" society; rather, training was conducted behind closed doors, away from official scrutiny, reflecting the sensitive nature of combative practices under foreign oversight. Following the Satsuma invasion in 1609, martial training, particularly with weapons, could easily be misconstrued as preparation for rebellion, inviting severe repercussions from the Shimazu clan's occupying forces. Consequently, direct instruction in these arts was typically conducted in private homes, courtyards, or secluded areas, minimizing visibility. Furthermore, the very concept of formal public training institutions, such as dedicated martial arts schools or dojo, was virtually non-existent in Ryukyu until well into the Meiji era[3]. Knowledge transmission relied on deep, exclusive master-disciple relationships, where a master might accept only a handful of students over a lifetime, often after years of personal vetting and observation. This ensured loyalty, control over the dissemination of potentially dangerous knowledge, and the preservation of traditions within a trusted, insulated environment.

Familial Lines and The Role of Specialization

The transmission of Kobudo was thus predominantly an intimate affair, occurring within families or very select, trusted circles of students who often became akin to adopted family members, known as uchi-deshi (inside student). This familial bond ensured dedication, strict adherence to principles, and a profound understanding of the art's nuances passed down through generations or through exceptionally close tutelage. Within these private contexts, there was a historical tendency towards deep specialization in one, or very few weapons. A master might gain renown specifically for their unparalleled skill in bojutsu (staff techniques) or saijutsu (sai techniques), reflecting a lifetime dedicated to mastering the intricacies of a particular implement. This focused approach allowed for profound mastery and the development of highly effective techniques tailored to a specific weapon's unique characteristics.

However, while this deep specialization was undoubtedly common for achieving profound mastery, it is important to acknowledge that not all masters adhered strictly to this model. Some prominent martial artists did indeed possess proficiency across multiple weapon types, as well as empty-hand arts, demonstrating an integrated understanding of various combative principles. Nevertheless, the overarching concept of "Kobudo" as a unified curriculum encompassing a diverse array of weapon types, where practitioners are expected to learn bo, sai, tonfa, nunchaku, kama, and other implements as part of a single, comprehensive system, is a more modern development. This shift reflects the later formalization and popularization of these arts, driven by different pedagogical and preservationist goals than those that shaped their initial, discreet transmission.

The Path to Public View: Modernization and Systematization

The early 20th century marked a pivotal shift for Okinawan martial arts, as both empty-hand karate and weapon arts began their transformation from discreet, privately transmitted disciplines into publicly recognized and systematized curricula. This modernization drive, often mirroring the developments seen in karate, was fueled by a confluence of social, political, and pedagogical imperatives, fundamentally altering how Kobudo was preserved, taught, and understood.

The Preservationist Movement

As Okinawa transitioned further into the Japanese nation-state, and traditional ways of life began to erode, there arose a growing impetus in the 20th century to formalize, standardize, and preserve old martial traditions. Fears that these unique cultural and martial legacies might be lost amidst societal changes, the rise of modern education, and the decline of the old master-disciple paradigm spurred a concerted effort to document and disseminate these arts. This movement aimed to ensure the survival of techniques and forms that had previously existed largely within isolated lineages, often facing the risk of being lost with the passing of a single master. The impetus was not merely to maintain ancient forms, but to adapt them for a new era, ensuring their relevance and accessibility to a broader audience.

Key Figures in Modern Kobudo

This era saw the emergence of pivotal figures who dedicated themselves to the daunting task of collecting and systematizing disparate weapon kata. Among the most prominent were Shinken Taira (1897-1970) and Inoue Motokatsu (1918-1993). Shinken Taira, a diligent researcher and practitioner, traveled extensively throughout Okinawa, meticulously collecting kata from various old masters and preserving them from obscurity. He compiled a significant repertoire, documenting forms that might otherwise have vanished. Inoue Motokatsu, inheriting Shinken Taira's work and further developing his own extensive knowledge, played a crucial role in codifying these collected kata into cohesive systems. Their contributions were monumental: they not only preserved a vast array of techniques but also provided a structured framework that allowed kobudo to be taught more systematically and widely, moving beyond its fragmented, lineage-specific existence.

From Specialization to Comprehensive Curriculum

The efforts of individuals like Taira and Inoue facilitated a transformative shift from the traditional model of individually transmitted, weapon-specific training. Whereas historical practice often saw masters specializing deeply in one or a few weapons (e.g., being a bojutsu or saijutsu expert), the modern systematization introduced a more broad, multi-weapon "Kobudo" curriculum. This new approach aimed for comprehensive instruction, where students would typically learn forms for the bo, sai, tonfa, nunchaku, and kama as part of an integrated program. This systematized approach was designed for public instruction and broader dissemination, fitting into the emerging dojo culture alongside karate. It facilitated the teaching of kobudo to larger groups, streamlining the learning process and making these once-exclusive arts accessible to a global audience.

Impact on Original Intent and Pedagogy

While the systematization and public promotion of Kobudo were vital for its survival and spread, this transformation was not without its implications for the arts' original combative intent and methods. Mirroring the trajectory of empty-hand karate, the process of formalization often involved a degree of standardization and simplification for mass instruction. The intricate, often brutal, applications (bunkai) inherent in traditional forms, honed for real-world defense, could sometimes become diluted or reinterpreted to fit a more generalized curriculum or to emphasize aesthetic appeal for demonstration. The focus might shift from raw combative efficiency to pedagogical progression, safety, or even sportification, potentially leading to the de-emphasis or abstraction of certain aspects crucial to their original purpose. While modernization ensured the continuity of kobudo, it also presented the ongoing challenge of preserving the profound depth and combative essence of techniques forged in a vastly different historical context.

The Evolving Legacy and the Imperative of Critical Inquiry

The journey through the historical landscape of Ryukyu Kobudo reveals a narrative far more intricate and compelling than popular lore often suggests. We have endeavored to disentangle the realities from the romanticized tales, demonstrating that the contemporary understanding of Kobudo benefits immensely from a nuanced and critically informed perspective.

Crucial to this is the critical re-evaluation of the pervasive "weapons ban" narrative, revealing it as a series of specific, targeted historical restrictions, imposed by King Sho Shin and later by Satsuma, that primarily controlled military arms and firearms, rather than universally disarming the common populace of their essential livelihood tools. This understanding positions the bans as contributors to the discreet nature of training, but not the sole or primary impetus for tool adaptation. Additionally, the profound impact of international exchange, particularly the dominant influence of Chinese martial arts (quanfa), points to the adaptation of local tools often occurring as a conscious effort to find functional analogs for the sophisticated foreign weapon forms to which Okinawan practitioners were exposed.

The "hidden practice" of traditional Kobudo transmission, characterized by a discreet, private ethos primarily within familial lines or very select master-disciple relationships, was shaped by the socio-political climate and the absence of public training institutions. This era also witnessed a historical tendency towards deep specialization in one or a few weapons, a stark contrast to the comprehensive, multi-weapon "Kobudo" curriculum that is a hallmark of its modern systematization. The eventual path to public view in the 20th century, led by figures like Shinken Taira and Inoue Motokatsu, formalized and preserved these disparate kata. While vital for its survival and global dissemination, this modernization, mirroring karate's trajectory, invariably impacted the original combative intent and pedagogical methods, raising questions about the balance between standardization and the preservation of raw, functional applications (bunkai).

The history of Okinawan martial arts, including Kobudo, is a testament to human ingenuity, resilience, and the fascinating interplay of culture, politics, and practical necessity. The complexities inherent in this history underscore the imperative of applying critical scholarly approaches, allowing us to differentiate verifiable historical fact from the layers of cultural mythology that have accumulated over time. By engaging with this past rigorously, we not only honor the true legacy of these arts but also deepen our understanding of their enduring essence.

Kobudo's continued evolution, from its humble, pragmatic origins to its global recognition today, is an ongoing journey, inviting practitioners and scholars alike to perpetually seek a richer, more authentic connection to its rich and layered past.

Notes

1.   The Pechin (親方) were a prominent class within the Ryukyu Kingdom, serving as both scholar-officials in administrative government roles and as a gentry-warrior class responsible for law enforcement and defense. They held a respected position in the social hierarchy and were closely associated with the development of "Te," the indigenous Ryukyuan fighting style that predates modern karate.

2.   The Aji (or Anji) class represented the highest tier of the Ryukyuan aristocracy, second only to the King and his direct heirs. These influential individuals were typically local lords who governed specific territories within the kingdom, often tracing their lineage directly back to the royal family or prominent historical figures. As regional nobility and key figures in the administrative and feudal structure, the Aji held substantial influence and wealth. Their esteemed status led them to be patrons and practitioners of various cultural arts, including the indigenous fighting style known as "Te," thereby playing a crucial role in its preservation and development within their domains. Their authority was essential in maintaining the centralized power of the Ryukyuan monarchy while overseeing the daily affairs and defense of their respective territories.

3.   The Meiji era (1868–1912) marks a period of rapid modernization and centralized imperial rule in Japan. For the Ryukyu Kingdom, this period came to a head with its formal annexation by Japan in 1879, which effectively ended its unique dual tributary relationship with both China and Japan. This integration significantly transformed Okinawa's political, social, and cultural landscape, leading to the implementation of Japanese assimilation policies that also affected the public presentation and organization of Okinawan martial arts.

Ryukyu's Arsenal
From Tools to Weapons

Ingenuity in Iron and Wood

When one thinks of Okinawan martial arts, they often envision focused strikes, powerful stances, and the precise choreography of empty-hand kata. However, this perspective overlooks a crucial aspect of Okinawa's traditional weapons arts known as Kobudo, the martial heritage of the Ryukyu Islands.

Contrary to being secondary to Karate, Okinawan Kobudo exemplifies the resourcefulness and adaptability of a people shaped by political oppression, cultural fusion, and a pragmatic need for self-defense. The weapons used in Kobudo are not relics of a samurai class but rather creative adaptations of everyday tools, including farm implements, fishing gear, and household items, transformed into effective extensions of the body. This evolution was not spontaneous; it was largely driven by the Yukatchu, an educated scholar-official class that, through contact with Chinese martial traditions and formalized training, codified these improvised tools into sophisticated systems of combat.

In this study, we will explore the development and design of Okinawan Kobudo weapons such as the bo (staff), eku (oar), nuntibo (gaff), tonfa (grinding handle), sai (metal truncheon), kama (sickle), nunchaku (flail), and tekko (hand-held striking enhancer). By tracing their trajectory from necessity to refined martial systems, we reveal not only technical ingenuity but also the cultural resilience that enabled a small island kingdom to forge a distinct martial identity under the influence of powerful foreign empires. Through Kobudo, we witness the convergence of survival, scholarship, and creativity—where the ordinary becomes martial and necessity shapes legacy.

The Bo: Foundation of Reach and Rythm

Long before the bo staff was formalized into martial kata, it was an essential tool in everyday life in Okinawa. Commoners used it as a walking stick to navigate the island's rugged terrain and as a tenbin (carrying pole) to balance heavy loads, such as buckets of water, baskets of crops, or firewood across their shoulders. Its simplicity and widespread use made it an ideal concealed weapon: practical, unobtrusive, and entirely unthreatening in appearance.

During the Satsuma occupation, when weapon ownership was restricted for Okinawans, the everyday bo became a subtle form of defense. It was never outright banned, and this loophole was exploited by generations of martial artists who recognized its potential for adaptation and combat utility.

Foreign Inspirations: The Chinese Gùn and Beyond

Exploring the primary weapons of Okinawan Kobudo reveals a rich legacy of creativity and adaptability. These self-defense tools are not just specialized weapons; they represent the impressive transformation of everyday items such as farming tools, fishing gear, and household implements into refined instruments of combat. This evolution was not merely a random discovery of their martial potential; it was a thoughtful and informed adaptation, often inspired by the fighting principles and designs of weapons encountered through Okinawa's extensive cultural exchanges, particularly with China.

Each weapon tells a unique story, ranging from the fundamental bo and its various extensions like the eku and nuntibo, to the distinctive tonfa, the versatile sai, the agricultural kama, the dynamic nunchaku, and the hand-reinforcing tekko. These weapons were born out of practical needs and demonstrate creative martial development. Their original civilian uses provided a discreet advantage for Okinawan practitioners, enabling them to carry and train with tools that, in skilled hands, could serve as formidable means of protection. The connections to other Asian weapons, such as the Chinese gun, Thai mai sok san, and Chinese tai chi, highlight the awareness and influence of Okinawan martial artists in their development.

Japanese influences may also have played a secondary role. Although less directly impactful, knowledge of sojutsu (spear techniques) and naginata-jutsu (halberd arts) introduced additional insights into the use of long weapons, particularly in areas such as distance control, angular defense, and pivoting strikes.

Variants and Evolutions: The Staff Principle Expanded

The bo, characterized by its principle of extending the body's reach through a balanced shaft, laid the foundation for various tools that adapted its effective design. One such tool is the eku, originally a boat paddle, which evolved to embody the bo principles in a heavier and asymmetrical form. The broad blade of the eku can deliver crushing blows, while its unique shape allows for sand-throwing techniques, particularly useful in shoreline combat. More than just a novelty, the eku demands advanced control due to its mass and fluidity, providing distinct tactical advantages in battle.

Another tool reflecting this evolution is the nuntibo, believed to have originated from a fisherman's gaff or harpoon. This weapon features a hook-like protrusion at one end, which can be used in various ways during combat. The hook allows practitioners to trap weapons or limbs, disrupt attackers' balance, and assist in joint manipulations, demonstrating how Kobudo extracts martial value from the challenges of seafaring life.

Additionally, the shorter variants of the bo, known as the jo and hanbo, further illustrate the versatility of this martial concept. The jo measures approximately four feet long, while the hanbo is around three feet. These shorter staffs carry the principles of the bo into closer ranges. Their reduced length facilitates faster transitions, tighter angles, and more compact movements, making them especially suited for confined spaces or close engagements. Like their full-length counterpart, both the jo and hanbo emphasize precision and fluidity over brute force, showcasing the adaptability of the bo across different contexts and combat scenarios.

Why the Bo Endures

The enduring appeal of the bo lies in its universality and elegance. Unlike bladed weapons that require specialized metallurgy or complex designs, the bo is simple, just wood, symmetry, and intention. It helps train posture, power generation, and fluidity of motion while refining timing and distance. Most importantly, it embodies the philosophy of Kobudo: to take the ordinary and make it extraordinary.

The Tonfa: Handle of Control and Power

The tonfa is an impressive weapon that embodies the practical principles of Kobudo, particularly in close-quarters control. Among all the Okinawan Kobudo weapons, the tonfa (or tunfa) stands out as one of the most mechanically ingenious. With its unique perpendicular handle and compact design, the tonfa effectively serves as both a tool and a weapon, showcasing efficiency and adaptability. Initially used as a practical implement, it has been transformed into a highly versatile device for striking, blocking, trapping, and joint control, reflecting the innovative spirit of Okinawan martial culture.

From Millstone to Martial Precision

The most widely accepted theory regarding the origin of the tonfa suggests that it began as a grinding handle. This handle was mounted through a hole in a millstone used for processing rice and grains. Farmers would grip the perpendicular handle and rotate the stone in laborious circles. Some believe that the tonfa may have also served as a lever to draw water from wells.

In either scenario, its ergonomic design, featuring a stout handle perpendicular to a longer shaft, was intended for functional use rather than combat. However, within its simplicity lies hidden potential. Its compact size, natural grip, and rotational axis are easily translated into effective martial techniques.

Combat Mechanics of Shield and Lever

The tonfa's design allows for a variety of effective combat applications, showcasing its versatility as a weapon. One of its primary functions is blocking; when held against the forearm, the tonfa can absorb and redirect incoming strikes, significantly enhancing the user's defensive capabilities. Its unique curved movement facilitates active parrying, providing not only passive defense but also a means to effectively deflect attacks.

In addition to blocking, the tonfa serves as a powerful striking tool. The extended shaft, which reaches beyond the elbow, allows for dynamic whipping strikes that utilize centrifugal force. This enables the user to deliver impactful blows with considerable speed and power. The butt end of the tonfa can also provide focused, bone-breaking impacts when necessary, while the short end of the tonfa becomes an effective thrusting tool, allowing for precise targeting of vital areas with pinpoint accuracy.

Furthermore, the tonfa is invaluable for executing joint locks and traps. Its perpendicular handle offers excellent leverage, making it an effective instrument for immobilizing joints and pinning limbs. This aspect of the tonfa is particularly beneficial in grappling situations, where control and compliance techniques are essential.

Together, these techniques demonstrate that the tonfa is not merely a striking tool; it also serves as a means of non-lethal control. This characteristic aligns with the historical needs of Okinawa's administrative class, who often sought to subdue opponents without resorting to lethal force.

Inspirations and Parallels: A Weapon Across Borders

The tonfa's distinctive shape is not unique to Okinawa. Similar designs appear in various Southeast Asian and East Asian martial traditions, suggesting either shared origins or parallel evolution based on similar functional needs.

- In Thailand, the Mai Sok San closely resembles the tonfa in both structure and usage, serving as a tool of both agriculture and self-defense.
- In China, the weapon called guai, a crutch-like implement, shares linguistic and physical similarities. Likewise, the Malay word topang translates to "crutch," indicating regional patterns of dual-use tools evolving into combat gear.

What distinguishes the Okinawan tonfa is the depth of its systematization. Through kata and partnered drills, its use was elevated from intuitive improvisation to a fully developed martial discipline.

A Weapon of Discipline, Not Desperation

The common belief that Okinawan peasants secretly turned their farm tools into weapons in response to oppressive bans has proven to be a myth. In reality, the tonfa was intentionally integrated into martial arts systems with a strategic purpose. Its use requires strength, coordination, and rotational control, all qualities that reflect the benefits of formal training rather than spontaneous development.

The tonfa's lasting significance in Kobudo, along with its contemporary use by police forces worldwide as the PR-24 baton, highlights its effectiveness. It represents more than just a remnant of Okinawa's agricultural history; it is a weapon of sophisticated design and tactical versatility, shaped by necessity, refined through knowledge, and preserved through tradition.

The Sai: Trident of Control and Restraint

Among Okinawan Kobudo weapons, the sai stands apart; sleek, symmetrical, and forged from metal rather than carved from wood. With its central shaft flanked by two curved prongs (yoku), the sai is often misunderstood as a simple agricultural tool-turned-weapon. In truth, its design suggests a deliberate martial origin, one deeply connected to law enforcement, restraint, and the ability to neutralize an adversary without resorting to lethal force.

More Than a Farmer's Tool

Popular legend often depicts the sai as a farming tool used for planting rice or digging soil. However, this theory quickly falls apart upon closer examination. In pre-modern Okinawa, metal was both scarce and expensive, making it an unlikely choice for everyday agricultural tasks. Wooden tools would have been sufficient for these purposes, and there are no historical records or archaeological findings that support the sai's use in farming.

In contrast, historical and structural evidence suggests that the sai was a weapon from the beginning, specifically, a tool for policing and control. Its design is more suited for subduing rather than harming. The sai's non-lethal potential, durable construction, and versatility in both defense and restraint indicate that it may have been used by officials and retainers to maintain order under the rule of local lords or Ryukyuan magistrates.

Precision, Restraint, and Versatility

When wielded by skilled practitioners, the sai becomes an extension of the body, providing a versatile combination of control, targeted strikes, and effective defense. Unlike weapons primarily designed for cutting, the sai emphasizes precision over brute force. Its sturdy structure and outward yoku (side guards) make it ideal for catching and redirecting attacks from various offensive tools, including sticks, blades, and fists. A practitioner can quickly twist their wrist to trap an opponent's weapon or limb within the yoku, gaining a mechanical advantage to control or disarm them.

In addition to trapping, the sai can deliver concussive strikes using its shaft and butt end. The blunt metal tip acts similarly to a truncheon, enabling practitioners to target nerve centers, bones, or soft tissue with disabling force without necessarily breaking the skin. The central prong is designed for precise thrusts into pressure points, joints, or the solar plexus, aiming to disable rather than to destroy.

Moreover, the unique design of the sai allows for exceptional joint manipulation. Practitioners can pin wrists, elbows, or ankles using the curved yoku, or apply pressure with the shaft to force compliance. This ability to trap, lock, and control truly elevates the sai beyond a simple baton or truncheon, making it a complete grappling weapon for those trained in its intricate mechanics.

Forged in a Broader Asian Context

The presence of the sai in Okinawa is not unique; rather, it reflects a broader regional lineage of similar three-pronged metal weapons found throughout Asia. For example, the Chinese Tie Chi, also known as the Iron Ruler, is a comparable metal baton used in close-quarters martial arts for both defensive purposes and control. Meanwhile, the Japanese Jutte, a single-pronged iron truncheon, holds historical significance as it was carried by police during the Edo period. This tool was specifically designed to capture and subdue swordsmen without causing fatal injuries.

Additionally, the Indian Trishula, while primarily symbolic, shares a resemblance to the sai due to its iconic trident shape. However, its ceremonial role distinguishes it from practical combat applications. These cultural connections suggest that the sai was likely imported or adapted from existing military or policing tools, rather than having been independently invented as a simple farming implement.

The Scholar-Warrior's Baton

The sai, with its unique structure and effectiveness in non-lethal combat, fits seamlessly into the Yukatchu toolkit. Literate scholars and Confucian-trained officials, tasked with maintaining order, required weapons that asserted authority without resorting to excessive violence. The sai was an ideal choice: intimidating, functional, and versatile, it met the nuanced demands of restraint rather than relying solely on raw power.

In today's practice of Okinawan Kobudo, the sai's combative depth is preserved through classical kata that emphasize timing, interception, and control rather than brute force. The weapon's elegance lies in its ability to neutralize threats without unnecessary harm, disarm opponents without injury, and assert authority without creating chaos.

As such, the sai remains one of the most intellectually and technically rich weapons in the Okinawan arsenal, standing as a quiet testament to the discipline, foresight, and cultural interconnectedness that defines classical Kobudo.

The Kama: Blade of the Fields

Of all the tools-turned-weapons in the Okinawan arsenal, none better embodies the blurred line between agriculture and martial arts than the kama. Its sickle-shaped blade, originally designed to cut crops at their base, became a symbol of transformation; of turning labor into lethality, survival into strategy. When wielded as a weapon, the kama offers both devastating slashing power and remarkable finesse, bridging the physical demands of rural life with the refined techniques of combative movement.

Harvesting Life from the Soil

The kama originated primarily as a harvesting tool. Widely used by farmers in Okinawa to harvest rice, sugarcane, and grains, it played a crucial role in agricultural survival. Its curved blade allowed for efficient cutting at ground level, while its compact size made it portable, easy to handle, and accessible even to the poorest villagers.

In addition to harvesting crops, the kama had secondary uses, such as clearing underbrush, cutting thatching for roofs, and weeding fields. Because it was so commonly found, it was often carried or kept nearby, making it an ideal choice for improvised self-defense during a time when the carrying of weapons was strictly prohibited under Satsuma rule.

However, the kama's transition into the realm of martial arts was not a spontaneous act of desperation. Instead, it represented a deliberate and strategic adaptation, likely initiated by educated martial scholars in Okinawa who recognized the potential to transform simple tools into effective instruments for structured combat training.

Cutting Precision and Grappling Versatility

The kama, recognized by its distinctive right-angled blade, is a unique weapon used in Okinawa. Its design allows practitioners to perform a variety of techniques that are both lethal and versatile. One of its primary offensive capabilities is the curved blade, which enables clean, arcing slashes that can effectively sever muscles, arteries, or tendons. When wielded in pairs, a practitioner can execute a series of rapid slashes that may overwhelm even the most skilled opponent.

In addition to its slashing abilities, the sickle shape of the kama facilitates hooking and trapping maneuvers. This feature allows practitioners to catch or deflect incoming weapons and limbs, effectively pulling opponents off balance or redirecting their energy. Moreover, the kama's blade can be employed for joint manipulation and disarming techniques. By hooking around critical points such as wrists or elbows, practitioners can apply pressure to joints, using leverage from the handle to execute joint locks or entrap limbs, a skill that distinguishes the kama from other bladed instruments.

Additionally, while the kama's edges are sharp, practitioners can also utilize the flat or spine edge to block or parry incoming strikes, provided they maintain precise control over the angle. This dual nature—combining offensive strikes with controlling techniques—makes the kama a particularly dangerous weapon. It demands skillful timing and emphasizes the importance of angle manipulation and spatial awareness, allowing practitioners to navigate the complexities of combat effectively.

A Global Tool

The kama is arguably the most universal of all Kobudo weapons, as its basic form can be found in agrarian cultures worldwide. Similar curved blades used for harvesting are present throughout East and Southeast

Asia, Europe, and Africa. However, Okinawa's formalization of the kama into structured martial kata distinguishes it from these other forms.

Although the Okinawan kama may not be directly modeled on any specific foreign weapon, it likely absorbed principles from Chinese southern weapon systems, which also utilize sickle-like blades in paired applications. For example, the Chinese lian dāo (a sickle with a chain) demonstrates how similar tools were creatively adapted for combat, though its flexible chain sets it apart in practice.

More significant than any foreign influence is the philosophy of adaptation itself. Okinawan martial artists, especially the Yukatchu, observed functional designs from various cultures and applied those insights to their available tools. The evolution of the kama into a weapon was an intellectual act of synthesis, driven not merely by necessity, but by a thoughtful integration of ideas.

From Fields to Forms

The use of the kama in formal kata clearly demonstrates evidence of scholarly codification. The movements are carefully structured around angular cuts, positional traps, and fluid transitions between offense and defense. This reflects a deliberate effort to elevate the kama beyond mere instinct, situating it within the broader, interconnected framework of Okinawan Te and Kobudo.

Unlike other weapons in the arsenal, the kama exudes a sense of dangerous elegance. Its blade is curved like a crescent moon, and its movements are compact yet lethal. It does not rely on brute force; instead, it emphasizes mechanics, deception, and precision; principles that are deeply rooted in Okinawan martial philosophy.

The Nunchaku: From Flail to Fury

Few weapons from the Okinawan arsenal have captured the global imagination quite like the nunchaku. Immortalized in popular media and martial arts demonstrations, its dramatic whipping strikes and blurred arcs embody fluidity, speed, and danger. However, beneath its flashy appearance lies a weapon with practical origins and a surprisingly sophisticated history of adaptation.

Originally used as an agricultural or equestrian tool, the nunchaku showcases the Okinawan talent for improvisation. It was reimagined through the lens of Chinese flexible weapon theory and refined into a combat system within the broader framework of Kobudo.

Original Use: Flail or Bridle? The Debate of Origins

The nunchaku's exact origin remains contested, but two primary theories prevail:

- **Rice Flail Theory**: The more common interpretation places the nunchaku's roots in farming, as a tool for threshing grain. The two sticks connected by rope or chain resemble a traditional flail, used to beat rice stalks and separate husks from grain. This design allowed for mechanical leverage and repetitive striking; concepts later adapted for martial use.

- **Equestrian Bit Theory**: A less discussed but plausible theory suggests that the nunchaku began as a horse bridle or control bit. In this version, the sticks formed part of the reins or control mechanism, with the rope aiding in restraint and guidance. This is supported by Okinawa's use of horses and the practicality of adapting tack hardware for defensive purposes.

Regardless of its original function, the nunchaku shares a consistent trait with other Kobudo weapons: it was accessible, inconspicuous, and easily transformed into a means of protection, especially in a society where overt weapons were restricted.

Dynamic Striking and Entanglement

The nunchaku stands out in the martial arts world due to its unpredictable movement and flexible dynamics. Unlike rigid weapons, its dual-stick design allows practitioners to harness explosive energy and redirect forces in ways that can be challenging for opponents to counter.

A key technique involving the nunchaku is the use of whipping strikes. By leveraging centrifugal force, practitioners can deliver powerful, high-velocity strikes from various angles, adding speed and deception to their attacks. Additionally, the cord or chain connecting the two sticks enables a range of control techniques. This allows users to wrap, trap, or entangle their opponent's limbs or weapons, creating opportunities for follow-up techniques that can shift the momentum of a confrontation.

In close-range encounters, the nunchaku can be particularly effective for applying joint locks by encircling an opponent's arm, wrist, or neck, the practitioner can exert pressure and leverage, establishing dominant control over the opponent's movements. Furthermore, even when used in a single-stick configuration, the nunchaku can serve as a bludgeoning tool. Strikes can be delivered using either the shaft or the pommel, similar to a short baton or truncheon.

Ultimately, mastering the nunchaku requires a strong sense of timing, flow, and kinesthetic awareness. The weapon rewards precision over brute strength, with its effectiveness relying on factors such as momentum, angle control, and rhythm. This dynamic nature makes the nunchaku akin to a flail used in agricultural settings, showcasing the beauty of its movement in martial practice.

The Flexible Arsenal of Asia

The nunchaku, while distinctly Okinawan in its development, shares conceptual similarities with several weapons across East Asia, including the Two-section Staff, Three-section Staff, Rope Dart, and Meteor Hammer.

The Chinese Two-section Staff, known as the Shuang Jie Gun, is a flail-like weapon used in various southern Chinese martial arts. It is especially effective for striking and entangling opponents due to its high rotational energy. Its design and functionality likely inspired the later development of the nunchaku.

Another important Chinese weapon is the Three-section Staff, or San Jie Gun. This variant features additional articulation, enhancing its versatility while still utilizing the core mechanics of centrifugal motion, wrapping, and manipulation through chain-like movements.

Additionally, the Rope Dart and Meteor Hammer are flexible weapons that require a high level of skill and offer unpredictability in combat. Both can be used to bind and strike from unexpected angles, making them effective for long-range attacks. Although they differ structurally from the nunchaku, they embody the same fluidity and adaptability present in nunchaku practice, showcasing the diverse range of weaponry found in Chinese martial arts.

Through cultural exchange and trade, Okinawan scholars may have observed these weapons firsthand or encountered their concepts through written materials or direct instruction. As a result, the nunchaku likely emerged as a localized response to these influences, adapted to the available materials and the social context of the Ryukyu Islands.

The Scholar's Refinement From Tool to Kata

The nunchaku, like other Kobudo weapons, did not develop solely through random trial and error. Its incorporation into structured kata, particularly within systems such as Matayoshi Kobudo, demonstrates purposeful refinement in teaching methods. The movements are codified, transitions are clearly mapped, and striking sequences highlight both the realism of martial arts and the importance of physical control.

Although often perceived as flashy or challenging to handle, the nunchaku, when wielded by a skilled practitioner, exemplifies principles such as flow, range manipulation, and transitional power. These concepts are central to the Okinawan martial arts philosophy.

The Tekko: Reinforced Fist, Relentless Impact

Among the more understated weapons of Okinawan Kobudo, the tekko occupies a unique position as both a practical tool for improvisation and an extremely effective enhancement to unarmed techniques. Compact and easily concealed, the tekko serves not as a standalone weapon but as an extension of the fist itself, increasing the power of every strike with devastating efficiency.

Its development highlights a central theme in Okinawan martial culture: the transformation of everyday materials into tools for survival, shaped by necessity, ingenuity, and external influences.

Repurposed from Equestrian Gear

The tekko, sturdy, curved iron implements that could be modified to fit around the knuckles, are widely believed to have been repurposed from horse stirrups or horseshoes. In a society where metal was scarce and often reused, these durable items offered both availability and practicality.

The curved structure of the stirrup naturally aligned with the shape of the human fist, allowing it to enhance punches without compromising the hand's flexibility. Some variations of tekko were likely made from wood or carved coral, shaped to fit comfortably in the palm and extend slightly beyond the knuckles.

Their non-threatening civilian appearance made them an ideal choice in an environment where carrying weapons could raise suspicion under the watchful eyes of authorities.

Amplifying the Natural Weapon

A distinctive martial arts weapon that enhances the striking power of the human hand without significantly changing the mechanics of a punch, the tekko focuses and concentrates force while also providing protection. Their design includes a striking surface reinforced with metal or dense wood, which increases the impact of a punch. This reinforcement concentrates the energy into a smaller area, resulting in greater tissue damage; even a glancing blow can incapacitate an opponent.

Beyond its offensive capabilities, the curved frame of the tekko serves a vital defensive role. It can intercept or deflect incoming strikes, functioning like a small shield that protects the knuckles and forearm from injury.

Furthermore, some designs of the tekko feature protruding edges or hooks, allowing practitioners to employ trapping and limb control techniques. These features enable the effective snaring or hooking of an opponent's wrist or weapon, making for a seamless transition between striking and grappling.

Certain variations of the tekko also incorporate sharpened or ridged points, making them suitable for raking or tearing flesh. This design blurs the distinction between blunt force trauma and cutting attacks, providing the user with versatile options in combat situations.

When used alongside traditional kata or empty-hand techniques (te), the tekko become a natural enhancement within the Okinawan martial arts system, rather than merely an accessory.

Global Knuckle Weapons

The concept of reinforcing the fist is not exclusive to Okinawa; it has been present in various forms across different cultures and historical periods. For instance, in traditional Chinese martial arts, practitioners use a tool known as Tie Quan, or Iron Fist. This device consists of iron rings or guards that serve dual purposes: conditioning the hands and enhancing combat effectiveness. Similarly, in Western history, brass knuckles have been used in Europe and America as practical tools to maximize punching power in close-quarter confrontations.

Japan also has its own version of hand reinforcement called the kakute. Although more specialized, the kakute is designed to enhance control and deliver damage in tight situations, often worn discreetly.

What sets the tekko apart is its unique adaptation within the Ryukyuan context. Typically made from scavenged or reshaped materials, the tekko became an integral part of the kata systems in various Kobudo lineages, showcasing a rich tradition of martial arts innovation.

Strategic Simplicity

The simplicity of the tekko hides its strategic value. It requires no complicated techniques to function effectively, yet it demands discipline and restraint. In the wrong hands, its amplified force can cause unintended harm; in the right hands, it acts as a precise tool for control and protection.

Its ongoing use in Okinawan Kobudo today serves as a reminder of martial pragmatism: that the art of fighting is not always about flair or size, but rather about intent, adaptation, and efficiency.

A Legacy Forged in Necessity

The legacy of Okinawan Kobudo is not merely inscribed in steel and ceremony but manifests itself in the quiet ingenuity of survival. It embodies the transformation of everyday items, farming tools, fishing gear, and simple implements, into sophisticated instruments of self-defense. Far from being an eccentric footnote to Karate, the traditional weapons of Okinawa reflect the resourceful and resilient spirit of the Ryukyuan people, particularly in the face of external occupation and political suppression.

These weapons are not mere relics; they represent embodied principles of leverage, adaptation, and strategy, passed down through kata, oral tradition, and hands-on instruction. Each weapon carries the imprint of daily life repurposed into combat insights, echoing the broader narrative of a culture that found ways to endure, protect, and refine its martial identity despite external limitations.

The bo, originally a water-carrying pole, becomes a long-range tool for reach and redirection. The tonfa, originally a grinding handle, transforms into a weapon that utilizes rotational force and joint control. The sai, which lacks any practical farming function, stands as a reminder that some tools were always intended as weapons, deliberately adapted from outside sources to fulfill internal needs. The kama, a sickle from the field, evolves into a blade of close-quarters lethality. The nunchaku, with its centrifugal chaos, and the tekko, known for its amplified impact, illustrate how motion and form can be reimagined for martial purposes.

A significant influence on this martial landscape was the Yukatchu class, the educated elite who possessed the means, exposure, and motivation to study foreign systems and formalize their adaptations into kata. While the myth of "peasant weapons" continues to capture modern imaginations, historical records indicate a deliberate, literate, and strategic synthesis of martial arts, deeply informed by Chinese military theory, trade contacts, and the challenges of self-governance under foreign rule.

In exploring these weapons, we delve deeper than just learning how to strike, trap, or defend; we engage with the lived experiences of Okinawa's martial innovators. Their inventiveness, adaptability, and pragmatism remind us that martial arts are not merely collections of techniques; they are cultural expressions of resilience.

Today, the study of Kobudo encourages practitioners to look beyond the surface, allowing us to comprehend how environment, necessity, and creative spirit converge in the act of martial creation. This legacy is not only worthy of preservation but also of active engagement, both on the dojo floor and within the broader scholarly conversation about the evolution of martial traditions.

In the end, the greatest weapon of Okinawan Kobudo may not be the bo, the sai, or the kama. Rather, it is the mind that recognized potential in the mundane and the hand that dared to transform it.

Beyond the Surface
Re-framing Karate as an Extension of Kobudo

Rediscovering the Integrated Warrior

In the vast and diverse landscape of global martial arts, Okinawan Karate stands as a towering and widely recognized discipline. Its dynamic strikes, disciplined forms, and emphasis on self-improvement have captivated millions, propelling it from a secretive island tradition to a dynamic art practiced across continents. The pervasive modern perception often casts Karate as a purely weaponless martial art, a system developed in isolation, distinct from the intricate weapon-based practices known as Kobudo. This popular image often portrays the "empty hand" warrior as fundamentally distinct from their armed counterpart, with each evolving along independent paths.

However, a closer examination reveals that this widely held notion of separate development for Okinawan Karate and Kobudo is often unsubstantiated and oversimplified. It is a perspective that overlooks the deeper historical and conceptual connections that bind these two facets of Ryukyu's combative heritage. This paper argues that Karate didn't develop in isolation, but rather evolved as an extension of a broader, integrated Ryukyu martial culture that incorporated weapon training

(Kobudo). This integrated view suggests a shared lineage, common core principles, and intertwined training methodologies that later historical narratives and modernization processes have obscured.

To illuminate this integrated legacy, we will embark on a journey to reframe the relationship between Okinawa's empty-hand and weapon arts. We will begin by challenging prevalent myths surrounding their origins, and then explore the historical evidence that indicates their deep intertwining. Subsequently, we will detail their shared foundational roots in Chinese martial traditions and analyze the common body mechanics and training methods that transcend the distinction between armed and unarmed combat. Finally, we will examine the impact of modernization and systematization on their perceived separation, ultimately arguing for a more complete understanding of the Ryukyu martial tradition.

Myth of the Weaponless Warrior

The popular narrative surrounding the genesis of Okinawan Kobudo often paints a romanticized, yet largely inaccurate, picture. It suggests that, following historical weapon bans in Okinawa, the disenfranchised peasant class secretly developed fighting techniques using everyday farm implements, such as the bo (staff), sai (three-pronged truncheon), and nunchaku (flail), as improvised weapons to defend themselves against the armed samurai. This "peasant weapons" narrative, while compelling, has unfortunately permeated public understanding and contributed significantly to the perception of Kobudo as a distinct, folk-based art, separate from the more formalized empty-hand practices. However, critical analysis of historical evidence reveals this to be a pervasive myth, one that obscures the actual, more sophisticated origins of these martial traditions.

In reality, evidence strongly suggests that Kobudo, and by extension the indigenous empty-hand fighting art known as te, were indeed practiced by the nobility (Aji), aristocrats (Ueekata), and scholarly warrior class (Pechin) within the Ryukyu Kingdom[1]. Far from being crude peasant improvisations, these weapon arts were sophisticated combative systems, often influenced by the martial traditions of China and Japan. The weapons themselves, such as the bo and sai, were not merely farm tools but legitimate instruments of war and defense, requiring specialized training and intricate knowledge of leverage, distance, and anatomy. This aristocratic and martial background reflects a level of complexity and formal instruction that contradicts the notion of their spontaneous emergence from agricultural necessity.

To really understand the roots of Okinawan martial arts, we must first embrace the concept of a complete Ryukyuan martial culture. Within this integrated framework, weapon and empty-hand skills were not viewed as disparate or opposing disciplines but as complementary components of a complete fighting system. A practitioner was not simply a "weaponless warrior" or an "armed combatant," but rather an integrated martial artist capable of adapting their skills to various combative scenarios, whether armed or unarmed. This reframing lays the groundwork for understanding Karate not as an isolated development, but as a natural extension of this comprehensive and interconnected martial heritage.

Weapons and Empty-hand's Shared Lineage

Moving beyond the myth of separate development, historical indications strongly suggest that Karate and Kobudo did not evolve in isolation, but rather in a parallel and complementary fashion. Evidence points to a martial landscape where practitioners frequently trained in both disciplines, viewing them as two sides of the same combative coin. This perspective is reinforced by the observation that modern Okinawan Karate and Kobudo are often considered two sides of the same coin, a testament to their deep-rooted symbiosis. This is no mere modern connection, but a historical intertwining that reflects a practical reality where a truly skilled warrior would cultivate proficiency in both armed and unarmed methods, seamlessly transitioning between them as necessity dictated.

The secretive nature of early martial arts transmission in Okinawa further supports the idea that comprehensive training, encompassing both empty-hand and weapon skills, was likely the norm within specific lineages and master-disciple relationships. Far from specializing in one over the other, masters would impart a holistic understanding of combat. A good example of this mix can be found right in traditional weapon forms. For instance, Soeishi No Kun Dai, a prominent bo form, is notably one of the few authentic Okinawan Kobudo kata to incorporate an empty-hand technique (a kick) as a penultimate movement. This inclusion within a dedicated weapon form directly demonstrates that even within weapon-specific training, the principles and applications of empty-hand combat were recognized and integrated, signifying a unified approach to martial development.

Indeed, the historical reality of integrated training is vividly demonstrated through the lives of prominent Okinawan martial arts masters renowned for their proficiency in both empty-hand and weapon arts. Figures such as Chatan Yara[2] (1668–1756) stand out as pivotal examples. Credited with disseminating te throughout Okinawa, Yara was a celebrated weaponry master, exceptionally skilled in the use of the bo, tonfa, and particularly the sai. Similarly, Kojoshiku Shinpo[3] (1647-1721) is recognized for his profound influence on the development of both Karate and Kobudo, especially bojutsu. Historical accounts indicate that he taught both kobudo and empty-handed martial arts, further solidifying the image of masters who imparted a complete combative curriculum.

Even later figures like Matsumura Sokon[4] (1809–1899), a foundational figure in modern Shorin-ryu, is understood to have synthesized various empty-hand te styles with Chinese Shaolin influences, building upon a lineage that included masters like Sakugawa Kanga[5], who developed bo kata and was known for combining Chinese kenpo with Okinawan te, and even Japanese kenjutsu (Jigen-ryu). These examples collectively illustrate that the historical "weaponless warrior" was often, in practice, a comprehensively trained martial artist whose empty-hand skills were deeply informed by, and an extension of, their armed expertise.

Chinese Root of the Okinawan Martial Arts

The deeper we delve into the historical currents of Okinawan martial arts, the more undeniable the influence of various Chinese martial arts becomes, serving as a common and foundational point of origin for both Karate and Kobudo.

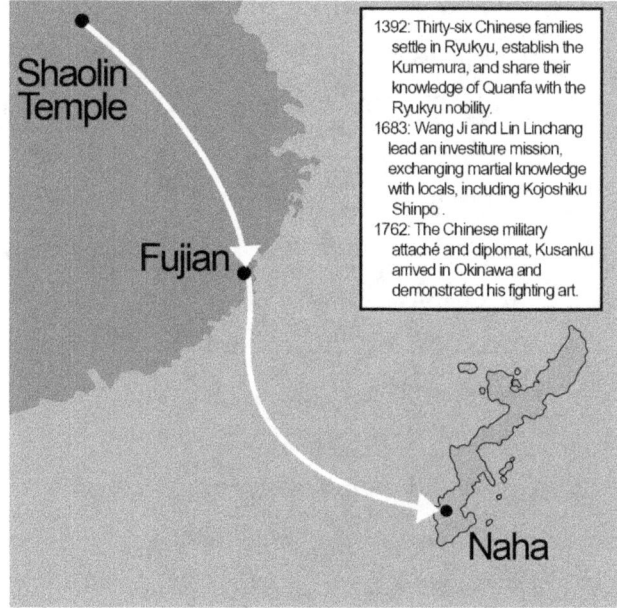

1392: Thirty-six Chinese families settle in Ryukyu, establish the Kumemura, and share their knowledge of Quanfa with the Ryukyu nobility.
1683: Wang Ji and Lin Linchang lead an investiture mission, exchanging martial knowledge with locals, including Kojoshiku Shinpo.
1762: The Chinese military attaché and diplomat, Kusanku arrived in Okinawa and demonstrated his fighting art.

Systems like Baihe Quan[6] (Fujian White Crane Fist) and Luohan Quan[7] (Shaolin Arhat Fist) represent the rich tapestry of Chinese combative systems that flowed into the Ryukyu Kingdom over centuries of trade, diplomacy, and cultural exchange. This influx of knowledge provided a shared wellspring from which many of the fundamental principles and techniques of both empty-hand and weapon arts emerged. From stances and footwork to power generation and strategic application, the echoes of Chinese methods resonate through the Okinawan traditions, establishing an integrated heritage long before any perceived separation.

A Universal Principle: Integration Across Martial Traditions

The integration of weapon and empty-hand combat is not a peculiar characteristic confined solely to the Ryukyu Kingdom or its Chinese influences; rather, it represents a universal principle of martial development, one that is echoed across diverse societies and throughout history. Around the world, complete training, both armed and unarmed, was seen as necessary for real combat skill.

- **Chinese Wushu:** Within historical Chinese martial arts, the distinction between armed and unarmed combat was often fluid, with weapon training inherently integrated into empty-hand methodologies. Masters of various Wushu styles viewed weapons—be it the sword (jian, dao), staff (gun), or spear (qiang)—as direct extensions of the body. The same fundamental body mechanics, footwork, balance, and power generation cultivated through extensive empty-hand practice were seamlessly transferred and applied to weapon manipulation. This integrated approach meant that a practitioner's unarmed skill directly informed their armed prowess, and vice versa, creating a unified and adaptable fighting system.

- **Japanese Koryu Budo:** Classical Japanese martial arts schools, collectively known as Koryu Budo, similarly provided integrated systems of combat, particularly for the samurai class. Disciplines such as Kenjutsu (swordsmanship), Jujutsu (unarmed grappling and close-quarters combat), and Bojutsu (staff fighting) were rarely taught in isolation. Instead, they developed a cohesive curriculum designed to prepare warriors for any combative scenario. The sophisticated body movements, strategic principles, and cultivation of maai (combative distance) learned with a blade were directly applicable to unarmed encounters, and the grappling techniques often served as the crucial link in disarms or transitions between weapons.

- **Indian Martial Arts (e.g., Kalaripayattu):** Ancient Indian martial traditions, epitomized by the southern Indian art of Kalaripayattu, offer another compelling example of seamless weapon-empty-hand integration. Training typically begins with rigorous physical conditioning and unarmed combat, focusing on strikes, locks, and vital point attacks. This foundational empty-hand mastery then progresses to the use of various weapons, including the sword, shield, spear, dagger, and flexible sword (urumi). The profound understanding of human anatomy, leverage, and body control developed in unarmed practice is directly and continuously applied to weapon mastery, affirming both aspects as intrinsically linked facets of the same combative art.

- **Other Traditions:** This principle extends even further across global martial landscapes. In Filipino martial arts, such as Arnis, practitioners often learn weapon techniques (e.g., stick and knife) first, with the understanding that these skills are directly transferable to empty-hand combat; the weapon is simply a "longer arm." Similarly, Indonesian martial arts, like Silat, frequently integrate weapon training (like the kris or staff) as a natural extension of their fluid empty-hand movements and close-quarters grappling. Even in the historical martial arts of Europe, medieval and Renaissance fighting manuals often depicted integrated training that combined swordplay with wrestling, dagger fighting, and unarmed grappling, demonstrating a comprehensive approach to self-defense that transcended the simple armed/unarmed dichotomy.

These diverse examples illustrate that the integrated development of weapon and empty-hand skills is not merely an incidental feature but a testament to a universal understanding of effective combat, rooted in efficiency, adaptability, and a holistic view of the human body as the ultimate weapon, capable of extension.

Mechanics & Methods: Weapons as Limb Extensions

Building upon the understanding that weapon and empty-hand integration is a universal principle woven into the fabric of effective martial traditions globally, we now turn to the specific manifestations of this synergy within the Okinawan context. Here, the profound connection between Karate and Kobudo becomes evident through their shared underlying principles, body mechanics, and mutually reinforcing training methodologies.

At its core, the concept of weapons as limb extension is central to understanding the seamless relationship between Kobudo and Karate. Many Kobudo techniques are not distinct combative innovations but rather direct applications of the same body mechanics and principles found in empty-hand Karate, simply augmented by a weapon. The staff (bo), for instance, often follows the same trajectories and generates power from the same core rotation and hip movement as a Karate punch or block. The sai can be wielded with the wrist rotation and internal drive reminiscent of shuto uke (knife-hand block) or nukite (spear hand). This perspective clarifies that the weapon is not an external tool grafted onto the body, but rather an integral extension, requiring the same foundational body control, balance, and kinetic chain generation inherent in unarmed techniques.

This integration is underpinned by universal principles cultivated in both empty-hand and weapon training. Essential attributes such as rootedness (grounding through the feet), internal power (efficient transfer of force from the core), and precision of movement are not specific to either armed or unarmed combat, but are foundational to both. A strong, stable stance, vital for generating power in a Karate punch, is equally crucial for delivering a devastating bo strike or maintaining balance when wielding nunchaku. The development of a connected body, where movement initiates from the center and extends efficiently to the extremities (whether a fist or a staff tip), is the shared objective, demonstrating that the training for one inherently builds the capacity for the other.

Consequently, there is a remarkable degree of transferable skills between empty-hand and weapon training, creating a symbiotic loop that enhances overall martial prowess. Training extensively with kobudo weapons significantly enhances empty-hand skills; for instance, the continuous manipulation of a sai or tonfa builds exceptional grip strength and wrist conditioning, invaluable for grappling or close-quarters striking in Karate. It also refines one's understanding of range, leverage, and timing; critical elements for both armed and unarmed combat. Conversely, the precise footwork, balance, and explosive power generation honed through dedicated empty-hand kata and kihon practice directly translate to more effective and powerful applications with weapons. The ability to move efficiently, generate force from the ground up, and maintain a strong core, developed through unarmed training, is indispensable for wielding any weapon with true mastery. This reciprocal relationship highlights that, rather than being separate entities, Karate and Kobudo are fundamentally interlinked, with each discipline enriching and reinforcing the other within a unified combative framework.

Shared Principles

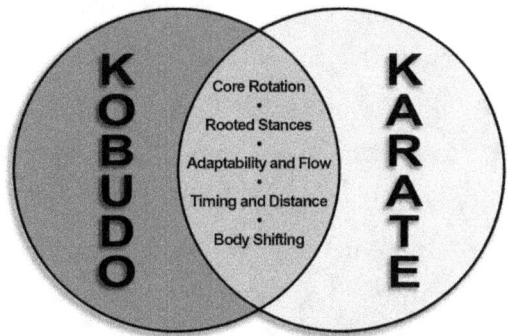

K
O
B
U
D
O

Core Rotation
•
Rooted Stances
•
Adaptability and Flow
•
Timing and Distance
•
Body Shifting

K
A
R
A
T
E

# of Karate and Kobudo

Divergence Through Modernization

Despite the compelling historical and functional evidence of an integrated martial tradition, the modern era witnessed a profound shift that led to the gradual de-emphasis and, ultimately, the explicit separation of Kobudo from Karate. This divergence can be largely attributed to the modernization and institutionalization of Karate, beginning primarily in the early 20th century. When Karate transitioned from secretive family or village traditions to public instruction, specifically its introduction into the Okinawan public school system and its subsequent emphasis as a form of physical education, its very nature began to transform. This shift, coupled with the later development of sport Karate, inadvertently cultivated a specialized, weaponless identity that gradually overshadowed its comprehensive roots.

The need for broader accessibility and safety in public instructional settings was a primary driver for this simplification. Teaching weapon arts to large groups of schoolchildren or new, untrained practitioners posed obvious safety concerns and required specialized equipment that was not readily available. Consequently, weaponless forms were prioritized, leading to a marginalization of integrated training. This process was further exacerbated by the post-World War II period, where, under the Allied occupation, there was a general discouragement of martial arts and weapon training. While not a direct ban, the prevailing atmosphere and the desire for karate to be seen as a harmless, character-building physical exercise rather than a combative art, solidified its public identity as purely empty-handed. This era cemented the perception that weapons were a distinct and separate discipline, effectively removing them from the mainstream karate curriculum for mass instruction.

This modern specialization stands in stark contrast to the comprehensive, integrated training approach characteristic of older (koryu) traditions, not only in Okinawa but also in the global martial arts we explored previously. In the formalized dojo setting or the competitive arena, the intricacies of weapon handling became secondary, if not entirely absent, from the focus, only seeing a resurgence in the late 20th century. The rigorous, holistic development that encompassed both armed and unarmed techniques, once a hallmark of the serious martial artist, gave way to an emphasis on codified empty-hand kata and competitive kumite. This divergence fundamentally reshaped public understanding and the practical transmission of Okinawan martial arts, paving the way for the "weaponless warrior" archetype to become the dominant image of Karate.

Reclaiming the Complete Warrior

The journey through the historical currents and underlying principles of Okinawan martial arts reveals a truth often obscured by modern perceptions: Karate, far from being a purely weaponless and independently developed discipline, is fundamentally an extension of a cohesive Okinawan martial culture that historically integrated both empty-hand and weapon skills. The "weaponless warrior" archetype, while compelling, is ultimately a simplified portrayal that belies the rich, comprehensive nature of these fighting traditions.

Our exploration has sought to systematically dismantle the pervasive myth of Kobudo's origins as crude "peasant weapons," demonstrating instead its sophisticated practice within the Ryukyu nobility and warrior class. We have seen how historical indications consistently point to the parallel and complementary development of empty-hand te and weapon arts, with prominent masters renowned for their proficiency in both, as exemplified by figures like Chatan Yara and Matsu Higa. The profound and undeniable influence of Chinese martial arts on both Karate and Kobudo further establishes a common ancestral lineage, rooting them in a unified combative philosophy. Moreover, by examining the universal principle of weapon-empty-hand integration across diverse global martial traditions, from Chinese Wushu and Japanese Koryu Budo to Indian Kalaripayattu and beyond, we have underscored that Okinawa's integrated approach was not an anomaly but a logical and effective method for comprehensive combative training. Within this framework, the concept of weapons as "extended limbs" highlights the shared body mechanics and universal qualities like rootedness and internal power, fostering a remarkable degree of transferable skills between armed and unarmed practice. Ultimately, it was the pressures of modernization, institutionalization in public education, and the rise of sportification, particularly in the post-World War II era, that led to the gradual de-emphasis and perceived separation of these once-unified disciplines.

This reframed understanding carries significant implications for contemporary research, enhancing historical accuracy and offering profound insights for practical training in Okinawan martial arts today. By acknowledging and embracing the integrated heritage, practitioners and scholars alike can move beyond superficial distinctions to grasp the true depth and versatility of these traditions. It encourages a return to a more holistic approach to studying and practicing Okinawan martial arts—one that bridges the perceived gap between the "weaponless warrior" and their armed counterpart, thereby reclaiming the complete legacy of the integrated Ryukyu warrior.

Notes

1.   Nobility (Aji), Aristocrats (Ueekata), Scholarly Warrior Class (Pechin): The Ryukyu Kingdom's social structure featured a distinct upper class composed of scholar-officials and warriors who served the monarchy. At its apex were the Aji, high-ranking lords often with royal lineage, governing regional territories. Below them were the Ueekata, influential state ministers holding key positions in the central government. The Peichin constituted a broad class of scholar-officials and feudal warriors, responsible for administration and defense, with internal ranks like Chikudun Pechin, Satunushi Pechin, and Pekumi denoting their standing.

2.   Chatan Yara (1668–1756): Remembered as a pivotal figure in Okinawan martial arts, credited with disseminating te (the indigenous empty-hand art) throughout Okinawa. He was a celebrated weaponry master, exceptionally skilled in the use of the bo, tonfa, and the sai, in particular. He is notably associated with kata such as Chatan Yara no Sai, which are recognized for their seamless blend of empty-hand techniques alongside weapon applications, showcasing a holistic combative philosophy.

Though comprehensive historical documentation from his lifetime is scarce, Yara's lasting influence is preserved through the kata attributed to him and their practical application. Legends surrounding his martial prowess reflect deep reverence for foundational Okinawan masters, solidifying his stature as a key figure in the integrated development of Okinawan martial traditions.

3.   Kojoshiku Shinpo (1647-1721) also known as Matsu Higa or Matsuhiga: Remembered in Okinawan oral tradition as a formidable martial artist and a possible early codifier of bojutsu in the Ryukyu Kingdom. He is often associated with the legendary kata Matsuhiga no kon, tonfa, and sai, which persist today in many Ryukyu Kobudo systems, particularly the Matayoshi and Taira lineages.

Though little historical documentation survives, Matsu Higa is said to have studied under Chinese emissaries, including Wang Ji (Wanshu), who led a known diplomatic mission to Okinawa in 1683. This cultural exchange may have introduced elements of Chinese Quanfa into the local fighting arts, influencing what would become Okinawa Te.

Legends about Matsu Higa's combat skill, including his famed use of the bo during an encounter with a master of the weapon known as an Iron Ruler (what many believe is the precursor to the modern sai), reflect the rich folklore surrounding foundational Okinawan martial figures. While these stories serve to highlight his stature, there is no direct historical evidence to confirm many of the more colorful details.

4.   Matsumura Sōkon (1809–1899): Widely regarded as a foundational figure in modern Shorin-ryu Karate, Matsumura Sōkon was a highly influential martial artist who served the Ryukyu Kingdom. He is remembered for his significant role in synthesizing various empty-hand te styles with Chinese Shaolin influences, laying much of the groundwork for what would become contemporary Okinawan Karate. His training lineage included masters such as Sakugawa Kanga, through whom he inherited and further developed an integrated understanding of martial arts.

Matsumura's teachings emphasized comprehensive combative principles, suggesting a lineage where empty-hand skills were deeply informed by, and an extension of, armed expertise. He is noted for incorporating elements from Japanese kenjutsu, specifically the Jigen-ryu school, into the evolving Okinawan martial arts.

5.   Sakugawa Kanga (1786-1867): A key figure in the lineage leading to modern Okinawan Karate, Sakugawa Kanga was a significant predecessor and teacher to masters like Matsumura Sokon. He is remembered for his contributions to the development of bo kata and for his crucial role in combining Chinese Quanfa with local Okinawan te.

6.   Baihe Quan (白鶴拳), or Fujian White Crane Fist, is a prominent Southern Chinese martial art style originating from Fujian province. Characterized by its unique emphasis on short-range power generation, deceptive footwork, and precise hand techniques that mimic the movements of a white crane, it often employs internal principles for generating explosive force (fa jin) and engaging in close-quarters combat. Baihe Quan is historically significant for its profound influence on the development of Okinawan martial arts, particularly the Naha-te lineage that gave rise to styles like Goju-ryu and Uechi-ryu, making it a crucial link in the history of Karate.

7.   Luohan Quan (羅漢拳), or Shaolin Arhat Fist, is a classical Northern Chinese martial art style deeply associated with the Shaolin Temple. Named after the Arhats (Buddhist enlightened disciples), its forms often embody a strong, dynamic, and fluid fighting methodology. Luohan Quan is characterized by powerful stances, extensive hand techniques, and dynamic footwork, often incorporating both long-range striking

and close-quarter applications. Its principles and techniques are considered to be among the Chinese influences that shaped the development of the Shorin-ryu system of Okinawan Karate. Philosophically, it integrates Buddhist principles of self-cultivation and discipline, making it a foundational and influential style within the broader spectrum of traditional Chinese martial arts.

Traces of Steel in Ryukyu Wood
Questioning Jigen-ryu's Influence on Okinawan Bo-jutsu

The Influence of the Sword on the Staff?

The rich tapestry of Okinawan martial arts is woven from indigenous development, profound Chinese influence, and subtle connections to the martial traditions of mainland Japan. While the Satsuma[1] occupation undeniably shaped the essence of Te and Kobudo, an intriguing and often debated question arises regarding the influence of a specific Japanese sword art: Jigen-ryu[2]. Was this powerful, aggressive kenjutsu style a significant factor in the evolution of Okinawan bojutsu? If so, how deeply did its principles penetrate the island's unique weapon traditions?

Jigen-ryu, a distinctive school of swordsmanship, originated in the Tohoku region of Japan before migrating south and establishing a notable historical presence in the Satsuma Domain. Known for its explosive, single-strike philosophy and rigorous training methods, it fostered an almost fanatical dedication to delivering a decisive, overwhelming blow. A central figure in this potential cross-cultural exchange is often cited as Matsumura Sokon (c. 1809–1899), a pivotal Okinawan martial artist and royal bodyguard, who allegedly encountered and trained in Jigen-ryu during his time in Satsuma. This connection has sparked speculation that elements of Jigen-ryu's aggressive striking and body mechanics may have influenced the development of Okinawan staff forms.

To explore this possibility, we must critically examine the technical characteristics of Jigen ryu and compare them with the established methodologies of Okinawan bojutsu. This discussion goes beyond mere historical curiosity; it delves into the very foundations of Okinawan martial arts, impacting lineage claims, the understanding of technical principles, and our interpretation of the complex cultural exchanges that shaped these combative traditions. Unraveling this historical knot requires careful analysis, distinguishing verifiable facts from compelling but unproven folklore. To understand whether Jigen-ryū left an imprint on Okinawan bōjutsu, we must first examine the art on its own terms. This begins with a closer look at its origins, technical structure, and philosophical foundation within the Satsuma domain.

Jigen-ryu: The Fierce Sword of Satsuma

To accurately assess the potential influence of Jigen-ryu on Okinawan bojutsu, it is crucial first to establish a clear understanding of Jigen-ryu itself. This unique school of Japanese swordsmanship is more than just a collection of techniques; it embodies a distinct philosophy and rigorous training methodology that sets it apart from many other kenjutsu traditions.

Historical Development and Characteristics

Jigen-ryu's origins trace back to the late 16th century in the Tohoku region of northern Japan, founded by Togo Chui. However, its true prominence and the development of its most distinctive characteristics occurred after it migrated south, becoming the official swordsmanship school of the Shimazu clan[3], the powerful daimyo of the Satsuma Domain. This deep integration into Satsuma's samurai class meant that

Jigen-ryu was not merely a martial art but a vital component of the domain's military and cultural identity. The style was forged in an environment that valued decisive action and unwavering spirit, reflecting the fierce independence and combative prowess for which Satsuma samurai were renowned.

At the heart of Jigen-ryu's technical approach lies an emphasis on delivering a single, overwhelming, and decisive blow to incapacitate an opponent immediately. This philosophy eschews prolonged engagements or intricate parrying in favor of raw, unyielding power. The primary method for achieving this is the diagonal downward strike, often initiated from a high, almost overhead position. This powerful, arcing cut aims to cleave through an opponent's guard and body with maximum force, embodying the principle of "one cut, one kill." The focus is on generating immense momentum and delivering a crushing impact rather than relying on finesse or multiple rapid attacks.

Cultivating this explosive power is central to Jigen-ryu's demanding training methodology. Perhaps its most iconic practice is tachimaki, a form of repetitive striking against a wooden post or tree. Practitioners strike the post hundreds, even thousands, of times daily, developing incredible grip strength, wrist power, and the ability to channel their entire body weight into a single, devastating blow. This relentless repetition ingrains the muscle memory necessary for executing the decisive strike. Accompanying this physical exertion is the pervasive use of shouting or kiai[15], not merely as a vocalization but as an integral part of power generation, focusing energy, intimidating the opponent, and synchronizing breath with movement. The tachi-maki[11] makiwara (a specialized striking post for sword practice) is therefore a fundamental tool, distinct from the Okinawan makiwara[18] used for empty-hand striking, yet sharing the concept of developing impact through dedicated practice.

Philosophical Underpinnings

Beyond its physical techniques, Jigen-ryu is deeply rooted in a philosophy of aggression, dominance, and overwhelming psychological pressure. Significantly influenced by Bushido, its rigorous and often brutal training is meticulously designed to cultivate an unshakeable resolve and a mindset that relentlessly pursues victory through a single, decisive action. This aggressive posture aims not only to inflict physical damage but also to shatter the opponent's will and spirit, ideally before or during the initial engagement. Practitioners are

instilled with the unwavering loyalty and discipline to move forward relentlessly, strike with absolute commitment, and eliminate all doubt and hesitation. This profound psychological intensity, combined with the technical effectiveness and a focus on fearlessness and rigorous mental and physical preparation, molded the Satsuma samurai into a formidable force, capable of achieving victory through a singular, overwhelming strike.

If any Okinawan martial artist was in a position to absorb, adapt, and transmit the principles of Jigen-ryu, it was Matsumura Sokon. His role as a royal bodyguard, diplomat, and martial innovator places him at the intersection of Ryukyuan, Chinese, and Japanese martial traditions.

Crossroads of Cultures: Matsumura Sokon

Matsumura Sokon (c. 1809–1899) stands as a figure of immense historical significance in the development of Okinawan martial arts. Holding the prestigious and convenient position of royal bodyguard to the last three kings of the Ryukyu Kingdom, he was widely acknowledged as a Bushi[6], a term signifying a warrior or military man who embodied the highest standards of martial and ethical conduct within the kingdom's gentry class. His scholarly background, evidenced by his mastery of classical Chinese texts and calligraphy, was as profound as his martial skill, underscoring the warrior-scholar ideal[7]. Given his prominent role and exposure to both Okinawan and Chinese martial traditions, his alleged connection to the Japanese Jigen-ryu school of swordsmanship becomes a critical point of inquiry for understanding the influences on Okinawan bojutsu.

Historical Context and Allegations

Matsumura Sokon's introduction to Jigen-ryu is deeply rooted in his service to the Ryukyu Kingdom. Upon his return from China in 1832, King Sho Iku specifically sought a bodyguard proficient in swordsmanship, a critical need Matsumura was destined to fulfill. Matsumura subsequently ascended to become the chief martial arts instructor and bodyguard, serving King Sho Ko, King Sho Iku, and King Sho Tai[5]. Given Satsuma's pervasive influence over the kingdom, formal training in their formidable martial art would have conferred a significant advantage and legitimacy upon the king's chief protector. It was during Matsumura's documented diplomatic missions to Satsuma, including a notable five-year sojourn in modern-day Kagoshima[4], that he immersed himself in Jigen-ryu. His dedication culminated in the prestigious Menkyo Kaiden[8] from his sensei, Yashichiro Ijuin, signifying a profound and successful period of study that ultimately enabled him to integrate Jigen-ryu principles into Ryukyu Kobujutsu.

While Matsumura's frequent, obligatory travels to Satsuma accompanying the king provide the historical context for this cross-cultural martial exchange, the exact extent and nature of his formal Jigen-ryu instruction remain subjects of scholarly discussion. Prominent researchers such as Patrick McCarthy, Thomas Quast, and Hokama Tetsuhiro have explored this connection, though their interpretations vary regarding the verifiable depth of his training. Matsumura's presence in Satsuma is undeniable, but primary historical documents explicitly confirming his enrollment or mastery of Jigen-ryu are scarce. Consequently, much of our understanding of this crucial link relies on oral traditions passed down through generations of martial artists, providing valuable insight into lineage and perception, yet requiring careful critical analysis to distinguish it from definitive historical fact.

Intriguingly, an account from Okinawan karate master Nagamine Shoshin[9] offers a compelling, albeit tragic, anecdote that lends further credence to these oral traditions. Nagamine recounted visiting the home of Matsumura's great-granddaughter in Naha in August 1942. During this visit, he reportedly discovered a menkejo (master's license) in Jigen-ryu kenjutsu, alongside a colored paper bearing verses[10], housed within the family's Buddhist shrine. These documents were purportedly granted to Matsumura by his Jigen-ryu master, Ishuin Yashichiro, upon Matsumura's departure from Satsuma after achieving the highest level of Jigen-ryu techniques. While these valuable documents were reportedly destroyed when Matsumura's home was lost during World War II, Nagamine Shoshin's eyewitness account suggests that tangible evidence of Matsumura's menkyo kaiden in Jigen ryu indeed existed within his family's possession at one point, offering a vital, if indirect, link to the veracity of the oral accounts.

Comparing Martial Methodologies

To assess the credibility of Jigen-ryu's influence on Matsumura Sokon's martial systems, a detailed comparison of their striking methods, body mechanics, footwork, and combative mindset is essential. Shuri-te, as shaped by Matsumura, is known for its powerful, direct techniques, often emphasizing rooted stances and explosive execution. This combative intensity aligns conceptually with Jigen-ryu's hallmark principle of delivering a single, decisive blow. However, a closer examination of body torque, attack angles, and overall kata rhythm reveals essential distinctions. Jigen-ryu emphasizes relentless forward pressure and overwhelming aggression, while Matsumura's kata also incorporate evasive maneuvers and nuanced defensive strategies; adaptations shaped by Okinawa's specific environmental and societal context during the Satsuma occupation.

Exploring Matsumura Sokon's potential training in Jigen-ryu provides an insightful perspective on the technical development of Okinawan bōjutsu. If Matsumura did indeed achieve menkyo kaiden in this influential sword system, his role as a transmitter of knowledge, whether intentionally or through adaptation, becomes more than just biographical information; it may serve as a key connection for incorporating Japanese sword

principles into Okinawan weaponry. To investigate this possibility, we will conduct a detailed comparative analysis of the core techniques and tactical philosophies of Jigen-ryu alongside those found in traditional Okinawan bojutsu. This examination will help us determine whether any significant traces of Jigen-ryu are present in the kata and combative logic of the Okinawan staff.

Striking Parallels: Jigen-ryu and Okinawan Bojutsu

Having established the core tenets and historical context of Jigen-ryu, we now turn to the important task of identifying technical parallels, or the lack thereof, between this formidable Japanese sword art and the distinctive forms of Okinawan bojutsu. This comparative analysis aims to determine whether the assertive and aggressive principles of Jigen-ryu resonate within the staff traditions of Ryukyu or if any similarities are merely superficial or coincidental.

Overview of Okinawan Bojutsu Striking Systems

Okinawan bojutsu developed as an efficient, highly practical, and versatile weapon art designed for defense in a civilian context, as opposed to large-scale military engagements. Its striking systems emphasize powerful, sweeping, and thrusting movements, often utilizing the full length of the staff to maintain distance and generate considerable force. Unlike the sword, which relies on cutting edges, the bo primarily delivers blunt force trauma, necessitating different biomechanical principles for maximum impact. Okinawan bojutsu forms frequently feature dynamic transitions, circular blocks, and rapid changes in direction, reflecting a need for adaptability in varied combative scenarios.

Technical Parallels and Divergences

When comparing the technical principles of Jigen-ryu kenjutsu and Okinawan bojutsu, several key points of convergence and divergence become evident. These similarities, whether structural, strategic, or philosophical, help illuminate the possibility of cross-influence while also highlighting the distinct identities of each system.

• Linearity and Engagement Strategy[20]

> Jigen-ryu is characterized by an uncompromisingly linear approach to combat. Its core tactic revolves around delivering a single, overwhelming strike, often through a downward diagonal cut intended to end the confrontation instantly. This strategy is reinforced by deep, stable stances that drive explosive forward momentum.
>
> Okinawan bojutsu also values committed, powerful first strikes, particularly in kata, where opening techniques are designed to assert dominance or preemptively stop an attacker. However, unlike the relentless forward pressure of Jigen-ryu, Okinawan methods often blend linearity

with circular motion and broader target engagement. The stance widths in bojutsu are more adaptable, facilitating rapid shifts in direction, counterattacks, and evasive footwork. This reflects the defensive ethos embedded in much of Okinawan martial culture.

- Body Mechanics and Weapon Posture

    Jigen-ryu's trademark tonbo no kamae[17] ("dragonfly stance"), in which the sword is held high above the right shoulder, prepares for its hallmark diagonal cut. Power is generated through total-body torque and an aggressive, committed lunge. While Okinawan bojutsu similarly employs body torque to power its strikes, the mechanics differ in execution. In Okinawan systems, practitioners frequently incorporate lateral movement and transitional stances to create openings, evade attacks, or reposition. Although some high-ready stances with the bo resemble the spirit of tonbo no kamae, they are less rigid and more tactically fluid, aimed at delivering versatile strikes from multiple angles.

- Rhythm and Tactical Cadence

    The rhythmic qualities of movement in each system reflect their distinct combat philosophies. Jigen-ryu training exercises, like tategi-uchi[12], are explosive and linear, culminating in a single, devastating moment. This style is not built for prolonged exchanges but is designed to overwhelm with immediacy.

    In contrast, Okinawan bojutsu kata often flow between hard and soft phases, alternating explosive strikes with fluid repositioning. This dynamic rhythm mirrors the utility of the staff as both an offensive and defensive tool, capable of sustained engagement. While strikes are delivered with the same intensity, Okinawan bojutsu offers a broader tactical repertoire suited to varying ranges and rhythms, rather than relying on a single decisive action.

Conditioning the Strike: Repetitive Impact Training

Both Jigen-ryu and Okinawan martial arts emphasize the cultivation of powerful strikes through repetitive impact training. In Jigen-ryu, this is exemplified by repeatedly striking a vertical wooden post with full-force sword cuts to develop muscular endurance, tendon strength, and mental focus, the goal of which is simple: to produce a single, decisive blow capable of ending a confrontation.

Okinawan systems, particularly in karate, adopted a similar training method through the use of the makiwara, or striking post. While there is little historical evidence that the makiwara was used in traditional bojutsu, the conceptual parallel remains; both practices are rooted in forging precision, structural alignment, and committed intent. Even if bojutsu did not employ a striking post in the same way, the principle of conditioning the body to deliver maximum impact remains a shared combative ideal.

These comparative lenses do not confirm a direct technical transmission, but they do highlight areas where underlying principles overlap, showcasing both unique identities and potential influences between the two martial arts. Yet even as these technical similarities appear persuasive, a rigorous historical approach demands that we examine alternative explanations. Could these parallels reflect coincidence, shared universal principles, or other influences entirely? Several scholars have raised important counterpoints worth considering.

Skepticism, Coincidence, and Cultural Drift

The assertion that Jigen-ryu significantly influenced Okinawan bojutsu is compelling but not without its scholarly skeptics and counterarguments. A balanced analysis necessitates a critical examination of these alternative perspectives, ensuring the narrative is grounded in verifiable evidence rather than excessive reliance on speculative connections or romanticized oral traditions.

Questioning Exaggerated Satsuma Influence

Prominent researchers and historians of Okinawan martial arts, such as Thomas Quast, Patrick McCarthy, and Hokama Tetsuhiro, have often cautioned against overstating the direct technical influence of Satsuma martial arts on Okinawan systems. While they acknowledge the undeniable political and economic subjugation, they suggest that the extent of direct martial cross-pollination may be exaggerated in popular narratives. Their position is not that no influence occurred, but rather that its depth and pervasiveness may be overstated or misunderstood, especially when looking for direct technical correlations.

One key aspect of this skepticism relates to the nature of bojutsu itself. While Jigen-ryu is a sword art, its principles may not translate directly to the staff, which is a weapon with fundamentally different mechanics, range, and striking methods. Some scholars speculate that if any Satsuma combative arts did influence Okinawan bojutsu, it might have come from other weapon systems, such as Naginata-jutsu[22] or Sojutsu.[23] These polearm traditions share more direct correlations with the bo in terms of length, leverage, and the types of targets they engage, making them potentially more relevant sources of influence than a sword art.[24]

The Distortion of Oral Narratives

Oral traditions play a vital role in preserving martial culture and heritage, but they are also inherently fluid. Over generations, details can change due to misremembering, reinterpretation, or the natural evolution of storytelling. In situations of political subjugation, such as Okinawa under Satsuma rule, this fluidity can be complicated by the influence of power dynamics. Narratives may have been unconsciously altered to align with dominant

social values, assert local legitimacy, or distinguish a unique Okinawan identity. This results in a complex historical landscape where distinguishing between authentic transmission, reinterpretation, and mythmaking is both essential and challenging. Understanding this dynamic is crucial when evaluating claims of influence, such as the alleged links between Jigen-ryu and Okinawan bojutsu, because what is preserved may reflect not only factual elements but also the aspirations and pressures of the era.

Coincidental Similarities and Chinese Parallels

Ultimately, it is crucial to acknowledge that any perceived similarities between Jigen-ryu and Okinawan bojutsu may be entirely coincidental, arising from universal principles of effective combat. Certain combative movements, such as powerful diagonal cuts or the emphasis on a decisive first strike, are not unique to Jigen-ryu. Many martial traditions across Asia, including various Chinese systems, employ similar principles. For example, some styles of Chinese Xinyi Quan[25] are known for their explosive, linear movements and focus on overwhelming the opponent with a single, committed advance. Given Okinawa's deep and long-standing martial connections with China, it is plausible that any shared characteristics with Jigen-ryu could stem from a common Chinese root or represent efficient combat solutions developed independently.

Therefore, while the alleged link between Matsumura Sokon and Jigen-ryu is intriguing, a rigorous scholarly approach requires us to weigh these counterarguments and consider all potential sources of influence before drawing definitive conclusions.

We now return to the central question: was Jigen-ryu a formative influence on Okinawan bojutsu, or merely a peripheral presence in a much larger web of cultural and martial exchange? Though definitive proof remains tenuous, a careful synthesis of the evidence reveals a nuanced answer.

Threads of Influence in Motion

While direct historical evidence is unfortunately elusive, the influence of Jigen-ryu on Okinawan bojutsu, particularly through the figure of Matsumura Sokon, emerges not as myth but as a plausible and meaningful cultural transmission, shaped by both documented practice and nuanced oral tradition, and Nagamine Shoshin's eyewitness account regarding the menkejo provide strong circumstantial evidence that deserves consideration.

Our comparative analysis reveals intriguing technical parallels between the two styles, particularly in their emphasis on powerful and decisive first strikes and the rigorous use of repetitive impact training, where the concepts of Jigen-ryu's ichi-no-tachi[16] and tategi-uchi resonate with the Okinawan pursuit of efficiency and devastating power. However, significant differences in body mechanics, footwork, and the broader tactical rhythms of kata suggest that any influence from Jigen-ryu was likely integrated and adapted into the existing Okinawan framework, rather than adopted in its entirety. Bojutsu forms, such as Sakugawa no Kun[20] and Soeishi no Kon[21], serve as living artifacts of this complex historical interplay, reflecting both indigenous Okinawan ingenuity and potential external influences.

Ultimately, this inquiry highlights the remarkable adaptability and systematization intrinsic to Okinawan martial arts. Faced with external pressures and new encounters, Okinawan masters like Matsumura Sokon selectively absorbed and integrated elements that enhanced their combative effectiveness while preserving the unique character of their traditions. The potential influence of Jigen-ryu on Okinawan bojutsu is not about rewriting history; it enriches our understanding of it. This underscores the importance of questioning established narratives, embracing complexity, and recognizing that martial traditions, like all cultural phenomena, are products of dynamic exchange and continuous evolution. This ongoing scholarly pursuit allows us to appreciate the profound depth and resilience of Okinawan martial arts, which emerged from a unique blend of necessity, innovation, and cross-cultural dialogue.

Notes

1   Satsuma Domain (薩摩藩) – A powerful feudal domain in southern Japan that invaded and controlled the Ryukyu Kingdom.

2   Jigen-ryū and Founder Togo Chui (東郷 重位) – Section II opens with Jigen-ryū's historical background. 3 Shimazu Clan – The ruling family of the Satsuma Domain.

3.   Shimazu Clan - The ruling family of the Satsuma Domain

4   Kagoshima – The capital city of the Satsuma Domain.

5   King Shō Kō, King Shō Iku, King Shō Tai (尚灝王, 尚育王, 尚泰王) – Discussed during the biography of Matsumura Sōkon.

6   Bushi (武士) – A term signifying a warrior or military man in the Ryukyu Kingdom.

7   Warrior-Scholar – The ideal of balancing literary/intellectual pursuits with martial arts mastery, known as   Bunbu Ryodo.

8   Menkyo Kaiden – A Japanese martial arts license signifying full transmission of a system's teachings. Refers to the full license allegedly awarded to Matsumura in Jigen-ryū.

9   Nagamine Shōshin – A prominent Okinawan karate master who is cited as the source of the menkyo discovery account.

10   Note on papers found with Menkyo certificate at Matsumura's family shrine – While the specific content of the verses remains unknown, their presence alongside Matsumura's menkyo kaiden in Jigen-ryū underscores the multi-faceted nature of martial arts training beyond mere physical technique. They point towards

the philosophical depth inherent in these traditions and hint at a lost piece of the historical and philosophical puzzle connecting Jigen-ryū and Ryukyu martial arts.

11   Tachi-maki makiwara – A specialized striking post used in Jigen-ryu for sword practice.

12   Tategi-uchi (立木打ち) – Jigen-ryū training method involving repetitive striking against a wooden post or tree.

15   Kiai (気合) – A Japanese term for a shout used in martial arts to focus energy, intimidate, and synchronize breath.

16   Ichi-no-tachi – Jigen-ryū principle emphasizing a single, decisive cut.

17   Tonbo no Kamae – Jigen-ryū's distinctive "dragonfly stance" ready position.

20   Makiwara – A striking post, wrapped in rice straw rope, used in Okinawan karate for conditioning and impact development.

21   It is also important to acknowledge that while Jigen-ryū places great emphasis on the power of the initial strike, it remains a comprehensive system. Its methods include varied footwork, angular attacks, and a full spectrum of combative techniques, not unlike those seen in Okinawan bōjutsu. Thus, identifying the subtle technical overlaps, while remaining cautious about drawing direct lines, is key to determining whether the similarities are due to actual transmission, shared martial logic, or coincidental evolution from common principles of effective combat.

22   Sakugawa no Kun – A classic Okinawan bōjutsu kata, often associated with Sakugawa Kanga. 23 Soeishi no Kon – A classic Okinawan bojutsu kata, often associated with Soeishi Ryotoku.   24 Naginata-jutsu – Japanese combative art focusing on the halberd.

25   Sōjutsu – Japanese combative art focusing on the spear.

26   Joachim Meyer's 1600 treatise, for example, treats the staff as the foundation and a training tool for all other polearms.

27   Xinyi Quan – often translated as "Form-Intent Fist," is a Chinese internal martial art known for its explosive linear power, direct entry tactics, and emphasis on overwhelming the opponent with committed forward pressure. It is one of the oldest internal systems and is historically linked to battlefield applications and spear principles. In the context of this paper, Xinyi Quan is mentioned as a possible alternate source for the striking similarities seen in Okinawan martial arts, particularly the emphasis on decisive first strikes and body-driven power. Given Okinawa's extensive historical ties to Chinese martial culture, including documented training exchanges with Fujian-based systems, it is plausible that the combative logic seen in Xinyi Quan may have influenced Okinawan bōjutsu as much as, or more than, Jigen-ryū kenjutsu. This underscores the necessity of evaluating all plausible vectors of influence, rather than attributing technical parallels solely to Japanese sources.

Tsuken Bo

Decoding Okinawa's Complex Martial Tapestry

This paper examines the historical complexity of Tsu'ken Bo, a name attributed to multiple distinct kata within Okinawan kobudo. Through linguistic analysis, lineage mapping, personal experience, and a critical view of oral tradition, I look to explore the separate but intertwined paths of the forms known as Chi'kun no Kun and Tsu'ken Bo.

Most martial artists are taught that a kata's name reveals something about its origin. But what happens when two completely different forms share the same name—and neither tells the full story? The confusion surrounding Tsu'ken Bo, or Chi'kun no Kun, often begins with a simple misunderstanding: that we're talking about just one kata with multiple names. In truth, we're dealing with two entirely different bo forms, developed in different areas and transmitted through separate lineages, that happen to share the same name due to linguistic overlap and cultural naming conventions. One version is preserved within the Matayoshi kobudo tradition and is commonly referred to as Tsu'ken Bo, while the other is linked to the Matsumura Seito line through Chi'kun Kraka and is known as Chi'kun no Kun. Here we seek to untangle the dual identity of these forms by exploring their origins, lineages, and the broader historical currents that shaped them.

So how can two different kata have the same name? And how can one kata have two names? To untangle this, we have to look at Okinawan linguistics, regional geography, naming customs, oral tradition, and martial lineage, all woven into one complicated history.

Same Word, Different Tongue

Let's start with the simplest layer: Tsu'ken and Chi'kun are actually the same word, just pronounced differently. Tsu'ken is the Japanese reading of the kanji 津堅, the name of a small island off the eastern coast of Okinawa. Chi'kun is how that same name would be pronounced in the native language of the Ryukyus, known as Uchinaaguchi.

This linguistic complexity is further compounded when we take into account the terminology different regions use to refer to the weapons themselves. In mainland Japanese, the six-foot staff is typically called "Bo," whereas in Okinawa (Uchinaguchi), it is traditionally referred to as "Kun" or "Kon." Although these terms have distinct origins, they are often used interchangeably in modern discussions of martial arts. This practice complicates the task of accurately identifying and discussing specific kata.

So depending on whether you're following Japanese or Okinawan linguistic conventions, you'll hear either Tsu'ken Bo or Chi'kun no Kun, or possibly even a combination of the two. This explains the two names for what might seem like the same kata, but that still doesn't explain why there are two different kata with the same name.

A Case of Parallel Evolution

Here's where things start to diverge. Tsuken Island is a small place, just a couple of square miles, but it's long been associated with bojutsu. Several major kobudo lineages claim kata connected to the island. At some point, at least two completely different forms were independently named Tsu'ken Bo (or Chi'kun no Kun, depending on the lineage). Was it intentional? Probably not. More likely, these kata developed separately, each named after either a member of the Tsuken family or the island itself, by practitioners unaware that someone else was using the same name for a different form.

This kind of parallel naming isn't unusual in Okinawan martial arts. Kata names were often passed down orally for generations before they were codified or written down. It wasn't until the 20th century, when systems were formalized and organizations like the Ryukyu Kobudo Hozon Shinkokai and the Matayoshi lineage began documenting kata lists, that attempts at systematization even began in earnest.

Beyond the Island: Could "Tsu'ken" Mean a Martial Tradition?

The name Tsu'ken is most often associated with Tsuken Island, a small but historically significant landmass off Okinawa's eastern coast. Yet, there is reason to believe that the term may have once referred to more than just a geographic location. What if "Tsu'ken" wasn't simply a place-name, but a reference to a distinct martial methodology, perhaps even a tradition of bojutsu informed by battlefield strategy and regional adaptation?

This possibility gains traction when we look into historical references of Matsumura "Bushi" Sokon, the legendary bodyguard to the Ryukyuan kings and one of the primary architects of Shuri-te. It is widely accepted, through both oral tradition and scholarly sources, that Matsumura studied Jigen-ryu, a hardline style of Japanese swordsmanship, during his time in Satsuma, where Ryukyuan envoys and officials were often sent as part of the island's tributary relationship with the Shimazu clan (Kerr, 1958; McCarthy, 1995; Quast, 2013). Jigen-ryu emphasized explosive, diagonal, linear strikes and aggressive forward movement; principles that have clear echoes in both Shuri-based karate and certain Okinawan weapons forms.

Some researchers suggest that Matsumura did not merely absorb these principles, but actively synthesized them into his own teaching, adapting sword-based movements to fit Okinawan weapon systems like bojutsu, creating the foundations of Tsu'ken bojutsu. In this view, the term "Tsu'ken" might represent not just where a form originated, but how it was practiced, an internalization of combative principles that distinguished it from other village or family styles. Understood this way, Tsu'ken bojutsu could be read not as a kata of island origin, but as a stylistic school of practice shaped by a hybrid of Ryukyuan and Japanese influences.

So... Who Was Chi'kun Kraka?

Now, some people will ask, "But isn't the kata named after a man, Chi'kun Kraka?"

It's a fair question, and one that brings us to the naming practices of Ryukyuan society. In traditional Okinawan culture, individuals of pechin (samurai) class often carried kamei, place-based names that indicated region, clan, or house affiliation. That's why we hear names like Chatan Yara ("Yara from Chatan") or Yomitan no Anko. These weren't nicknames, they were geographic and social identifiers.

Fortunately, there is growing evidence that "Chi'kun Kraka" was a real historical figure, not just an oral artifact. According to both oral traditions and lineage charts preserved within the Matsumura Seito and Kise family systems, Chi'kun Kraka, also known as Tsuken Mantaka, was born in 1829 and died in 1891. He studied under Tomigusuku Seiko no Ueekata (aka Tsuken Saisoku)[1], a bo and yari (spear) expert known for his mastery of horsemanship and for having trained under two important martial figures: Bushi Sakiyama Kitoku[2] and Gushi Peichin[3].

Chi'kun Kraka, in turn, taught Komesu Ushi no Tanmei (1854–1920)[4], who passed the teachings on to Soken Hohan Osensei(1889–

1982), founder of Matsumura Seito Shorin-ryu, who would go on to train Kise Fusei Hanshi.

Archival footage from the late 1960s or early 1970s, believed to be the oldest known video recording of Chi'kun no Kun, shows Soken Hohan Osensei performing the kata with precision and fluidity, offering a rare visual glimpse into how this kata was expressed within his lineage during that era. This footage not only substantiates the kata's continuity but also provides historical context for its transmission into the modern era through the Kise family.

So the lineage of Chi'kun no Kun, which many traditions attribute to Chi'kun Kraka (as the one who systemized the battlefield and village spear methods), can be seen as:

Lau Loon Kon → Sakiyama Kitoku → Tomigusuku Seiko → Chikin Kraka → Komesu Ushi no Tanmei → Hohan Soken → Kise Fusei

That same kata, passed down through this lineage, eventually came to me in 2003, at the hands of my instructor John Shipes Hanshi, who had trained extensively within the Matsumura Seito and Kise family traditions. That version, grounded in the teachings passed down through Komesu Ushi no Tanmei and Soken Hohan, was both structurally direct and tactically fluid, with a clear emphasis on the kata's spear-inspired roots. In 2008, I had the honor of reviewing and refining this form under Kise Isao Hanshi, the son and designated successor of Kise Fusei Hanshi. His guidance helped illuminate finer points of timing, grip transitions, and rotational mechanics that reflected not just technical precision, but generations of refinement within the Chi'kun no Kun lineage. That experience remains one of the clearest bridges I've felt between kata practice and its deeper historical current.

This paints a far more concrete picture than the "mystery figure" theory and lends significant historical weight to the practice of Chi'kun no Kun, especially in the Matsumura Seito tradition. It also explains why some traditions attach the name Chi'kun not just to the island, but to a person and a transmission line, potentially blending both meanings in a single kata name.

Different Lineages

While the Chi'kun no Kun preserved in the Matsumura Seito tradition traces its roots through Chi'kun Kraka and the teachings of Komesu Ushi no Tanmei, it is not the only kata to bear the name Tsu'ken Bo. In fact, entirely distinct versions of this form exist in other lineages; forms that share the name but differ in structure, movements, and origin. One such version appears in the Matayoshi Kobudo tradition.

It's tempting to think of the Matayoshi and Matsumura Seito versions of Tsu'ken Bo as variations on a theme, but they're not. These are two distinctly different kata, each with its own movements, tactical philosophy, and historical lineage. While both draw from Okinawan bojutsu principles and reference Tsuken Island either directly or symbolically, they evolved separately.

I was first exposed to the Matayoshi Kobudo version of Tsu'ken Bo in the early-to-mid 2000s by John Shipes Hanshi, who had learned it years earlier from a performance by Nishiuchi Mikio Sensei, captured on a now-rare video. I remember watching that footage with Shipes Hanshi and comparing details. It was clear this was a refined and well-practiced form, but notably different from the Chi'kun no Kun taught in the Kise family system.

Later, while reviewing a different video of the same kata (as performed by Matayoshi Shinpo Hanshi), Shipes Hanshi shared an anecdote from a conversation with Kise Fusei Hanshi-sei. When shown the kata, Kise Hanshi remarked that it was a version from the Akamine family kobudo tradition, claiming it as part of a lineage tracing back hundreds of years.

Akamine Family Connections and Crossovers

That observation isn't far-fetched, and it carries weight considering that near the end of his life, with no chosen successor, Akamine Seiyu, the final soke of the Akamine family tradition, entrusted his full body of knowledge to Kise Fusei Hanshi. While the Akamine lineage may not enjoy the international visibility of larger systems, it remains deeply rooted in Okinawan martial history.

Historically, martial arts transmission in Okinawa was shaped by deeply personal relationships, and this is especially important when examining figures like Matayoshi Shinpo. As the individual who formalized and promoted what we now recognize as Matayoshi Kobudo, Shinpo was known for actively seeking instruction from a wide range of teachers. He is also believed to have had familial ties to Akamine Seiyu. This kind of "cross-pollination" wasn't merely common, it was foundational to the fabric of Ryukyuan karate and kobudo, where instruction flowed through webs of mentorship and community, guided by longstanding norms of family allegiance, caste responsibility, and shared cultural duty. In this context, martial knowledge was not just transmitted, it was entrusted, woven into the broader social fabric of Ryukyuan life.

Given these connections, it is entirely plausible that Matayoshi adapted a version of Tsu'ken Bo from the Akamine family. Over time, this kata may have evolved under his teaching, refined through his experience and the Matayoshi system's structural framework, resulting in the version we see preserved in Matayoshi Kobudo today.

These familial links deepen when we consider that Matayoshi Shinpo's father, Matayoshi Shinko, had deep roots in the classical

Ryukyuan martial tradition. A member of the Ryukyu Kobujutsu Kenkyukai, Shinko trained alongside figures like Soken Hohan, Moden Yabiku, and Uehara Seikichi. He was also a student of "Tanme" Agena Shokuho, who himself was a direct student of Matsumura Sokon, the same foundational figure often credited with adapting Jigen-ryu sword principles into Okinawan bojutsu.

This lineage context underscores that both Matayoshi and Kise family traditions, though distinct, ultimately draw from a common martial ancestor. Their versions of Tsu'ken Bo may differ in technique and expression, but they are both reflections of Okinawa's evolving, interconnected bojutsu heritage.

Alternative Perspectives and Counterarguments

Of course, not all scholars or practitioners accept these lineage-based narratives at face value. Prominent researchers such as Andreas Quast and Patrick McCarthy Hanshi have repeatedly cautioned against placing too much weight on oral history in the absence of contemporaneous documentation5. They argue, rightly so in many cases, that Okinawan martial traditions are especially vulnerable to embellishment, especially when lineages are reconstructed generations after the fact. Over time, localized forms may be elevated to classical status, and the accomplishments of individuals can become exaggerated through the filters of loyalty, pride, or institutional legacy.

This skepticism is important. It acts as a necessary check on the natural human tendency to seek order in the past, to impose linear continuity where none may have existed, or to romanticize figures and events in service of modern legitimacy. When viewed uncritically, oral accounts can morph into a pseudo-historical framework; convenient but not always accurate.

And yet, we must also acknowledge that Okinawan martial history has survived in large part because of oral transmission. In a society where martial instruction was often private, undocumented, and deeply embedded in personal and familial relationships, teachers entrusted their students not just with techniques, but with context, philosophy, and stories. These oral lineages carried more than history, they carried meaning.

To dismiss oral tradition entirely is to risk discarding much of what gives Okinawan martial culture its richness. The practice of kata itself, codified movement passed from one generation to the next, is a kind of embodied oral tradition. These forms carry not only technique but echoes of the teacher's intent, the era's demands, and the community's identity.

Ultimately, the truth likely lies between these poles. The landscape of Okinawan kobudo is a mosaic: part archaeological, part folkloric, shaped by shared roots, evolving forms, regional adaptations, and the occasional case of parallel naming. In this light, the coexistence of multiple kata called Tsu'ken Bo (or Chi'kun no Kun) is not a historical error to be corrected, but a living reflection of Okinawa's dynamic, non-linear approach to martial preservation.

Conclusion: A Living History with Fragile Threads
So where does that leave us?

Tsu'ken Bo is still very much alive in the Matayoshi tradition, refined, preserved, and passed down through generations of dedicated instructors. Meanwhile, the Akamine family kobudo system, though once deeply influential, may no longer be a viable lineage, as Kise Fusei, now in his nineties and the Akamine material never publicly taught, that system teeters on the edge of extinction.

This is the delicate reality of Okinawan martial history: systems live and die not by their technical merit alone, but by the willingness and capacity of their inheritors to carry them forward.

Whether or not "Chi'kun Kraka" existed exactly as described may remain up for debate. But what is certain is that the kata—or katas—bearing his name reflect a deep entanglement of island geography, personal legacy, and regional martial philosophies.

And maybe that's the point. Okinawan martial arts were never static traditions etched in stone or locked away in scrolls. They were—and are—living practices, shaped by community, lineage, politics, and personal encounter. They evolved through need, mentorship, and adaptation, not just preservation.

In the end, Tsu'ken Bo, regardless of which version you practice, is more than just a sequence of techniques. It is a reflection of living history—one that reminds us not only of what has endured, but of what remains vulnerable to time.

The presence of both Chi'kun no Kun and the Matayoshi version of Tsu'ken Bo within the Kise family system, one passed through Hohan Soken, the other entrusted by Akamine Seiyu, underscores their shared significance. Though entirely different kata with distinct origins and methods, each deserves recognition as a valuable artifact of Okinawan martial heritage. Rather than being conflated or reduced to a naming coincidence, they should be understood as complementary expressions of the island's combative legacy, each preserving a vital thread in the fabric of Ryukyuan tradition.

Notes

1.   Tomigusuku Ueekata Seiko (1829–1893), also known as Tsuken Saisoku, was a highly esteemed warrior scholar and weapons master from Okinawa's pechin class. He is best known for his mastery of the yari (spear) and exceptional horsemanship, reflecting both military training and status in the Ryukyu Kingdom's aristocratic martial culture. Seiko's reputation grows more intriguing when viewed as a direct student of Sakiyama Kitoku, the Okinawan master who returned from Fujian, China with advanced bō and empty-hand methods, and Gushi Peichin, thus placing him at a crossroads of martial transmission.

Oral lineages credit him with passing the Tsuken no Kun (a variant of Chi'kun no Kun) to Chi'kun Kraka. In fact, one statement mentions that this kata has been preserved on Tsuken Island for generations, with Seiko recognized for codifying its "reverse and spear-counter techniques" after learning it locally. While formal documentation of his teaching methods is sparse, his presence on these lineage charts suggests he was a pivotal conduit between older spear and bojutsu traditions and later kobudo systems, especially within the Matayoshi and Kise lineages.

2.   Sakiyama Kitoku (1819–1888) was a renowned master of Tomari-te and Okinawan kobudo, whose expertise was validated by both oral tradition and historical records. He hailed from Wakuda Village in Naha and gained early repute as a proficient martial artist, so respected that he was invited to further his training in Fujian Province, China, under Lau Loon Kon, who served as a military-academy instructor. According to multiple dojo histories, Sakiyama spent over four years there (1839 to 1843) before returning to impart his knowledge in Okinawa, specializing in a blend of empty-hand kata, bojutsu, and paired-weapons kumite. He later passed these teachings to Shinkichi Kuniyoshi, who would become a prominent influence on practitioners like Shigeru Nakamura of Okinawa Kenpo (a pivotal instructor of Kise Fusei, Hanshi).

While specific documents from his time in China remain scarce, Sakiyama's influence in Okinawa's martial development is well-attested. His name is frequently cited among the generation that bridged Chinese military arts and Okinawan weapon traditions, and his legacy remains visible through the kata practices and lineage
lines stemming from Tomari-te schools. Historians and traditionalists alike regard him as a central node in the formation of modern kobudō.

3.   Gushi Peichin stands as a significant, if somewhat enigmatic, figure in the history of Ryukyu kobudo. Universally acknowledged in oral tradition as a master of the bo, he is most often associated with the preservation of the foundational form, Sakugawa no Kun; some lineages even suggest that Gushi received this form directly from Sakugawa or passed it on in parallel, though definitive documentation is lacking. Still, the consistency of this claim across multiple traditions gives it weight. The title "Peichin" places Gushi within the gentry class of the Ryukyu Kingdom, where martial training was part of an aristocratic education, especially among those tasked with law enforcement or civil service. While precise dates and student-teacher relationships remain murky, the enduring presence of his name in multiple lineages and kata traditions reinforces his legacy. He is frequently cited as the teacher of Ishimine of Gibo, a practitioner remembered in Okinawan oral accounts for his mastery of classical kata like Passai and Kūsankū. Moreover, Chibana Choshin named Gushi as his first teacher in a 1957 article, while Miyahira Chogi referenced him in 1973 as a formative influence in early Shuri-te. Taken together, these paint a picture of Gushi not as a marginal figure, but as a pivotal link in the transition from older weapons-based arts to the emergence of systems like Shorin-ryu and Shorei-ryu. His teachings, both in bojutsu and empty-hand kata, helped lay the foundations of the martial traditions still practiced today.

4.   Komesu Ushi no Tanmei (1854–1920) emerges as a pivotal figure in the late-19th-century evolution of Shuri based kobudo. A native of Nishihara village, he is typically described as a samurai-class martial artist skilled in the kobudo arts, particularly proficient with the bo. Although precise documentation is scarce, dojo lineage records consistently identify him as a key instructor of Hohan Soken, and oral traditions credit Komesu with teaching essential forms such as Sakugawa no Kun and Chi'kun no Kun, the latter linked to his mentor, Tsuken Mantaka (Chikin Kraka).

He is characterized as a large man of exceptional physical strength, with anecdotal reports comparing him to Okinawa's most renowned wrestlers, stories that suggest he may have trained with or emulated techniques from early judo or traditional grappling arts.

Komesu's significance is further reinforced by matched mentions in both Shuri-te and kobudo-revival communities, where he is frequently referenced in seminar notes, practitioner lineages, and dojo histories as a credible conduit connecting the era of Chi'kin Kraka to the post-war resurgence under Hohan Soken. Though still reliant largely on oral transmission rather than formal records, Komesu Ushi no Tanmei's placement in the lineage helps illuminate the continuity of Okinawan martial arts.

5.   Both Andreas Quast and Patrick McCarthy Hanshi have written extensively about the limitations of oral tradition in Okinawan martial history. Quast, in Karate 1.0: Parameters of an Ancient Martial Art (2013), argues that oral transmission often leads to conflicting or contradictory origin stories and cautions against overreliance on uncorroborated lineage claims. Similarly, McCarthy, in his annotated translation of the Bubishi (1995), emphasizes the need to distinguish between cultural mythology and verifiable history. Both encourage a respectful but critical approach to oral accounts, viewing them as culturally meaningful but not necessarily historically definitive.

The Evolving Lexicon of Okinawan Martial Arts

A Conceptual Transition from 'Te' to 'Karate'

The late 19th and early 20th centuries witnessed significant changes in the conceptualization and terminology of Okinawan martial arts. Originally known as "ti," these regional expressions evolved into "Tode" and "Karate" (meaning "China Hand") before finally becoming "Karate" (meaning "Empty Hand"). Further influencing this evolution was the introduction of Japanese-style "Ryu" classifications. These changes, influenced by a complex interplay of internal developments and external political pressures, most notably those stemming from Japan's Meiji Restoration and its subsequent political and social integration of Okinawa, ultimately complicate the understanding of the rich and diverse history of Okinawan martial arts, both before and during this transformative period.

Foundational Terms: 'Te' and Early Distinctions of Style

Yoshimura Chogi (1866–1945), of the Yoshimura Udun, offers a glimpse into the prevailing terminology of the late 1880s in his "Autobiography of Martial Arts" (1941). Writing decades after the fact, Yoshimura recounted: "Then, I don't know on what basis they began to say so, but people used to say Matsumura was Okinawa-te and Higaonna was tode."

As Yoshimura began his martial arts training around 1883, this statement likely reflects the "public" perception during his formative years (circa 1887-1888).

This anecdotal evidence, however, highlights a broader historical challenge: distinguishing "Okinawa-te" vs. "Tode" as explicitly distinct "schools of thought" with opposing ideas, rather than descriptive terms that evolved, is that historical evidence for a clear, formalized rivalry is often circumstantial or based on later interpretations. Consequently, most scholars now lean towards viewing these terms as descriptive labels that gained prominence in different contexts, rather than strict, opposing schools akin to modern rival dojo. The lines were often blurred, and masters frequently incorporated elements from various sources.

In the late 19th century, the overarching term was "Te" (Oki: Ti, hand), a common designation for the indigenous martial arts practiced across Okinawa. As these regional expressions began to evolve and formalize, various terms emerged to describe perceived differences or origins, though these terms were often fluid and subject to interpretation.

Within this evolving terminology, "Okinawa-te" (Oki: Uchinadi, Okinawa hand) became a descriptive label often associated with masters like Matsumura Sokon. This term generally referred to a synthesis of native Okinawan fighting methods with long-standing Chinese influences that had been integrated over generations. Matsumura's own teachings, as evidenced by his "Advice to His Last Formal Student," emphasized comprehensive martial virtues, rigorous physical conditioning through methods like makiwara, and a deep understanding of kata principles, highlighting a practical, combative art rooted in self-defense and ethical conduct.

Conversely, the term "Tode" (Oki: Todi, China hand) was often applied to martial arts perceived to have a more direct or recent connection to Chinese *quanfa* (kung fu). This term became particularly associated with masters such as Higaonna Kanryo, largely due to his extensive direct study of *quanfa* in Fuzhou, China. Higaonna reportedly spent approximately thirteen years in Fuzhou, studying under masters like RuRuKo[1] (often cited as a student of White Crane gongfu master Pan Yuba), and subsequently brought these "new" or more contemporary Chinese martial arts influences back to Okinawa. While "Tode" broadly denoted "Chinese hand," the idea of "new" Chinese martial arts likely referred to the specific *quanfa* influences that were continually arriving in Okinawa through ongoing diplomatic and trade exchanges with China.

It's also worth noting that terms like Yabu Kentsu's "Kamite" have been suggested by some to be nearly synonymous with "Okinawa-te"; however, explicit historical documentation directly substantiating this precise comparison remains elusive, highlighting the informal and often anecdotal nature of much of this early nomenclature.

This perceived distinction between "Okinawa-te" and "Tode," as observed by some contemporary chroniclers, such as Yoshimura, represented a public or regional understanding of the different prevalent forms. However, the precise nature of their "distinction," whether it was purely based on lineage, technical emphasis (e.g., Matsumura's more linear Shuri-te vs. Higaonna's more circular Naha-te), or simply a social perception of origin, requires deeper investigation beyond anecdotal accounts. The evolution of these terms reflects a dynamic period where Okinawan martial arts were both preserving tradition and continuously absorbing new influences.

The Evolution of 'Karate' and Stylistic Categorization

The early 20th century marked a significant conceptual shift in Okinawan martial arts, primarily catalyzed by prominent students of Matsumura Soken, such as Itosu Anko. In the early 1900s, the umbrella term "Te" began to diminish in formal usage, primarily replaced by "Karate" (唐手, China hand). Itosu's influential "Ten Precepts of Karate" (1908)[2] explicitly utilized this term. They structured the art under specific, newly introduced categories: "Karate is primarily derived from two different schools, Shorin-ryu and Shorei-ryu."

With this, the martial art became increasingly understood to be entirely of Chinese origin, simplifying its complex historical lineage. It is important to note that historically, neither "Shorin-ryu" nor "Shorei-ryu" existed as formalized "schools" or "styles" within the Ryukyu Kingdom period, nor are these specific "ryu" classifications known to exist in Chinese martial arts, which do not typically use the character "流" (*ryu*) in the same way as Japanese martial arts to denote distinct lineages.

This adoption of the "ryu" nomenclature in Okinawa subsequently led to common associations: Shorin-ryu became connected to northern Chinese *kenpo* and the Shuri-te tradition (characterized by hard, fast, linear techniques), while Shorei-ryu was associated with southern Chinese *kenpo* and the Naha-te tradition (emphasizing softer, more circular techniques, internal power aspects, as seen in styles like Goju-ryu and Uechi-ryu). These categorizations were further solidified in later, particularly post-war, interpretations.

This systematization and the eventual shift in the kanji for "Karate," was driven by a complex set of motivations rooted in the era's geopolitical landscape. It is theorized that Itosu Anko, recognizing the pressing need for Karate to gain wider public acceptance and integrate into the burgeoning Japanese educational system, strategically formalized the art. As recounted by Gichin Funakoshi, Itosu's student and the popularizer of Karate in mainland Japan, the explicit reference to "China" in "Tang Te" (唐手) became politically unacceptable in an era of rising Japanese nationalism and militarism, particularly after the Russo-Japanese War and leading into the Sino-Japanese conflicts. To facilitate its adoption into Japanese schools and society, Itosu, and later Funakoshi, strategically embraced the homophonous "Karate" (空手, Empty Hand). This change emphasized the art's unarmed nature, allowing it to be presented as a purely Japanese discipline, and represented a crucial move to "develop the combat form in Japanese style" and distance it from its overt Chinese roots.

Karate in the Curriculum: Pedagogy and Formalization

The deliberate shift to introduce karate into the public school system was crucial, driven by a confluence of internal desire for legitimacy and external geopolitical pressures. With the decline of the Ryukyuan samurai class, who had traditionally maintained the art, and Okinawa's integration into Japan, the very transmission of martial practices was at risk. Concurrently, the broader Japanese educational landscape in the Meiji era emphasized physical education as a means of "nation building," incorporating elements of Bushido and militarism to foster national objectives. For karate to survive and flourish within this new socio-political climate, shedding its "secretive, combative" image and embracing a role in character development became imperative.

Itosu Anko emerged as the pivotal figure in this transformation. In April 1901, he successfully introduced karate into the physical training curriculum at the Shuri Jingo Elementary School. His influence expanded significantly over the next few years as he became a part-time instructor at the Prefectural Daiichi College and, critically, at the Prefectural Teachers' Training College. Teaching future educators meant that Itosu's methods and vision for karate would be disseminated widely across Okinawan schools, effectively multiplying his reach.

Recognizing the need to adapt the art for mass instruction and children's physical development, Itosu meticulously developed and simplified existing techniques. He is widely credited with devising the Pinan (Heian) series of kata, drawing movements from more complex advanced forms like Kusanku, Passai, Chinto, and Jion. These five fundamental forms were designed to be more accessible for schoolchildren, simplifying intricate applications into mostly punch and block techniques suitable for group settings. His "Ten Precepts (Tode Jukun)" of 1908 further articulated karate's value, emphasizing its moral, physical, and educational benefits to the Okinawan government, providing a philosophical foundation for its inclusion in the curriculum.

Supporting Itosu's efforts was Yabu Kentsu, also a student of Matsumura and a former officer in the Japanese army. Yabu played a significant role in systematizing and, at times, militarizing karate training methods to suit the large-group instruction required in schools. He introduced various procedures, many of which are still observed in dojos worldwide, including bowing upon entering, lining up students by rank, incorporating sequenced training, and emphasizing loud acknowledgments to instructors. These innovations reflected a blending of traditional Japanese neo-Confucian ideals with contemporary European militarism and physical culture, all aimed at instilling discipline and nationalistic spirit. Furthermore, for broader public consumption and suitability for schoolchildren, many advanced techniques and the nuanced *bunkai* (explanations) of kata were systematically removed or simplified, reducing the curriculum to core punches, blocks, and kicks.

This move fundamentally changed the perception of karate. Historically, Okinawan martial arts, often referred to simply as "te," were taught primarily in secret, a practice reinforced by historical bans on weapons and a scarcity of written records. Knowledge was transmitted orally and through private teaching. The introduction of karate into public schools radically shifted this paradigm, transforming it from a secretive, combative art into a formalized system of physical and moral education. While this standardization facilitated its spread and acceptance, it also meant that some aspects of the traditional art, namely its emphasis on intricate self-defense applications, grappling, joint locks, and the "why" behind movements (as opposed to simply the "how" for execution), were either de-emphasized or lost in the process of adapting it for a broader, non-combative, pedagogical purpose. This created a divergence between the traditional practice and the emerging school-based curriculum, shaping how the art would be understood and practiced for generations.

Reconciling the Past: 'Te' as Legacy and the Challenge of Historical Understanding

As "Karate" (空手) was increasingly formalized and integrated into the Japanese educational system, a significant conceptual shift occurred not only in how older Okinawan martial arts were referenced but, more profoundly, in how they were understood and practiced. The indigenous term "te" or "di" (meaning "hand"), which had historically served as the foundational, overarching descriptor for Okinawan fighting methods, began to acquire a new, more specific connotation. It came to describe koryu (old-style) arts or those distinct Okinawan indigenous martial traditions that either predated or purposefully remained outside the scope of the newly systematized "Karate." While "te" literally means "hand" and undeniably forms the etymological root of all Okinawan fighting methods, its specific usage evolved to distinguish these traditional, often less codified, and privately transmitted practices from the standardized, pedagogically adapted "Karate" taught in public institutions. This rebranding created a linguistic and practical division between the past and the present forms of the art.

Crucially, this transformation was not merely terminological; it fundamentally altered the pedagogical emphasis of the art. Traditionally, the transmission of "te" was an intimate affair conducted in one-on-one or extremely small, exclusive groups. The focus of this instruction was deeply rooted in the principles of self-defense, encompassing not only the physical execution of techniques but also the underlying intent, strategic understanding, and practical application of every movement within a combative context. The emphasis was squarely on "what" was being done and "why," ensuring a comprehensive grasp of the art's combative efficacy. Traditional training often included grappling, joint locks, throws, and intricate *bunkai* (explanations of kata applications) that were honed for efficacy in real-world situations.

However, with the shift to mass instruction in the public school system, the teaching methodology had to change. The "new," modified, and simplified system developed for teaching children emphasized rote repetition, standardized movements, and a focus on physical exercise and moral development. Under figures like Yabu Kentsu, training became systematic and, at times, militaristic, prioritizing uniform execution and basic punches, blocks, and kicks suitable for large groups. In this environment, the nuanced *bunkai* and many of the more intricate or grappling-oriented techniques were systematically removed or de-emphasized. Consequently, as the vast majority of people were exposed to karate through this new, streamlined system, much of the original design and combative intent of "Te" its principles of defense, its holistic understanding of the body, and its deeper applications, became increasingly relegated to "lost" or "secret" principles, known only to a select few who continued to practice the older ways.

Such modifications and substitutions of terminology and, more significantly, pedagogy, while serving a critical purpose in modernizing and broadly disseminating the art, inevitably hinder our nuanced understanding of the history and evolution of Okinawan martial arts that came before this era of transformation. The imposition of later classifications and the politically motivated redefinition of terms can, often unintentionally, obscure original lineages, making it challenging to trace direct lines of transmission without careful deconstruction. This linguistic and practical re-framing can also subtly alter the perception of technical content, as complex or grappling-oriented techniques might be overlooked or miscategorized if they don't fit the simplified curriculum of formalized "Karate." Crucially, it risks diminishing the recognition of unique local contributions and the diverse martial traditions that flourished in Okinawa, separate from or even preceding the significant Chinese influences, by subsuming them under a singular, redefined umbrella. This ongoing challenge underscores the need for a critical and comprehensive approach to Okinawan martial history, moving beyond modern classifications to explore the original context and identity of these rich traditions.

Karate's Evolving Legacy and the Imperative of Critical Inquiry

The journey of Okinawan martial arts, from the informal "Te" to the formalized "Karate" known today, is a profound narrative of adaptation and transformation. As we have explored here, the late 19th and early 20th centuries witnessed a complex evolution, driven by both internal developments within the art and the irresistible currents of Japanese political and social integration. The transition from terms like "Okinawa-te" and "Tode" to the strategically chosen "Karate" (first "China Hand," then "Empty Hand"), accompanied by the adoption of Japanese "Ryu" classifications, was far more than a linguistic exercise; it was a deliberate reimagining of the art's identity for a new era.

Pioneering figures such as Itosu Anko, Gichin Funakoshi, and Yabu Kentsu, recognizing the imperative for martial arts to survive and thrive within this evolving landscape, were instrumental in systematizing "Karate" for inclusion in public education. This pivotal shift, while ensuring broader dissemination and public acceptance, fundamentally altered the art's pedagogical core. Where traditional "Te" emphasized intimate, principle-driven, and combatively nuanced self-defense for small groups, the school-based curriculum prioritized standardized, often militaristic, rote instruction designed for the masses.

Consequently, much of the original depth, design, and intent of Okinawan martial arts, its holistic understanding of the body, its intricate *bunkai*, and its more comprehensive defense applications, became either diluted or obscured. These once-central principles were increasingly relegated to "lost" or "secret" knowledge, passed down only by a dwindling few who maintained the older traditions. This historical trajectory, marked by necessary adaptations and politically expedient rebranding, inevitably complicates our contemporary understanding. It underscores the critical need to approach the study of Okinawan martial history with a discerning eye, moving beyond modern classifications to excavate the rich, diverse, and often hidden layers of its original context and identity. The true legacy lies not just in what was preserved, but in diligently seeking to comprehend what was subtly reshaped, or even, inadvertently, set aside.

Notes

1. The exact identity and direct lineage of RuRuKo (also transliterated as Ryū Ryū Ko) remain subjects of scholarly discussion. He is commonly cited in various historical texts as a master of White Crane *gongfu* and a teacher of Higaonna Kanryō. See, for example, Bishop, *Okinawan Karate: Teachers, Styles and Secret Techniques*, pp. 43-44, for further discussion.

2. Itosu Anko's "Ten Precepts of Karate" (唐手十訓, *Tode Jukun*), which he wrote in October 1908, is essentially a letter to the Prefectural Education Board in Okinawa. It was Itosu's effort to promote the inclusion of karate in the public school system. In it, he outlined his views on the art and its benefits, making it a foundational text for understanding the modernization and institutionalization of Okinawan karate.

Various translations of the Ten Precepts exist, and while the exact wording might differ slightly between them, the core idea that karate originated from two main schools (Shorin-ryu and Shorei-ryu) from China is a consistent point within the first or second precept in most versions.

Beyond the Kata
The Vanishing Core of Okinawan Martial Arts

What if the Karate we know today is only half the story?

Okinawan Karate is celebrated worldwide for its dynamic strikes, disciplined forms, and philosophical depth. But hidden beneath this polished, global art lies a more rugged, often forgotten legacy of a lineage of Ryukyuan fighting systems that once embodied close-quarters realism, tactile sensitivity, and body mechanics far more nuanced than the bulk of modern practice often reveals.

This paper argues that the very process that preserved Okinawan martial arts, the modernization, systematization, and public instruction, also diluted or buried many of its core combative principles. By exploring the faded methods of Kakidī and Kakedameshi, and the lost tactical depth of Meoto-de, Muchimi, Kakei, and Tuidi, we aim to reconnect with a more complete vision of what Okinawan martial arts once were, and what they might become again.

For centuries, Okinawan fighting systems evolved quietly, shaped by personal mentorship, regional influences, and pragmatic necessity. Techniques weren't taught in gyms, but passed from teacher to student in tight circles, embodied by knowledge honed through sweat and touch. As

Okinawan martial arts entered the modern world, many of those intimate, tactile methods were sacrificed for mass instruction, public respectability, and sportification. What was gained in preservation may have cost us something even more valuable: depth.

Modernization and the Loss of Okinawan Combative Principles

The early 20th century marked a profound turning point for Okinawan martial arts, initiating a period of rapid transformation that would fundamentally reshape their identity, practice, and public perception. This era, driven by the imperatives of modernization and the island's integration into the Japanese nation-state, inadvertently became the genesis of a subtle yet significant loss in the art's deeper combative principles.

How Okinawan "Te" Shifted from Secret Transmission to Public Education

Historically, the indigenous fighting art known as "te" (手, hand) was transmitted through discreet, often intimate channels. Knowledge was typically passed down within families, or through highly selective master-disciple relationships that resembled familial bonds, where a handful of inside students would receive personalized, in-depth instruction. This private mode of transmission, shaped by centuries of political realities and the absence of formal public training institutions, fostered a nuanced understanding of combative principles tailored to individual aptitudes and specific self-defense scenarios.

However, as Okinawa transitioned into a Japanese prefecture, the desire to preserve and legitimize "te" within the new social order spurred a shift towards formalized, institutionalized instruction. This was a critical move to ensure the art's survival and relevance in a rapidly modernizing society. Key figures emerged to champion this cause, most notably Itosu

Ankō (1831-1915), a prominent student of Matsumura Sōkon. Itosu was instrumental in introducing karate into the physical education curriculum of Okinawan public schools, beginning with Shuri Jingo Elementary School in 1901. His efforts, supported by figures like Kentsu Yabu (1866-1937), a former army officer and another Matsumura student, focused on standardizing the art for broader consumption. This process involved developing simplified pre-arranged forms (kata) like the Pinan (Heian) series, making them accessible for large groups of schoolchildren. Their vision was to transform "te" from a secretive, combative skill into a public discipline that contributed to physical fitness and moral development, thereby gaining official acceptance and popularity.

Why Standardization Stripped Away Depth

This shift from private, individualized instruction to public, mass pedagogy brought with it inherent imperatives that profoundly influenced teaching methods. The need for mass instruction meant that complex, nuanced techniques, often requiring extensive one-on-one guidance, had to be streamlined. Similarly, increased safety became a paramount concern when teaching large groups of children, leading to the de-emphasis or outright removal of techniques deemed "too dangerous" or "too rough" for a general curriculum. Furthermore, there was a strong drive to cultivate a more "respectable" public image for the art, aligning it with the ideals of Japanese budō which emphasized discipline, character building, and physical prowess, rather than raw, brutal combat.

While this process was undeniably successful in preserving the skeletal forms of the art and ensuring its widespread dissemination across Okinawa and eventually mainland Japan, it often came at a cost. Many deeper combative principles and traditional training methods, which were not easily conveyed in large classes or were simply deemed unsuitable for new social contexts, were either simplified, reinterpreted, or omitted entirely. This inherent tension between preservation through standardization and the retention of original combative depth forms the very genesis of the "lost" principles we will explore.

Meoto-de: The Lost Art of Dual-Handed Tactics

As Okinawan martial arts transitioned from private, personalized instruction to public, institutionalized pedagogy, certain foundational principles that once governed body movement and application began to recede from common practice. Among these, the concept of Meoto-de (夫婦手, Husband and Wife Hand) stands out as a fascinating example of a "lost" or significantly diminished principle. It encapsulates a profound understanding of simultaneous, integrated, and continuous hand action for both offense and defense within close-quarter engagement.

Definition and Principle

At its core, Meoto-de dictates that the hands do not operate in isolation or in a purely sequential, back-and-forth manner, but rather move in a coordinated, "married" fashion. As elucidated by the formidable Motobu Chōki (1870-1944), a master renowned for his practical fighting prowess, the essence of Meoto-de is that "in both attacking and defending, the hands are supposed to move together like a married couple, close together." This implies a constant, fluid interplay between the lead and support hand, ensuring that one is always ready to assist, reinforce, or seamlessly transition from a defensive posture to an offensive one, and vice-versa, without unnecessary pauses or telegraphing movements. It represents an economic and highly efficient approach to hand work, where both limbs are perpetually "online" and engaged in the combative exchange.

Counter to Modern Interpretations

This principle stands in direct contrast to many prevalent modern interpretations of kata, particularly regarding the "hikite" (引き手, pulling hand to the hip). In numerous modern styles, a striking hand is often accompanied by the opposite hand retracting forcefully to the hip. Motobu Chōki himself questioned this practice in actual combat, asserting that if one "take[s] the time and effort to do that, the opponent will attack you in the meantime. All attacks should be done immediately from wherever the hand is positioned." His critique underscored the idea that kata movements are not always literal representations of combat but often camouflage and conceal deeper, hidden applications (bunkai).

Through the lens of Meoto-de, seemingly simple or formalistic kata movements reveal a richer tactical landscape. For instance, a "morote zuki" (two-handed thrust) often seen in forms like Naihanchi (Tekki) might appear as a straightforward double punch. However, through the principle of Meoto-de, this motion can conceal a highly effective joint locking technique, with one hand controlling or seizing while the other applies leverage, or even strikes. The continuous, integrated movement allows for fluid transitions between striking, trapping, grabbing, and joint manipulation, emphasizing control and entanglement over purely linear power.

Loss and Implications

Regrettably, Meoto-de, along with the nuanced understanding it provides for kata application, has largely diminished in widespread practice within modern Okinawan martial arts. Its decline can be directly linked to the simplification necessitated by institutionalized training. As karate was adapted for large classes in schools, the intricate, often subtle, and continuously flowing principles like Meoto-de, which demand significant individual guidance and extensive partner work for mastery, were difficult to convey efficiently to scores of students. The emphasis shifted towards more standardized, often linear, and visibly distinct movements suitable for mass instruction and demonstration. This pedagogical transformation, while ensuring the art's survival and global dissemination, inadvertently led to a loss of dynamic, flowing, and simultaneous close-quarter combat principles, ultimately impacting the depth of combative understanding available to many modern practitioners.

Muchimi, Kakei, and the Disappearance of Okinawan Grappling

Beyond the overt mechanics of hand movement, older Ryukyu fighting arts emphasized a profound internal quality of the body, cultivated through rigorous training, which profoundly impacted close-quarter combat. This quality, often referred to as "Muchimi," was inextricably linked to sensitivity drills like "Kakei," which combined to facilitate the intricate grappling and control techniques known as "Tuidi."

The Pervasive Body Quality

Muchimi" (むちみ, often translated as "sticky body," "heavy hand," or "viscous power") refers to a foundational body quality that permeates the practitioner's entire physique. It's not merely about brute physical strength, but rather a deeply rooted, connected, and yielding yet powerful state that allows for seamless transitions between techniques. Imagine a body that, when impacted, feels like a dense, rooted tree, absorbing force without collapsing, or like thick, viscous liquid that molds around an object rather than resisting rigidly.

This unique quality is not innate but is cultivated through rigorous, specialized training methods such as the tension and breathing exercises found in sanchin kata, the conditioning of nigiri game (gripping jars), and specific body mechanics drills. Through such practice, a practitioner develops the ability to generate profound, rooted power from the ground up, absorb an opponent's impact efficiently, and maintain an almost unbreakable connection to them. This allows for subtle manipulation and control, enabling the redirection of an opponent's force, the initiation of devastating close-range strikes, or the fluid execution of grappling techniques from a grounded stance. Ultimately, muchimi is about being simultaneously grounded and fluid, capable of both absorbing and delivering force with remarkable efficiency in a combative context.

Continuous Contact and Tactile Sensitivity

Emerging directly from the cultivation of Muchimi is the concept of Kakei (かけい, literally "hooking hand" or continuous contact work), which represents a primary application and principle designed to leverage and refine the Muchimi quality, particularly in close-quarter engagement. Its fundamental function is to maintain continuous, tactile contact with an opponent's limbs. Through this unbroken connection, the practitioner can "read" or sense the opponent's intentions, balance, and lines of force. This tactile sensitivity allows for immediate adjustments, enabling the practitioner to disrupt the opponent's posture, trap their limbs, or create subtle openings for follow-up techniques before they can fully develop.

Conceptually, Kakei shares parallels with the "sticky hands" (Chi Sao) drills found in Chinese martial arts like Wing Chun, or the "Hubud Lubud" methodologies prevalent in some Filipino Martial Arts. All these systems emphasize the development of highly refined tactile sensitivity and the ability to control and unbalance an opponent through continuous contact. However, Kakei in the Okinawan context has its distinct historical and technical expressions, often rooted in specific kata principles and their corresponding applications. While its underlying principles are vital for true close-quarter efficacy, the primary means of cultivating and testing Kakei in Okinawa's indigenous martial traditions involved specific forms of partner practice that were distinct from later, more formalized sparring methods.

These traditional Okinawan training methods included Kakidī (掛け手, also commonly written as Kakete, meaning "hooking hands" or "bridging hands"). Kakidī was a foundational and often continuous-contact drill explicitly designed to develop the tactile sensitivity, balance, and the ability to feel and respond to an opponent's force inherent in Kakei. It typically involved two partners maintaining a continuous, fluid connection with their hands and forearms, probing for openings, controlling the opponent's center, and reacting instinctively to shifts in pressure. Importantly, it was not overtly competitive in the modern sense but was instead a highly interactive and sensory-rich learning environment, crucial for developing the nuanced feel for an opponent's energy and embodying Kakei.

The Culmination of Close-Quarter Principles

Tuidi" (取手, grabbing hand or seizing hand), represents the ultimate combative manifestation of mastered Muchimi and Kakei. It encompasses the traditional Okinawan grappling, joint-locking, throwing, and controlling techniques that were historically an integral part of the fighting art. These close-range applications reflect a lineage rooted in older Okinawan grappling forms, most notably Tegumi (手組, hand grappling), a type of folk wrestling often associated with festivals and community gatherings. This historical connection highlights Tuidi's deep roots in native Okinawan combat methods, allowing the practitioner to secure, manipulate, and neutralize an opponent at close range, moving beyond mere striking.

The mastery and embodiment of Muchimi and Kakei provide the essential physical and sensory platform for effective Tuidi. Without the pervasive rootedness and connected power of Muchimi, a practitioner would struggle to execute powerful throws or maintain controlling locks. Similarly, without the continuous tactile sensitivity of Kakei, it becomes nearly impossible to "feel" for the precise points of an opponent's balance, the subtle shifts in their limb tension, or the opportune moments to apply a joint lock or sweep. Kakei allows for the precise "reading" of the opponent necessary for effective Tuidi, enabling accurate control and manipulation at close range.

However, as Karate underwent its strategic formalization for integration into the public school system in the early 20th century, the teaching of Tuidi applications, alongside its foundational body mechanics and sensitivity drills (Muchimi, Kakei), was progressively de-emphasized. This shift was likely a deliberate choice, as historians and researchers such as Thomas Feldmann and Patrick McCarthy theorize as the intricate and potentially dangerous control aspects of Tuidi were deemed unsuitable for general school-age children. It's theorized that the lack of mature understanding among young students regarding the principles of control, combined with the risk of injury during practice, led instructors like Ankō Itosu to prioritize simpler, safer, and more visible linear striking techniques. This contributed directly to the reduction and, in many cases, the misunderstanding of Tuidi applications within modern practice. The art began to lose its full, multifaceted combative vocabulary, prioritizing overt striking over the intricate, often subtle, close-quarter control inherent in its koryu roots.

Kakedameshi: The Forgotten Sparring That Made It All Work

Beyond the individual principles of hand and body mechanics, the very method of training in Ryukyu fighting arts was instrumental in cultivating the deep understanding that has largely been lost. The absence of specific, dynamic partner drills in many modern contexts represents a critical missing link in the chain of transmission, particularly concerning the internalizing of Meoto-de, Muchimi, Kakei, and Tuidi.

Koryu Forms of Continuous Sparring

Kakedameshi (掛け試し), meaning "testing hands" or "challenging hands," referred to a more free-form, continuous-contact sparring match format. Unlike later point-based or limited-contact *kumite*, Kakedameshi involved a much broader range of techniques, including strikes, grappling, joint locks (Tuidi), and throws, executed at a realistic level of intensity. It was a rigorous and often unscripted exchange where practitioners could test their skills and principles, including Kakei, in a dynamic, unpredictable environment. Both Kakidī and Kakedameshi were characterized by their focus on continuous flow and adapting to an opponent's spontaneous movements, making them unique to the practical, combative nature of Okinawan koryu.

Cultivating Core Principles

This dynamic and experiential learning environment was absolutely crucial for developing, testing, and internalizing the deep-seated principles central to Okinawan martial arts, far beyond what static solo kata practice could achieve alone.

The principle of Meoto-de (夫婦手, husband and wife hands), emphasizing the simultaneous use of both hands (one for defense, one for offense, or both working in concert), was intrinsically cultivated through Kakidī and Kakedameshi. The continuous contact forced practitioners to coordinate both limbs seamlessly, transitioning instantly from a block to a grab, or a parry to a strike, without conscious thought, embodying the idea of two hands working as one.

Similarly, the development of Muchimi (むちみ, sticky body/viscous power) was directly reliant on these continuous-contact drills. Through the constant give-and-take of Kakidī, practitioners learned to maintain a heavy, rooted, yet yielding connection. This allowed them to absorb force without collapsing, mold around an opponent's movements, and transmit powerful energy from their core, making them incredibly difficult to move or unbalance. Kakedameshi further tested this quality under live, unscripted pressure, honing the ability to stay connected yet unmovable.

The principle of Kakei (かけい, continuous connection/tactile sensitivity) was, in fact, the very essence of Kakidī. By maintaining constant physical contact, practitioners refined their ability to "read" subtle shifts in an opponent's weight, tension, and intention, anticipating their moves and feeling for opportune moments to exploit vulnerabilities. Kakedameshi then provided the ultimate test for the real-time application of this high level of sensitivity in a dynamic, combative exchange.

By extension, Kakidī and Kakedameshi were the primary vehicles for the natural discovery and practical application of Tuidi (取手, grabbing/ seizing hand). As practitioners learned to maintain continuous connection (Kakei) and embody rooted power (Muchimi), the transition into grappling, joint-locking, and throwing became organic. The drills fostered an environment where seizing an opponent, manipulating their balance, and applying control techniques were not isolated movements but natural extensions of the continuous flow, making Tuidi an inherent and deeply integrated part of their combative vocabulary.

Loss and Implications: Erosion of Core Understanding

The historical records and modern observations suggest a significant alteration, if not outright disappearance, of true Kakidī and Kakedameshi in many modern karate practices. This profound shift is inextricably linked to the art's strategic formalization and move towards standardized, less combative, and often more linear training formats for public schools.

As discussed previously, the complex, full-contact, and potentially dangerous nature of Kakedameshi and deep Tuidi applications made them unsuitable for general physical education classes, especially for children. Simplification for mass instruction led to the prioritization of solo *kata* and basic, often simplified, striking drills that could be taught safely to large groups. Furthermore, the subsequent rise of competitive sport karate, with its emphasis on limited-contact rules, point scoring, and often linear, explosive techniques, further marginalized the continuous-contact, grappling-oriented methods. Modern *kumite* (sparring) often lacks the continuous connection and close-range manipulation inherent in Kakidī and Kakedameshi, favoring speed and power over subtle control.

This progressive de-emphasis directly led to the erosion of a deep understanding and practical application of the very technical principles that these older sparring formats cultivated. Without the constant, tactile feedback and the need for seamless transitions provided by Kakidī and Kakedameshi, practitioners struggled to internalize Muchimi, Kakei, and the organic integration of Tuidi. The art's full, multifaceted combative vocabulary was gradually diminished, favoring visible, linear striking over the intricate, often subtle, close-quarter control inherent in its koryu roots. The consequence is that many modern karate practitioners, despite extensive training, may lack a complete grasp of the core body mechanics and combative applications that defined traditional Okinawan martial arts.

Recovering What Karate Once Knew

The journey of Okinawan martial arts from secretive island traditions to a global phenomenon is a testament to its enduring appeal and adaptability. However, as noted here, the strategic modernization and systematization essential for its widespread dissemination and acceptance in new social contexts, came at a discernible cost. The imperatives of public instruction and standardization led to an educational shift, simplifying complex, nuanced principles and marginalizing vital training methodologies in favor of more linear, visibly distinct, and safer forms of instruction.

We have seen how this transformation impacted the understanding and practice of key combative principles. The dual-purpose mechanics of Meoto-de, once integral to dynamic, simultaneous hand action in close-quarter engagement, became obscured by a more literal interpretation of kata movements. Similarly, the pervasive body quality of Muchimi and the sophisticated tactile sensitivity of Kakei, fundamental to absorbing force, maintaining connection, and initiating control, suffered a de-emphasis. Crucially, the decline of traditional continuous-contact drills like Kakidī and free-form sparring such as Kakedameshi deprived practitioners of the experiential learning environment essential for internalizing these principles organically. Consequently, the comprehensive close-quarter grappling and control applications known as Tuidi, which are the natural culmination of perfected Muchimi and Kakei in a dynamic context, were gradually diminished and misunderstood as striking became the dominant public image of the art.

Understanding these "lost" elements is not merely an academic exercise in nostalgia; it is crucial for a more authentic, profound, and holistic appreciation of Okinawan martial arts' original combative intent and depth. Recognizing what was deliberately or inadvertently set aside in the pursuit of modernization allows us to reconnect with a richer, more integrated system of self-defense that extended far beyond linear striking. It highlights a complete martial art designed for real-world efficacy, emphasizing control, balance disruption, and continuous engagement at all ranges. This deeper understanding invites both scholars and dedicated practitioners to engage in continued critical research, historical re-evaluation, and dedicated practical exploration. By actively seeking to comprehend and embody these multifaceted principles, we can strive to truly honor and reclaim the full legacy of Ryukyu's ancient fighting arts; bridging the gap between its romanticized past and its enduring, profound essence for future generations. For Okinawan karate to reclaim its rightful depth, we must not only preserve its forms, but recover its feel, its weight, its grip, its subtlety. That means not just practicing more, but practicing deeper.

More Than a Teacher
The Master-Disciple Bond in Okinawa's Martial Arts

Karate's Deepest Lessons

In the early years of the 19th century, a young man named Kyo Sokon stood patiently in attendance before his master, Sakugawa Kanga. This young man would later become the legendary Matsumura Sokon, a central figure in the history of Okinawan martial arts. Their training was not a public display but a private, rigorous ritual, reflecting a bond that transcended mere instruction and forming the very foundation of the art itself.

The master-disciple relationship, known as shisho-deshi, in Okinawan martial arts has always been more than just functional; it represents a moral, social, and often spiritual contract. This bond is essential for transmitting not only techniques but also values, identity, and an entire cultural legacy. Through this personal, demanding, and often lifelong commitment, the arts of Te and Kobudo were both forged and preserved.

This exploration will examine the evolution of this master-disciple relationship from classical Ryukyu society through the tumultuous Satsuma occupation, the Meiji educational reforms, and into the modern era, focusing on its main pillars: trust, secrecy, ethical shaping, embodied practice, and social structure.

Historical Context: Forged in Secrecy

To truly understand the depth of the bond between master and disciple in classical Ryukyu society, we must first examine the historical context from which it originated. The social structure of this society was significantly influenced by Confucian ideals, particularly through the aristocratic warrior-scholar class known as Yukatchu. These ideals emphasized values such as loyalty, filial piety, and self-cultivation, all of which were integral to the master-disciple relationship. For many young men, their martial master became a surrogate patriarch, and the bond they shared was as strong as familial ties; they formed a chosen family, united by a common pursuit of excellence and a shared moral code.

This bond was strengthened by the secretive nature of early martial arts training, known as Te. In a time before public dojos existed, instruction was a private and guarded affair. A master might only teach one or two students, creating a small circle of trust. To earn a place in this select group, a disciple had to undergo rigorous testing, not only for physical abilities but also for their kokoro, meaning heart or character. The master needed to trust their student implicitly, as they were sharing dangerous and potentially lethal knowledge. This art was something to be earned through unwavering dedication and the demonstration of a strong moral compass, rather than something that could be bought.

Following the Japanese Satsuma clan's occupation of Okinawa in 1609, this selective and secretive nature of training became even more pronounced. The carrying of weapons was prohibited, forcing Okinawan martial culture to go underground. The master-disciple relationship transformed into a crucial means of preserving not just combative skills but also the sense of Okinawan cultural identity amid political suppression. Dojos became sanctuaries, quiet spaces where history, philosophy, and self-defense were quietly passed down through whispers and subtle movements, away from the eyes of the occupiers. The trust between master and student became essential, serving as a matter of survival, not only for the art itself but also for the spirit of the people.

Shaping More Than Technique: The Role of the Shisho

In this unique cultural context, the master served as more than just a technical instructor. Figures like Higaonna Kanryo and Matsumura Sokon were not only teachers; they were life mentors, community leaders, and moral exemplars. The dojo and the master's household often overlapped, blurring the line between training and daily life. A disciple's apprenticeship became an immersive and comprehensive experience.

This role made the master an architect of ethics, responsible for shaping the disciple's character as much as their physical abilities. Training sessions were rigorous and included lessons on proper family life, conduct, humility, and the importance of perseverance. The training served as a moral compass, teaching not just how to fight, but also when to refrain from fighting.

The master's role also included that of a filter and custodian. In this selective tradition, they did not share everything with everyone. Their responsibility was to safeguard the art, revealing knowledge selectively based on a disciple's demonstrated trust, loyalty, and readiness. Certain teachings, such as the deepest applications, the most esoteric principles, and the "secret" techniques, were often reserved for the most dedicated students, those expected to carry the lineage forward. The master acted as a mirror, reflecting the disciple's character back to them, and as a guardian, ensuring the integrity of the art for generations to come.

The Path of the Deshi: Duty and Devotion

For the disciple, the path involved loyalty, service, and profound transformation. This role was characterized by the concept of giri, a deep sense of duty, unwavering respect, and a willingness to serve without the expectation of immediate reward. Service could take many forms, such as performing household tasks like cleaning the master's home or dojo, bringing him food, or assisting with various aspects of the master's daily life outside of formal training. These tasks were not seen as demeaning but as sacred acts, a way of repaying the master for the invaluable gift of their knowledge and mentorship.

The training itself was a journey through hardship. Physical discomfort, relentless repetition, and constant correction were not viewed as punishments but as necessary rites of passage. Endurance, cultivated through countless hours of hard training, fostered resilience, humility, and mental fortitude. This process involved breaking down the ego and rebuilding the self from a foundation of strength and discipline. This internal work was guided by the concept of Shoshin sho no kokoro, or "the beginner's mind."

This mindset, central to both martial arts and Zen Buddhism, emphasizes approaching every session with openness, eagerness, and a lack of preconceptions. It requires a conscious effort to set aside existing beliefs and judgments, viewing the art as a source of infinite possibilities. A disciple, even after years of practice, is expected to engage with each lesson as if experiencing it for the very first time, discovering new depths and meanings. This cultivation of humility and modesty serves as an antidote to arrogance, preventing complacency and ensuring a lifetime of continuous learning and refinement. The practice of Shoshin allows the disciple to let go of the need to be "right," embracing the opportunity to learn from every source and fostering true mastery without the constraints of a fixed mindset.

Through years of intense, holistic immersion, the student did not merely mimic the master's movements; they became a living vessel of the tradition. This model of transmission was not about a curriculum being delivered to a student but rather person-to-person, a lineage of embodied knowledge passed from one individual to another. The disciple's body, mind, and spirit became a seamless extension of the art, embodying the master's legacy.

Sacred Space Where the Art Was Forged

The dojo embodied the values of its martial arts tradition, although its design often differed greatly from that of a modern, purpose-built gymnasium. Early training spaces were flexible and often discreet, reflecting the need for secrecy and practicality. Training sometimes took place in a master's home or a quiet area within a temple, and many historical accounts describe training occurring in secluded clearings or even in the courtyards of tombs and graveyards.

These unconventional locations served several important purposes. First, they provided secrecy and concealment. With the official ban on weapons and public martial practice in Okinawa, training in remote areas allowed practitioners to safely develop and pass on their techniques. Second, practical considerations played a role; training at night in elevated, windy graveyards offered cooler temperatures and better airflow, offering a welcome relief from Okinawa's hot climate. Beyond these practicle considerations, these spaces carried significant spiritual meaning, as graveyards, where the boundary between life and death is confronted, provided a powerful backdrop for a martial art that emphasizes the value of life. Training in such an environment could help focus the mind and foster a deeper understanding of the art's seriousness. In some traditions, it was also viewed as a way to train under the watchful spirits of past masters, offering a deeply humbling experience for any dedicated student.

Regardless of the location, the dojo was more than just a training space; it was a blend of classroom, temple, and family dining room. This sacred space would also functioned as a moral incubator, where disciples formed close-knit brotherhoods, reinforcing their master's teachings and supporting one another. It served as a microcosm of the society the master sought to build; one grounded in mutual respect, hard work, and a shared moral code.

Living Legacies: Lessons from the Lineage

The historical record contains many powerful examples of the master-disciple bond, with one of the most famous being the relationship between Higaonna Kanryo and his student Chojun Miyagi. Miyagi's lifelong commitment to his master, which included caring for him in his old age, exemplified the virtues of filial piety.

Miyagi's dedication extended far beyond the dojo; he lived and served alongside Higaonna, bringing him food and assisting with household tasks. This relationship was not transactional but rather a significant act of service (giri) that fostered a deep, familial trust. Through this devotion, Miyagi gained a rich understanding of his master's character and philosophy, forming the basis of Goju-ryu's principles, which emphasize a balance of hard and soft techniques as well as a strong ethical code.

Another notable example is the connection between Matsumura Sokon and his disciple Itosu Anko. Matsumura embodied the secretive, combative master archetype, while Itosu emerged as a public reformer. Through his revolutionary efforts, Itosu brought Karate into the school system, transitioning from individualized mentorship to group instruction. Nevertheless, he credited Matsumura's legacy, ensuring that his master's foundational knowledge was preserved even as the method of instruction evolved. This demonstrated a disciple's loyalty while paving a new path for the art.

This dynamic reflects a significant transition in Karate's history. Matsumura, as a warrior-scholar, represented the private, secretive nature of Karate before the Meiji Restoration, with his teachings reserved for a select few. Itosu, honor bound to carry on that lineage, realized that the art needed to adapt to survive in a new era characterized by nationalization and militarization. His decision to modify his master's teachings for a public educational context marked a radical departure, but it was fundamentally an act of loyalty to the spirit of the art itself. Instead of betraying his master, Itosu honored him by ensuring that his techniques would endure, even as the teaching methods changed.

Finally, the mentorship of Funakoshi Gichin by masters like Azato Yasutsune and Yamakawa illustrates the seamless blend of intellectual, ethical, and combative ideals in pre-Meiji Okinawan mentorship. Funakoshi gained not only technical skills but also philosophy and character development from these masters, providing him a comprehensive education that later enabled him to introduce Karate to mainland Japan as a means of self-cultivation.

The relationship between Funakoshi and his mentors embodies the ideal of the yukatchu or "warrior-scholar." Azato, a respected noble, was proficient in both calligraphy and karate. He mentored Funakoshi not just in martial techniques, but also in classical Chinese and Japanese literature. This multifaceted training allowed Funakoshi to present Karate to mainland Japan not as merely a brutal martial art, but as a pathway to self-improvement (Karate-do), focusing on moral development and philosophical principles. The legacy of his masters was reflected not only in the kata he taught but also in the ethical framework with which he introduced the art to the world, a framework shaped by his intellectual mentorship.

Carrying the Flame: Evolution of the Teacher's Role

The profound relationship between master and disciple, rooted in tradition, has shown remarkable adaptability over time. Itosu Anko's innovative approach was not a disruption but a brilliant act of preservation. By introducing Karate into the school system, he ensured the art's survival in a rapidly modernizing society. He traded the exclusivity of private mentorship for the accessibility of public instruction, allowing Karate to reach a much wider audience and planting the seeds for its global growth and popularity.

This evolution has continued into the modern era. While dojos now operate in a more structured, pedagogical format, many instructors have successfully created a hybrid model. This approach balances the practical needs of running a contemporary school with a deep respect for traditional values. The role of the master has expanded beyond merely being an instructor; they are now community builders, mentors, and custodians of the art's ethical core. In these dojos, students learn not only techniques but also receive guidance toward personal development, self-discipline, and a deeper understanding of the art's history and philosophy.

Today, the master-disciple relationship thrives in a new form. It is often a bond forged through years of shared training and trust, even within group settings. Teachers continue to select and groom students who demonstrate a genuine commitment to the art's values, preserving the lineage while making the foundational principles of Karate accessible to all. This new model ensures that the rich legacy of Okinawan martial arts endures, not as a static historical relic, but as a living, breathing tradition that continues to shape lives around the world.

Loyalty, Legacy, and the Path Forward

The legacy of Okinawan martial arts is found not only in its powerful techniques but also in the deep, reciprocal bond between master and disciple; a relationship built on mutual devotion. The disciple's commitment goes beyond learning physical movements, encompassing the master's entire philosophy. This philosophy includes not only the "how" of fighting but also the crucial lessons of when and why to engage in conflict and when and why to refrain.

In turn, the master's devotion is equally significant. He is not merely a teacher of combat but a guide committed to shaping a student's character, ensuring they grow into an upstanding member of the next generation and a leader in their community. This enduring partnership, where loyalty meets guidance and technique balances with ethics, is the true essence of the art. The profound transformation that occurs in this sacred space holds timeless value, reminding us that the journey of martial arts is one of self-mastery best traveled with a devoted guide.

Unlocking Tuite
Rediscovering Okinawan Karate's Vanishing Core

Karate's Other Half

For many, Okinawan Karate is associated with explosive strikes, powerful punches, devastating kicks, and unyielding blocks made famous in cinema. It is often seen as a purely percussive art, a symphony of impact intended to overwhelm an opponent through sheer force. However, beneath this striking exterior lies a profound and often overlooked aspect: Tuite. This intricate element of Ryukyuan martial arts is not a mere add-on; rather, it represents a fundamental core of control and close-quarters engagement, integral to the art's traditional approach to combat.

Tuite, which comes from the Okinawan term meaning "hand seizing" or "grappling hand," is a crucial aspect of Okinawan karate. It emphasizes joint manipulation, pressure point control, and the use of body mechanics to subdue or control an opponent, adding a practical dimension to defense that extends beyond the striking techniques typically associated with karate. Unlike the more well-known Japanese grappling arts such as Judo or Jujutsu, Tuite is not a separate discipline; rather, it is an integral part of the holistic Te[1] system.

Historically, Tuite was not practiced in isolation. Its principles and applications were deeply incorporated into the kata that define Okinawan karate, serving as a subtle layer of combative strategy.

This exploration aims to delve into the historical origins and diverse influences that have shaped Tuite, outline its core principles and applications, and emphasize its vital yet often underappreciated importance in the overall effectiveness of Okinawan Karate. We will argue that a proper understanding of Tuite is essential for grasping the traditional essence of the art, revealing a sophisticated system designed not just for striking, but for comprehensive self-defense. To achieve this, we will trace Tuite's roots from early Okinawan Te and its significant Chinese influences, dissect its underlying mechanics and hidden applications within the kata, and examine the reasons for its historical neglect, as well as contemporary efforts to reclaim this essential core, ensuring that the comprehensive legacy of Okinawan Karate endures.

As a lifelong student and teacher of Okinawan Karate, I have come to view Tuite as one of the most meaningful and insightful aspects of this martial art. It represents the intersection of theory and physicality, where the intricate mechanics of control and leverage transform kata from abstract forms into practical, functional combat systems. For me, Tuite is not an obscure branch of Karate; rather, it is its hidden backbone. It embodies the original purpose of the art: not just to strike harder or faster, but to understand and resolve conflict with precision, restraint, and a deep understanding of the human body. This paper serves not only as an academic exploration but also as a personal journey into the part of Karate that I value most.

Okinawa's Early Controls

To understand the comprehensive nature of Tuite, one must journey back to the formative periods of Okinawan martial arts, long before they were systematized publicly. The roots of control and seizing techniques are deeply embedded in the pragmatic realities of early Te and its profound connections to Chinese martial traditions.

Tegumi and Te: Okinawa's Original Close Quarters

The indigenous martial art of Okinawa, known simply as Te, was a highly pragmatic and comprehensive system of self-defense. Unlike the specialized military arts of larger nations, early Te developed within a society where personal safety often depended on versatile, adaptable combative skills. It was not merely about striking; it encompassed a full spectrum of close-quarters engagements, including grappling, seizing, and controlling an opponent. This implied versatility is evident in the historical practice of tegumi[2], a form of Okinawan wrestling that served as both a recreational activity and a foundational method for developing practical grappling skills. A common part of growing up in the Ryukyu Kingdom, particularly for boys and young men, Tegumi helped foster an understanding of balance, leverage, and body manipulation; elements crucial to the later development of Tuite. Its influence can still be seen in the grappling techniques present within traditional karate kata.

The Fujian Connection

The most significant external influence on the grappling core of Okinawan martial arts comes from Chinese martial arts, particularly those originating from Fujian Province in Southern China. Okinawa's long-standing tributary relationship with China, along with extensive trade and diplomatic exchanges, fostered a continuous flow of cultural knowledge, including combative methods. This connection laid the groundwork for a deeper integration of Chinese martial principles into native Okinawan fighting systems.

Among these influences, Fujian White Crane, Monk Fist, and other Southern Chinese Quanfa[3] systems stand out. These styles are characterized by their emphasis on close-quarters combat and incorporate precise hand techniques, joint locks, off-balancing methods, and strikes to vital points. In contrast to many Northern Chinese systems, which are known for their wide stances and high kicks, Southern systems favor rooted stances and tactile sensitivity, optimizing both power and control at grappling range. Their techniques focus on manipulating an opponent's structure rather than relying solely on brute force.

Okinawan Yukatchu-class[o] martial artists, educated warrior-scholars tasked with civic defense, played a crucial role in absorbing and adapting these systems. Figures such as Matsu Higa, Takahara Peichin, Chatan Yara, Sakugawa Kanga, Matsumura Sokon, and Kosaku Matsumora exemplify this integration. Through study abroad and interactions with Chinese envoys residing in Okinawa, they adopted a holistic approach to martial training. Their responsibilities often included maintaining order and protecting the aristocracy, requiring a skill set that included non-lethal control and restraint techniques. In this context, Chinese locking and seizing methods were not only effective but essential. The fluid yet penetrating movements, emphasis on tactile responsiveness, and joint manipulation strategies derived from Chinese sources helped form a vital foundation for what would later become Tuite.

The Bubishi: Karate's Secret Manuscript

The Bubishi[5] is a classical Chinese martial arts text that plays a crucial role in understanding the deep influences of Chinese martial arts on Okinawan Te. This invaluable historical document has been studied extensively by Okinawan masters over generations, serving as a direct link to the theoretical and practical foundations of many techniques. In modern times, its accessibility has improved significantly thanks to the dedicated efforts of Patrick McCarthy[6] Hanshi. His seminal work, "Bubishi" (1st edition, published by IRKRS in 1990), marked a pivotal moment in the study and dissemination of this text. McCarthy Hanshi has spent decades researching and interpreting the Bubishi, sharing its insights with a global audience.

The chapters within the Bubishi explicitly detail principles and applications related to Tuite, including sections on pressure points (kyusho), vital targets, seizing methods, and even resuscitation techniques for unconscious opponents. Its presence and diligent study in Okinawa clearly demonstrate that concepts such as joint manipulation and control were not peripheral but central to the combative knowledge being transmitted from China.

Messengers of the Hidden Hand

Many Okinawan martial arts masters either traveled to China or studied under Chinese martial artists who had settled in the region. These men played a crucial role in transferring Chinese combat knowledge to the Ryukyu Kingdom, especially in the areas of close-quarters control and grappling techniques.

One notable figure is Sakugawa Kanga, who is thought to have studied under the Chinese military envoy Kusanku; a master we know to have practiced grappling techniques. A well-known account from the Oshima Hikki[7] describes Kusanku demonstrating a technique in which he placed one hand on his opponent's lapel and executed a takedown using a scissoring leg motion. While detailed records of their broader grappling curriculum are limited, the comprehensive nature of Chinese martial arts suggests that seizing, control, and close-quarters manipulation were central to what was transmitted.

Later, masters such as Kanryo Higaonna continued this exchange. Higaonna trained intensively in Fuzhou, China, under the guidance of Ru Ru Ko[8], which led to the development of highly refined close-quarters combat systems. The techniques he brought back, including locks, holds, and pressure-based control, became foundational to the formation of Goju-ryu karate, integrating Chinese grappling principles into Okinawan martial arts. These contributions formed a direct and influential root for what would later evolve into Tuite.

Survival Tactics Under the Watchful Eye

These Chinese methods were not simply copied but were skillfully assimilated and adapted into the unique Okinawan context. The development of Tode (a term that evolved from Te to specifically denote the "China Hand" influence) saw grappling elements become intricately interwoven with striking. This was a natural evolution, as Okinawan martial artists sought to create a holistic defense system.

The social conditions under Satsuma occupation[9] further necessitated this "hand-to-hand" nature of combat. With conventional weapons restricted and the consequences of lethal force against Satsuma samurai being severe, there was a pragmatic need for methods of control and non-lethal incapacitation. Tuite provided the means to subdue an opponent, apply pain compliance, or create openings for escape without resorting to overtly violent or fatal measures that could lead to dire repercussions for the practitioner and their community. This emphasis on control, precision, and the ability to manage a close-quarters confrontation without necessarily escalating to deadly force became a hallmark of Okinawan martial arts, reflecting a shrewd adaptation to their unique socio-political environment.

Cracking he Code: How Tuite Works

Having explored the historical roots of Tuite, we now focus on its fundamental principles and practical applications. Tuite is not merely a system based on brute force; instead, it is a sophisticated art that emphasizes leverage, precise body mechanics, anatomical knowledge, and meticulous technique to achieve control over an opponent. Its effectiveness lies in understanding how to exploit the body's natural weaknesses, making it a powerful component of traditional Okinawan Karate.

From Grip to Lock

Tuite encompasses several distinct but interrelated principles designed to achieve control or incapacitation through specific anatomical vulnerabilities:

Seizing/Grabbing: Tuite involves controlling an opponent by grasping their clothing, hair, or limbs. This is not merely holding; it is about disrupting balance, restricting movement, and setting up further techniques. By seizing a wrist, lapel, or even a finger, a practitioner can dictate the opponent's posture, create openings, or initiate a joint lock or throw. The grip is often accompanied by a pull or push that off-balances the opponent, making them vulnerable.

Joint Manipulation: This focuses on forcing a joint beyond its normal range of motion, leading to pain, instability, or dislocation. Techniques involve hyperextension (e.g., bending an elbow backward), hyperflexion (e.g., folding a wrist sharply inward), and rotation (e.g., twisting a shoulder or knee). Examples include various wrist locks (kote-gaeshi variations), elbow locks (often seen in applications from Naihanchi), and shoulder locks, which can be applied from standing or on the ground. The effectiveness of Kan setsu waza lies in understanding the anatomy of the joint and applying precise pressure.

Pressure Point Application: This highly specialized aspect of Tuite involves applying pressure or striking specific anatomical points on the body to elicit pain, control, or disorientation. These points, often located along nerves, arteries, or muscle attachments, can be sensitive even to light touch. When struck or pressed correctly, kyusho[10] can cause temporary paralysis, extreme pain, loss of balance, or even unconsciousness. The Bubishi explicitly details many of these points and their effects, underscoring their historical significance in Okinawan martial arts.

Chokes/Strangles: While not always the primary focus of Tuite, some control techniques can seamlessly transition into chokes, strangles, or cranks. These often involve restricting an opponent's airflow or blood flow to the brain, leading to unconsciousness. While direct chokes and strangle holds might be less prevalent as standalone techniques in traditional Karate compared to striking or joint locks, the ability to control an opponent's neck or posture through seizing techniques creates opportunities for such applications, particularly in close-quarters grappling.

The Hidden Language of Kata

A profound understanding of Tuite is essential for unlocking the true combative meaning of Okinawan Karate kata. Many of the seemingly abstract or ceremonial movements within kata are, in fact, encoded applications of joint locks, arm bars, seizing techniques, and pressure point strikes. These applications were often deliberately "hidden" or obscured within the kata for various reasons, including the secretive nature of training under occupation and the desire to protect dangerous knowledge.

For example, movements in Naihanchi (known as Tekki in mainland Japan) are rich with Tuite applications, including wrist locks, elbow breaks, and methods for controlling an opponent's arm while simultaneously striking. Similarly, sequences in Passai (or Bassai) can be interpreted as techniques for seizing an opponent's wrist and applying a joint lock, or for trapping and manipulating their limbs. Even forms like Seisan (or Seishan), known for their powerful strikes, contain movements that, when analyzed through a Tuite lens, reveal opportunities for close-range control, throws, and pressure point attacks. A deeper understanding of Tuite transforms the perception of kata from mere physical exercises into dynamic, multi-layered combative manuals. Once this concept is grasped, the ideas of bunkai and Tuite become almost synonymous.

Tuite and the Total Fighter

Tuite is rarely, if ever, isolated from striking in traditional Okinawan Karate. Instead, it is used in a dynamic and fluid interplay. A strike can serve as a distraction or a setup for a joint lock, creating an opening by momentarily stunning or unbalancing the opponent. Conversely, a joint lock or seize can create an opening for a devastating strike, controlling the opponent's posture and exposing vital targets. This seamless combination is encapsulated in the concept of Tuite, where the practitioner might strike to gain control, then use a seize to manipulate a joint, and finally deliver another strike to finish the encounter. This holistic approach ensures that the Okinawan martial artist is prepared for all ranges of combat, from long-range striking to close-quarters grappling and control.

Lost in Transmission: The Disappearance of Tuite

Having established the historical roots and fundamental principles of Tuite, we now confront a crucial question: if Tuite was so integral to traditional Okinawan Karate, why did it become largely obscured, even "vanish," from common practice in the past century? Here we will explore the complex reasons for its decline and highlight the contemporary efforts to revive this vital aspect of the art.

From Dojo to Schoolroom: Karate's Safe Repackaging

The marginalization of Tuite can be traced back to significant socio-political changes in Okinawa and Japan that followed the Meiji Restoration[11] in 1868 and the annexation of the Ryukyu Kingdom in 1879. One of the critical turning points was the formal introduction of Te into the Okinawan public school system, primarily led by influential figures such as Itosu Ankō[12]. While Itosu's reforms were essential for the art's survival and broader acceptance, they required a considerable systematization and simplification to accommodate mass instruction. As a result, complex and potentially dangerous elements such as intricate joint locks, pressure point applications, and grappling techniques were largely de-emphasized or even removed from the curriculum. This restructuring shifted the focus toward physical education, basic striking techniques, and character development, making the art safer and more accessible for the general student population, which aligned with the broader Japanese educational ethos. Unfortunately, this pedagogical change inadvertently stripped much of Tuite's practical emphasis from the curriculum.

As Karate made its way to mainland Japan and eventually gained international popularity, a strong trend towards sportification emerged. The growing desire for competition led to the establishment of standardized rules and a clear scoring system, which further marginalized grappling elements. Within this competitive environment, the more complex joint locks and pressure point techniques were often deemed too dangerous, difficult to judge, or simply not conducive to the stand-up striking format that became the hallmark of sport Karate. This evolution prioritized dynamic and often linear striking exchanges, pushing the close-quarters, control-oriented aspects of Tuite further into obscurity.

Additionally, even within Okinawa, Tuite was predominantly taught as a part of private, advanced lessons that were reserved for dedicated students who had already mastered foundational striking techniques. This inherent secrecy, a remnant of the occupation era, meant that as Karate became more public and widespread, the deeper and more dangerous elements like Tuite remained largely obscure. Without explicit instruction and dedicated practice, the bunkai of many kata movements became misinterpreted. Consequently, their grappling implications were lost to generations of practitioners who focused solely on striking interpretations, causing each subsequent generation to drift further away from the original intent of the art.

A Dangerous Art in a Safe World

The historical de-emphasis of Tuite has had a profound impact on contemporary Karate practice, and one significant consequence is the lack of formal instruction in Tuite techniques. In many modern dojos, there is either minimal or no teaching of these vital techniques. This is often due to instructors themselves not having received comprehensive training in Tuite, which results in a curriculum that focuses primarily on striking. Such a scenario creates a cycle where the knowledge and practice of Tuite continue to diminish over time.

Additionally, the inherent nature of Tuite techniques presents challenges for safe training. These techniques involve the manipulation of joints and the application of pressure to sensitive areas of the body. To train them safely and effectively, a high degree of control is required, along with trust between training partners and experienced guidance from instructors. Without proper supervision and a thorough understanding of human anatomy, there is a significant risk of injury, which understandably makes many dojos reluctant to delve deeply into these elements of training.

Revivalists of the Seizing Hand

Despite the fragmentation and obscurity that Tuite has experienced in the modern era, a growing movement of dedicated researchers and practitioners is working to recover and reintegrate its principles into contemporary Okinawan Karate. These efforts are not merely theoretical; they represent a living attempt to restore a vital component of classical martial practice.

One of the most influential figures in this revival is Seiyu Oyata[13], often credited with reintroducing the concept of Tuite to modern Karate audiences. Oyata developed Ryukyu Kempo, a system that emphasizes the practical application of kata, including joint manipulation, pressure point strikes, and close-quarters control. His legacy includes early instruction of American servicemen stationed on Okinawa in the 1950s and 60s, significantly helping to transmit Tuite concepts internationally.

Another key figure in this movement is Patrick McCarthy, the founder of the International Ryukyu Karatejutsu Research Society (IRKRS). Through his extensive translations of classical martial texts, including the Bubishi, and the development of his system, Koryu Uchinadi Kenpo-jutsu, McCarthy has played a central role in decoding the combative logic embedded within kata. His work has helped contextualize and reconstruct the original intent of Okinawan Karate, bringing grappling and control techniques back into the curriculum.

Within the traditional Okinawan sphere, Kise Isao[10], the son of Kise Fusei and a student of Hohan Soken, stands out as a practitioner who has carried forward a deep knowledge of Tuite as part of the broader Matsumura Seito tradition. His teachings emphasize the lock-based and tactile sensitivity components of Okinawan Karate that are often missing from modern iterations.

John Shipes[15], a senior student and close associate of the Kise lineage, has continued these efforts with dedication. For over two decades, Shipes has systematically worked to preserve, refine, and transmit Tuite as a distinct but integral part of traditional Karate. Similarly, Allan Amor[16], a longtime direct student of Seiyu Oyata, has carried forward Oyata's teachings with precision and commitment, ensuring that the principles of Tuite remain an active and evolving part of the Ryukyu Kempo legacy.

Collectively, the efforts of these and other committed practitioners are reshaping modern understandings of Karate, helping to restore its original purpose as a complete self-defense system, not only focused on strikes, but encompassing the full spectrum of human movement, control, and survival strategy.

Bringing the Hands Back to Karate

The exploration of Tuite's history and principles clearly shows that it is an essential part of traditional Okinawan Karate, rather than a peripheral or optional addition. Tuite's roots are deeply connected to the practical self-defense needs of early Te and are significantly influenced by the comprehensive grappling and control techniques found in Southern Chinese martial arts. This influence is particularly evident in texts like the Bubishi and through the teachings of prominent masters such as Kanryo Higaonna. The core principles of Tuite, focusing on seizing, joint manipulation, and pressure point application, exhibit a sophisticated art that relies on leverage and anatomical knowledge, seamlessly integrating with striking techniques to create a holistic combative system.

However, over the past century, Tuite has been unfortunately marginalized; a "vanishing core" resulting from the Japanization of Karate, its introduction into public schools, and the subsequent emphasis on sportification. While this shift has contributed to Karate's global popularity, it has also stripped away much of its close-quarters control and grappling depth, leading to a widespread misunderstanding of its true combative potential.

The narrative does not end with its decline, though. Contemporary revival efforts led by dedicated masters and researchers such as Seiyu Oyata, Patrick McCarthy, and Kise Isao, along with proponents like John

Shipes and Allan Amor, are crucial in this restoration process. Their relentless work in researching, teaching, and promoting the reintegration of Tuite is not merely an academic pursuit; it is a vital effort to reclaim the authenticity and full spectrum of Okinawan martial traditions.

Understanding Tuite goes beyond historical accuracy; it enriches our appreciation of Karate's profound depth. This understanding transforms the interpretation of kata from mere abstract movements into dynamic and multi-layered self-defense scenarios. It is essential for preserving the authenticity of Okinawan martial traditions and ensuring that the complete legacy, including both striking and control techniques, is passed down to future generations. A comprehensive understanding of Tuite also significantly enhances modern defense applications, providing practitioners with a broader and more versatile skill set for real-world confrontations. This extends beyond purely percussive solutions to include effective control, manipulation, and incapacitation. The ongoing journey to rediscover and integrate these vital elements ensures that the comprehensive legacy of Okinawan Karate endures, reflecting its historical resilience and timeless relevance as a complete system of self-protection.

As someone form whom Tuite represents not just a technique but a philosophy, I believe its revival is not merely a technical endeavor, but a reclaiming of Okinawan Karate's soul.

Notes

1. The term Te (手), meaning "hand," was the original term for Okinawan martial arts before the influence of Chinese Quanfa prompted the alternate reading Tode (唐 手, "China hand").

2. Tegumi (手組) was a native Okinawan form of wrestling and play-fighting among youth. It laid the physical and strategic groundwork for later grappling systems and Tuite, often seen as Okinawa's indigenous grappling heritage.

3. Fujian White Crane, Monk Fist, and other Southern Quanfa systems emphasized tactile sensitivity, joint control, and short-range power, all of which became central to the Okinawan Tuite concept.

4. The Yukatchu were the educated aristocracy of the Ryukyu Kingdom, trained in Confucian scholarship, civil administration, and martial arts. They served in bureaucratic and protective roles, receiving instruction in both Chinese and indigenous martial systems to guard dignitaries and maintain order. Their dual expertise made them essential transmitters of Te, blending Chinese concepts like joint locking and control into Okinawa's martial culture.

5. The Bubishi, a classical Chinese martial text, contains sections on vital points, seizing techniques (Qinna), and anatomical diagrams that have directly influenced the development of Okinawan Karate's grappling methods.

6. Patrick McCarthy's decades-long research into the Bubishi and translation of classical texts have been central to decoding Tuite and its applications in kata through his system, Koryu Uchinadi.

7. The Oshima Hikki recounts Kusanku demonstrating a leg scissor takedown after seizing an opponent's lapel—an example of integrated grappling methods taught to Okinawan martial artists.

8. Ru Ru Ko (also spelled Liu Liu Ko or Lu Lu Ko) was a 19th-century martial arts master from Fuzhou, Fujian Province. He is recognized as the teacher of Kanryo

Higaonna, a key figure in Okinawan martial arts and the founder of Goju-ryu Karate. Although historical details about Ru Ru Ko are limited, his teachings likely included Southern Chinese systems like White Crane and Monk Fist boxing, focusing on close-range techniques such as joint manipulation, tactile sensitivity, and pressure point control, which influenced Okinawan Tuite.

9. The Satsuma occupation of Okinawa (1609-1879) imposed strict weapons bans, which led to an increased emphasis on empty-hand control methods like Tuite to deal with physical conflict under tight constraints.

10. Kyusho-jutsu, the art of pressure point manipulation, is closely related to Tuite and involves targeting nerves, arteries, and muscle insertions to control or incapacitate an opponent.

11. The Meiji Restoration (明治維新, Meiji Ishin) was a political and social revolution in Japan that began in 1868, marking the end of the Tokugawa shogunate and restoring imperial rule under Emperor Meiji. This era initiated rapid modernization and centralization, dissolving the samurai class and absorbing the formerly semi-independent Ryukyu Kingdom into Japan as Okinawa Prefecture by 1879. These sweeping reforms dramatically altered Okinawa's political and cultural landscape, including the formalization and Japanization of local martial arts traditions such as Te, which would eventually become known as Karate.

12. Itosu Ankō (糸洲 安恒, 1831-1915) was a pioneering Okinawan martial artist credited with systematizing and popularizing Karate during the late 19th and early 20th centuries. A student of Matsumura Sōkon, Itosu introduced Karate into the Okinawan public school system in 1905, emphasizing simplified kata for physical education and moral development. While this move preserved the art and broadened its appeal, it also led to the omission of many combative and grappling elements; favoring a safer, more athletic form suited for mass instruction.

13. Seiyu Oyata is widely credited with reviving the practice and terminology of Tuite in the post-WWII era. His Ryukyu Kempo system emphasized locks, pressure points, and control techniques embedded in kata.

14. Kise Isao, son of Kise Fusei and student of Hohan Soken, is an important figure in the preservation of Matsumura Seito Karate and Tuite as part of his traditional teachings.

15. John Shipes has worked extensively under the Kise lineage to preserve and teach Tuite with precision, including systematized instruction and public seminars through the OSMKKF.

16. Allan Amor, a longtime direct student of Seiyu Oyata, continues to preserve and propagate Oyata's teachings on Tuite through seminars and private instruction, maintaining fidelity to the original Ryukyu Kempo system.

From Te to Tournament
The Evolution of Karate

From Hidden Art to Global Phenomenon

The martial arts of Okinawa, once a collection of secretive, privately transmitted combative methods known broadly as Te[1], embarked on a remarkable journey, transforming into the globally recognized discipline of Karate. This evolution, from clandestine practice to a worldwide phenomenon, is a compelling story of adaptation, strategic redefinition, and the complex interplay between cultural identity and global aspiration. It is a story marked by both its global spread and the gradual, often unintentional, erosion of its original combative essence.

At the heart of this global dissemination lie the pivotal contributions of two men, each often recognized as a "father of modern Karate" in their own right. The initial transformation began in Okinawa with Itosu Anko, whose visionary reforms introduced Te into the public school system, necessitating significant pedagogical innovations and simplifications. This crucial shift laid the groundwork for the art's broader accessibility. Following this, Gichin Funakoshi spearheaded its crucial transition to mainland Japan, where a distinctly Okinawan art was meticulously "Japanized" and integrated into the broader Budo[2] framework. Their combined efforts set the stage for Karate's dramatic internationalization.

This journey explores how Karate navigated changing socio-political landscapes, ensuring its survival and unprecedented reach. Yet, these adaptations also led to a significant de-emphasis of its original combative principles, prompting ongoing efforts within the martial arts community to rediscover and reintegrate the profound depths of its historical heritage. The story of Karate is thus a dynamic testament to an art constantly redefining itself, balancing its rich past with its diverse global present.

Itosu Anko: Reforming Te for the Modern Era

The transition of Okinawan Te from a secretive, privately transmitted combative art to a component of the public school system's curriculum represents a pivotal moment in its history, fundamentally reshaping its form and function. Central to this transformation was the vision and tireless efforts of Itosu Anko (1831–1915).

Itosu's early life and upbringing were steeped in the traditional Ryukyuan elite culture. Born in Shuri, the capital of the Ryukyu Kingdom, into a keimochi[3] (family of position), he received a rigorous education in Chinese classics and calligraphy, typical of the scholarly class. Though described as small in stature and introverted as a child, he dedicated himself to martial arts study under prominent masters early in life, including Nagahama Chikudun Pechin[4] and the legendary Matsumura Sokon[5]. This dual path of intellectual and martial cultivation prepared him for a life of service within the kingdom's administration, where he served as a secretary for the Administrative Office of the last Ryukyuan king, Sho Tai[6]; a position that placed him at the heart of the kingdom's governance.

However, Itosu's life, like that of many Ryukyuan officials, was dramatically altered by the Meiji Restoration[7] in Japan and the subsequent abolition of the Ryukyu Kingdom in 1879. With the end of the native monarchy and Okinawa's incorporation as a Japanese prefecture, the traditional roles and social structures of the Pechin class were dismantled. Stripped of his governmental position, Itosu faced a new reality. Leveraging his scholarly training and intellectual acumen, Itosu pivoted to a career as a teacher within the burgeoning public school system. It was in this transformative period, marked by a rising tide of Japanese nationalism and, by extension, an increasing anti-Chinese sentiment within Japan and its newly annexed Okinawan prefecture, that he recognized the potential of Te.

His extensive knowledge, deeply rooted in Chinese culture and classical texts, became less valued in this new climate, and this provided a powerful motivation for him to reframe Te not merely as a fighting method but as a powerful tool for physical education; its character development, and a subtle form of nationalistic discipline, aligning with Japan's broader goals of strengthening its populace. Notably, around 1905, Itosu also played a key role in changing the kanji for Karate[8] from 唐手 (Tang Hand, or China Hand) to 空手 (Empty Hand), further distancing the art from its Chinese origins and promoting a more indigenous Okinawan or Japanese identity.

A Curriculum for the Nation: Pedagogy and Public Karate

With a clear vision for the future of Te, Itosu Anko embarked on a profound pedagogical reform, fundamentally altering the art to suit the demands of public instruction. A cornerstone of this transformation was the creation of the Pinan kata. These five simplified forms were meticulously designed to address the practical challenges of safely and effectively teaching large groups of children in a school environment.

Beyond the Pinan series, Itosu is also credited with modifying and systematizing several older kata to better suit the public education curriculum. This is said to include breaking down the extensive

Naihanchi kata into three distinct forms: Naihanchi Shodan, Naihanchi Nidan, and Naihanchi Sandan. This division made the complex kata more digestible for students and easier to teach in a progressive manner. He also revised other classical kata such as Kusanku, Passai, and Chinto, adapting their movements to be more linear, standardized, and safer for group instruction. Furthermore, Itosu is sometimes credited with the creation or heavy modification of the Rohai kata, further expanding the foundational curriculum. These innovations aimed to create a systematic method of teaching Karate techniques that are still in practice today.

This shift in curriculum necessitated a profound simplification of training methodologies. The rigorous, often brutal, and unscripted close-quarter combat drills of traditional Te, such as the continuous-contact of Kakidī[9] and the free-form sparring of Kakedameshi[10], along with the practical grappling of Tuidi[11], were largely set aside. These methods, which demanded a high degree of maturity, resilience, and a willingness to engage in potentially injurious contact, were deemed unsuitable for a public school setting. In their place emerged safer, more visible, and directly obvious striking techniques, often practiced in isolation or in highly formalized, non-contact drills. This adaptation, while understandable for the context, inadvertently contributed to a disconnect from the immediate, fluid realities of self-defense.

Lost Principles, New Priorities

The most significant impact of this simplification was on the core principles that defined the older martial art, the nuanced body mechanics that cultivated Muchimi[12] and Kakei[13], qualities essential for close-range control and grappling, were gradually neglected. While still present in the underlying structure of the kata, their practical application and the methods for their internalization were often diluted or lost in the pursuit of standardized, easily reproducible movements. Concurrently, the concept of sparring began its evolution. Early kumite formats within the school system largely consisted of pre-arranged sparring and other highly controlled drills. These replaced the more free-form, continuous contact methods of the past, prioritizing safety and a visible demonstration of technique over the unpredictable, adaptive engagement that characterized traditional Ryukyuan combat arts.

Itosu's foresight, however, was not limited solely to curriculum reform; it extended to a clear philosophical vision for the art's future. His seminal "Ten Precepts of Karate" (Tode Jukun)[14], penned in 1908 and addressed to the Prefectural Educational Department (and the Ministry of War), served as a powerful blueprint for the art's public legitimacy. These precepts explicitly articulated a vision of Karate (now explicitly referred to by its new kanji) as a means of building strong bodies for national service, fostering moral character, and promoting health. This document was profoundly impactful, demonstrating Itosu's strategic thinking in aligning the art with broader national goals, thereby legitimizing its place in the public sphere and setting a formative direction for the next generation of Karate-ka.

The Bridge Between Eras

Itosu's profound influence transcended his direct pedagogical innovations; he also played a vital role in preserving and transmitting the older traditions by continuing the instruction of many of Matsumura Sokon's students. This ensured a critical bridge between the secretive, combative lineage of the past and the new, public instruction he championed. Among his most prominent students were Gichin Funakoshi (1868-1957), Kenwa Mabuni (1889-1952, founder of Shito-ryu), Choshin Chibana (1885-1969, founder of Shorin-ryu), Choki Motobu (1870-1944), Kentsu Yabu (1866-1937), Chomo Hanashiro (1869-1945), and Kanken Toyama (1888-1966). Each of these individuals would go on to propagate Itosu's vision and their inherited knowledge in various directions.

This era, therefore, marked a crucial pivot point in the history of Okinawan martial arts. Through Itosu's deliberate reforms, Te was transformed into a more palatable, yet fundamentally altered, art; one ready for its dramatic journey beyond Okinawa's shores. Gichin Funakoshi, deeply influenced by Itosu's pedagogical innovations and philosophical framing, would later play the pivotal role in introducing and popularizing Karate on mainland Japan, setting the stage for its dramatic expansion and global reach.

The Expansion of Karate to Mainland Japan

Having undergone a significant transformation under Itosu Anko's reforms in Okinawa, Te was poised for its next great leap: its expansion to mainland Japan. This crucial period saw a distinctly Okinawan martial art evolve into a "Japanese Budo," gaining wider recognition and setting the stage for its eventual global spread. Central to this monumental undertaking was the tireless dedication of Gichin Funakoshi (1868–1957), a direct student of both Itosu Anko and Anko Azato[15].

Gichin Funakoshi: Messenger of Karate

Funakoshi's youth was shaped by the dramatic shifts occurring in his homeland. Born into a Pechin family in Shuri, he began his martial arts journey the year after Japan annexed Okinawa, around the age of eleven. Introduced to the martial arts through his school friend, the son of the renowned Anko Azato, Funakoshi soon began formal training under Azato himself, and later, under Itosu Anko. Despite his intellectual prowess and a desire to attend medical school, the profound societal changes wrought by the Meiji Restoration, which dismantled the traditional Ryukyuan class system, closed that path to him. Consequently, Funakoshi followed a common route for educated men of his era, becoming a teacher. This background, combining deep martial training with an academic profession, uniquely positioned him to champion Karate's introduction to a new, broader audience.

Funakoshi's tireless efforts to promote Karate on the mainland began with humble circumstances, but his persistence led to significant opportunities for public demonstration. In 1917, he was invited to perform his martial art at a prestigious physical education exhibition sponsored by the Ministry of Education. His captivating display earned him a second invitation in 1922 when Jigoro Kano, the founder of Judo, invited Funakoshi to give a demonstration at the Kodokan dojo in Tokyo. This event was crucial in introducing karate to mainland Japan and fostering its subsequent growth, leading to the pinnacle of these early efforts came with a special, third performance: a demonstration of his art for the Emperor and the Imperial Family. This unprecedented exposure solidified Karate's legitimacy in the eyes of the Japanese establishment, prompting Funakoshi-sensei to make the momentous decision to remain in Japan and dedicate his life to teaching and promoting his art.

Shotokan and the Shaping of Modern Budo

This period was characterized by a deliberate process of "Japanization," driven by the rising tide of Japanese nationalism and militarism. To gain acceptance within the established Japanese Budo landscape, Karate needed to shed its foreign, "Chinese hand" (唐手) connotations; a symbolic shift that aligned the art with indigenous Japanese martial philosophy and emphasized its unique, weaponless nature. This transformation extended to terminology, with the adoption of established Budo concepts such as dojo (training hall), Karate gi[16], and the kyu/dan ranking system[17], further assimilating Karate into the formalized structure of Japanese Budo.

In this context of adaptation and integration, Funakoshi's teachings evolved into what would become known as Shotokan Karate. While he initially resisted naming his style, his dojo at Mejiro, Tokyo, was eventually referred to as "Shotokan" (松濤館), meaning "Pine Waves Hall," after his pen name, "Shoto." This marked the formalization of his particular interpretation of Okinawan Te into a distinct Japanese style. Funakoshi also laid the groundwork for the organizational structures that would facilitate Karate's spread, establishing associations that would eventually become instrumental in disseminating Shotokan across Japan and, later, around the world.

Forging the Path to Internationalization

Karate was meticulously presented to align with prevailing Japanese cultural values and the Budo ethos. The emphasis shifted beyond mere physical technique to encompass mental discipline, rigorous etiquette, and spiritual development. It was framed as a path to self-improvement and character building, resonating deeply with the Japanese concept of Do (道, "way" or "path"). This adaptation proved particularly effective in its introduction into universities, where Karate clubs swiftly gained popularity among educated youth. Influential early clubs at institutions like Keio, Waseda, and Takushoku Universities became vital breeding grounds for the art's expansion. Students, drawn by the promise of physical and mental discipline, embraced Karate, and these university hubs consequently produced many of the next generation of instructors who would carry the art across Japan and, ultimately, worldwide.

While Funakoshi's role was undeniably pivotal, it is important to acknowledge that he was not alone in this endeavor. Other prominent Okinawan masters also traveled to mainland Japan, contributing to the art's spread and diversification. Figures such as Kenwa Mabuni (founder of Shito-ryu), Chojun Miyagi (founder of Gojc-ryu), and Choki Motobu each brought their distinctive styles and interpretations of Te, enriching the nascent Japanese Karate landscape and ensuring a broader representation of its Okinawan roots. Their collective efforts cemented Karate's place as a recognized and respected martial art within Japan. Funakoshi's establishment of Shotokan and the organizational framework he pioneered, alongside the contributions of these other masters, laid the essential groundwork for Karate's eventual journey beyond Japan's borders, setting the stage for its dramatic internationalization following World War II.

Global Karate: Growth, Sportification, and Loss

Following its successful establishment and "Japanization" on the mainland, Karate embarked on its most expansive journey, globalization. This phase, particularly post-World War II, brought about unprecedented growth but also new challenges and ongoing debates about the art's fundamental identity and purpose.

Karate Goes Global: Post-WWII Spread and New Generations

The post-World War II era served as a critical catalyst for Karate's worldwide dissemination. To gain broader acceptance and thrive in this new global landscape, Karate strategically shifted its public image, presenting itself as a competitive sport and physical exercise rather than a combative art. This evolution further deemphasized its more aggressive aspects, including Kobudo (the study of weapons) and Tuiki (Okinawan grappling).

A vast new audience emerged through American servicemen stationed across Japan and Okinawa. Already accustomed to physical discipline, these young men often utilized their off-duty hours to train. Impressed by Karate's direct nature and effectiveness, many sought direct instruction from local masters. Upon their return home, these servicemen became Karate's first emissaries abroad, forming grassroots clubs that introduced the art to foreign audiences.

Simultaneously, a new generation of highly skilled and dedicated Japanese instructors began to travel internationally. These teachers, products of university Karate clubs and the standardized methodologies developed by Itosu and Funakoshi, were often two or three generations removed from the original Ryukyu Kingdom warrior-scholars and their koryu (old school) training practices. They carried their interpretations of Karate to North America, Europe, and beyond. This era marked a profound cultural transplantation, rather than just technical instruction, leading to the rapid proliferation of Karate schools across the globe.

From Kata to Competition

As Karate's popularity surged internationally, the need for standardization became apparent, leading to the formation of international organizations. Federations such as the Japan Karate Association (JKA), the World Karate Federation (WKF), and the International Traditional Karate Federation (ITKF) emerged, aiming to regulate techniques, establish ranking systems, and, significantly, standardize competition rules. This drive for uniformity paved the way for the rise of Sport Karate. The emphasis shifted towards competitive kumite and kata, with the development of specific rulesets, weight classes, and the introduction of safety equipment. A desire for broader appeal fueled this evolution and, ultimately led to Karate's inclusion in the Tokyo 2020 Olympic Games.

The Impact on "Traditional" Practices: A Fading Memory?

While the global spread and sportification brought unprecedented visibility to Karate, they also had a profound and often detrimental impact on "traditional" practices. The intense focus on competitive performance and adherence to sport-specific rules further sidelined the nuanced, close-quarter combative principles that defined early Okinawan Te. Traditional techniques, such as Tuidi and subtle body mechanics were increasingly de-emphasized or outright removed from mainstream curricula, and the dynamic, unscripted nature of traditional continuous-contact sparring was replaced by more formalized, point-based kumite. In many contexts, the art became a shadow of its former combative self, prioritizing aesthetics and athletic performance over its original self-defense efficacy. This shift has led to a situation where, arguably, most Karate practitioners worldwide today are not even familiar with these terms, let alone the profound concepts and practical applications they represent.

Rediscovering Karate's Soul

Following its successful establishment and "Japanization" on the mainland, Karate embarked on its most expansive journey, globalization. This phase, particularly post-World War II, brought about unprecedented growth but also new challenges and ongoing debates about the art's fundamental identity and purpose.

This divergence has ignited an ongoing and often passionate "Traditional vs. Sport" debate within the global Karate community. Proponents of traditional Karate argue for the preservation and rediscovery of the art's original combative principles, emphasizing its self-defense utility, philosophical depth, and historical integrity. As Choki Motobu famously asserted, "Nothing is more harmful to the world than a martial art that is not effective in actual self-defense." This sentiment reflects the concern that sportification has diluted the art, turning it into a mere game. Conversely, advocates for sport Karate highlight its benefits for physical fitness, discipline, and the global reach achieved through competition, arguing that adaptation is necessary for the art's continued relevance in the modern world. As Gichin Funakoshi himself stated, "The ultimate aim of karate lies not in victory nor defeat, but in the perfection of character." This ongoing discussion reflects a fundamental tension about Karate's identity.

In recent decades, however, there has been a growing and encouraging trend of re-evaluating roots. Researchers and dedicated practitioners, much like the reader engaged in this very study, are actively working to rediscover and re-integrate lost historical practices and principles. This involves meticulous study of old texts, analysis of foundational kata for their original applications, and a renewed interest in the training methodologies of the Okinawan masters. This movement seeks to bridge the gap between the modern, widely practiced sport and the rich, combative heritage of Te, ensuring that the full scope of Karate's legacy is understood and preserved for future generations.

A Dynamic Legacy of Adaptation

Karate's remarkable journey from the secluded Ryukyu Kingdom to its status as a global martial art stands as a testament to its inherent adaptability and the vision of its pioneering masters. This complex evolution began with Itosu Anko's strategic reforms in Okinawa, transforming Te into a public physical education discipline through simplified kata and training methods. This initial shift, born from the necessity of survival in a changing political landscape, laid the groundwork for the art's broader acceptance.

The subsequent expansion to mainland Japan, championed by figures like Gichin Funakoshi, marked a crucial phase of "Japanization." Here, Karate shed its foreign connotations, adopting Japanese Budo terminology and philosophical tenets to align with nationalistic ideals. The establishment of distinct styles like Shotokan and the introduction of Karate into university clubs cemented its place within Japanese society. However, the most significant transformation occurred post-World War

II, as Karate exploded onto the international scene. Driven by the interest of American servicemen and the dedication of Japanese instructors, the art spread worldwide, leading to the formation of international federations and the undeniable rise of Sport Karate.

This global dissemination, while ensuring unprecedented popularity and Olympic recognition, came with a profound cost: the gradual sidelining and, in many mainstream contexts, the near-oblivion of Karate's original combative principles. The nuanced body mechanics of Muchimi and Kakei, and the practical grappling of Tuidi, which defined the art's effectiveness, were often sacrificed for standardized, aesthetically pleasing, and safer sport-oriented techniques. This has fueled an ongoing "Traditional vs. Sport" debate, reflecting a fundamental tension within the community about Karate's true identity.

Yet, within this dynamic legacy of adaptation, there is also hope. The increasing trend of "re-evaluating roots" signifies a collective desire to bridge the gap between modern practice and historical intent. By meticulously researching and striving to reintegrate the lost combative principles, contemporary practitioners are working to reclaim the full scope of Karate's heritage. The story of Karate is, therefore, not just one of evolution, but of a continuing search for balance; and art poised between its historical combat roots and its contemporary global identity.

Notes

1. Te (手) Indigenous Okinawan hand-to-hand combat traditions, meaning "hand." These were the foundations of what later became known as Karate.

2. Budō (武道) Japanese term for martial ways or disciplines, encompassing Judo, Kendo, Karate-dō, and others. Emphasizes personal development and ethical practice.

3. Keimochi (or Chiimuchi) refers to a term used in the Ryukyu Kingdom (present-day Okinawa) to designate those individuals and families possessing a family lineage register

4. Research suggests that Nagahama Chikudun Pechin might be Nagahama Sohei, born in 1830, based on family records of the Nagahama family in Naha.

5. Matsumura Sōkon (1809-1899): Widely regarded as a foundational figure in modern Shorin-ryu Karate, Matsumura Sōkon was a highly influential martial artist who served as bodyguard to the Ryukyu King. He is remembered for his significant role in synthesizing various empty-hand te styles with Chinese Shaolin influences, laying much of the groundwork for what would become contemporary Okinawan Karate.

6. Shō Tai (1843-1901) The last reigning king of the Ryukyu Kingdom. He ruled until 1879 when Japan formally annexed Ryukyu and established Okinawa Prefecture.

7. Meiji Restoration (1868) A major political and social reform movement in Japan that ended the Tokugawa shogunate, centralized imperial power, and led to the annexation of Okinawa.

8. Chomo Hanashiro (1869-1945), a student of both Matsumura Sokon and Itosu Anko, is notably credited with being one of the first, to publicly use the kanji 空手 (meaning "empty hand") for Karate.

9. Kakidī (掛け手) A traditional Okinawan partner drill that develops tactile sensitivity and flow in close-range encounters. Known as "hooking hands."

10. Kakedameshi (掛け試し) - A sparring method evolving from Kakidī, allowing semi-free exchange of techniques emphasizing real-time adaptation.

11. Tuidi (取手) - "Seizing hand"; Okinawan joint-locking and control techniques similar to Chinese Chin Na or Japanese Aiki-jutsu. A key element of early Te.

12. Muchimi (むちみ) - "Sticky body" or "heavy movement." Describes whole-body movement that is grounded and connected—essential for grappling and striking power.

13. Kakei (かけい) - Continuous tactile connection that allows a practitioner to sense and respond to an opponent's movements in close contact.

14. Ten Precepts of Karate (Tode Jukun) - A document written by Itosu in 1908 outlining the moral, physical, and educational benefits of Karate, submitted to Okinawan authorities and the Ministry of War.

15. Anko Azato (1827–1906) - A Ryukyuan martial arts master and mentor to Funakoshi. Known for his precision and tactical intelligence in Karate practice.
    JKA (Japan Karate Association)
    Established in 1949, this was the first national organization for Karate in Japan and played a critical role in the sportification and international spread of Shotokan.

16. Karate gi - The training uniform for Karate practitioners, adopted and standardized in Japan along with the kyu/dan ranking system.

17. Kyu/dan ranking system - A belt-based ranking system originating in Judo and adopted across Japanese martial arts to denote progress and skill.

The Enduring Heart
Martial Arts and Cultural Identity in Modern Okinawa

A Living Tradition

In the hushed predawn light of an Okinawan beach, as the first rays of sun kiss the horizon, a lone figure moves through the precise, powerful motions of a kata, the only sound the whisper of the waves and the focused snap of his gi. This is not a performance for an audience, but a profound, personal communion with a tradition that runs as deep as the island's roots. These moments, often unseen by the casual observer, are vibrant testaments to the enduring presence of martial arts in contemporary Okinawa. While the global phenomenon of Karate often overshadows its island origins, such quiet dedication serves as a powerful reminder that the arts are not simply a historical curiosity, but a living, breathing part of the Ryukyu Islands' modern identity.

The journey of Okinawan martial arts, from the ingenious adaptation of everyday tools into formidable weapons to their clandestine development under the unique circumstances of the Satsuma occupation, has been a testament to human resilience and pragmatic innovation. These arts, shaped by the Yukatchu scholar-gentry and commoners alike, were never static historical artifacts. They were, and remain, dynamic traditions, passed down through generations, evolving yet retaining their fundamental essence.

Traditional Okinawan Karate and Kobudo are not merely from Okinawa; they remain deeply of Okinawa, held firmly in the hearts of its people and central to its modern cultural identity. This profound connection persists despite, and perhaps even because of, the global attention the arts now command. We will explore how this living legacy manifests through the intergenerational practice within Okinawan families and communities, the strategic safeguarding efforts by government and tourism initiatives, and the fierce collective pride that shapes its contemporary evolution and interaction with the world.

The Rhythm of Everyday Life: Karate and Kobudo in Okinawan Communities

To truly understand the enduring heart of Okinawan Karate and Kobudo, one must look beyond the grand international stages and into the intimate spaces where tradition truly lives: the dojos, the family homes, and the very fabric of local communities. Here, these arts are not just disciplines to be learned; they are a pulse, a rhythm passed from one generation to the next, embodying a continuity that defies the relentless march of modernity.

The Dojo as a Cultural Hearth

In Okinawa, the traditional dojo is far more than a mere training space for physical techniques. It is a vibrant community hub, a second home where bonds are forged, wisdom is imparted, and a shared cultural heritage is celebrated. Unlike the often commercial or purely sports-oriented gyms found in many parts of the world, an Okinawan dojo frequently serves as a nexus of mentorship and cultural transmission. Here, the emphasis extends beyond perfecting a punch or a kick; it encompasses the cultivation of character, the understanding of history, and the forging of lifelong relationships. Students, from toddlers taking their first tentative steps in a gi to seasoned elders still refining their kata, become part of an extended family, bound by mutual respect and a shared dedication to the do. This deep communal aspect fosters a sense of belonging and responsibility, ensuring that the art remains rooted in the lives of the people, not just in abstract theory.

Lifelong Learning and Family Transmission

The journey into Karate and Kobudo often begins remarkably early for Okinawan children, not as a structured extracurricular activity, but as a natural extension of family and community life. It is common to see children encountering these arts through local community centers, modest neighborhood dojos, or, most powerfully, through direct family traditions. Parents and grandparents, many of whom are practitioners themselves, actively encourage participation, seeing it not just as a physical pursuit but as a fundamental aspect of cultural upbringing and character formation.

This early immersion fosters a deep, intuitive understanding of the art. The relationship between sensei (teacher) and sempai (senior student) to kohai (junior student) in the local context transcends mere instructor-student dynamics; it is often akin to familial or clan bonds. The sensei is a paternal figure, guiding not just technique but life. The sempai assume a role of older siblings, mentoring and supporting their kohai. This intricate web of relationships creates an environment of continuous learning and mutual support, where knowledge flows organically, ensuring the art's living transmission.

Character as Curriculum

At the very heart of Okinawan martial arts lies a profound emphasis on character formation. Beyond the physical techniques, the arts are meticulously designed to instill discipline, perseverance, and, perhaps most crucially, respect (reigi) and humility. Every bow, every focused breath, every repetitive movement is a lesson in self-control and deference. This emphasis on reigi extends beyond the dojo, shaping interactions in daily life and fostering a harmonious society.

This dedication to ethical conduct and personal growth elevates the practice beyond mere combat to a "way" or "path"—the do. It is a lifelong journey of self-discovery and refinement, where technical mastery is inseparable from moral cultivation. Okinawan practitioners understand that the true strength of Karate lies not in brute force, but in the disciplined mind and spirit. These values, discipline, respect, perseverance, and humility, are seen as vital for the well-being of Okinawan society, embodying a quiet strength that has seen the islands through centuries of challenge. The martial arts, therefore, are not just about fighting; they are about living, about becoming a better human being.

Festival Demonstrations and Public Celebrations

The essence of this intergenerational practice is best captured through the voices and stories of those who embody it. You might hear tales of an elderly sensei, whose still agile body demonstrates a kata with a power that belies his years. His movements serve as a living archive of generations of knowledge. Alternatively, you may hear from a young girl, no older than seven, who proudly explains how practicing Karate helps her focus in school and respect her elders.

Consider the Kise family, whose dojo in Okinawa City stands as a vibrant testament to this living tradition. I recall visiting their dojo, where the air hummed with disciplined energy. There, I observed Kise Isao Sensei, a man whose movements carried the weight of decades of dedicated practice, guiding his young grandson through the intricate forms of their lineage. The grandson, perhaps eight or nine years old, mirrored his grandfather's precise footwork and powerful strikes with a seriousness that spoke volumes about his deep immersion in the practice. With gentle corrections and quiet encouragements, Kise Sensei was not just teaching techniques; he was transmitting a way of life; a direct link to the roots of Matsumura Seito. He often emphasizes that "Karate is not just about fighting; it is about building character, about understanding yourself and your place in the world." This multi-generational dedication, where the wisdom of the elder flows seamlessly into the eager spirit of the youth, encapsulates the very essence of how Okinawan martial arts endure. These personal narratives, rich with dedication and quiet pride, serve as powerful reminders that the heart of Okinawan martial arts beats strongest within the families and communities who continue to live and breathe its traditions.

This deep-rooted connection between martial arts and community finds some of its most vivid expression in the island's many cultural festivals, where tradition steps proudly into public view.

Across Okinawa, martial arts are not merely private disciplines, they are proudly and publicly performed, woven into the rhythm of daily life and celebration. Nowhere is this more evident than in the cultural festivals that punctuate the island's calendar. During these vibrant communal gatherings, Karate and Kobudo are as integral as the drums, dance, and food.

At the All-Okinawa Eisa Festival, the atmosphere comes alive with the thunder of taiko drums and the rhythmic movements of youth dancing in choreographed harmony. Amidst this celebration of ancestral spirits and youthful energy, local dojos often take the stage to perform traditional kata and weapons demonstrations. These acts connect the spiritual essence of Eisa with the focused discipline of martial arts heritage. Such performances are not merely ornamental; they serve as cultural affirmations that the spirit of Te continues to thrive within the younger generation.

Similarly, at the Naha Tug-of-War Festival, one of the largest and oldest celebrations in Okinawa, thousands gather for rituals and revelry centered around a massive symbolic rope pull. In addition to the tug-of-war and traditional parades, martial arts demonstrations take place in the streets and public squares. Children dressed in crisp gi and elders wielding polished sai or bo perform side by side, representing not only their dojos but also their neighborhoods, families, and the enduring pride of their island.

These public displays go beyond mere entertainment; they are deeply rooted rituals of cultural transmission and identity. To perform in a festival is to take one's place in a living lineage, to move with the memory of ancestors, and to declare, in motion and spirit, that Okinawa's martial flame has not dimmed, but dances vibrantly at the heart of its culture.

Stewardship and Strategy: Preserving a Living Legacy

Beyond the intimate sphere of family and community, the enduring presence of Okinawan martial arts is also shaped by a more institutional and strategic lens. In recent decades, the Okinawan Prefectural Government, recognizing the profound cultural and economic value of Karate and Kobudo, has actively engaged in safeguarding and promoting these traditions. This engagement, however, presents a delicate balancing act, navigating the opportunities and challenges that arise when a deeply rooted cultural practice meets the demands of modern tourism and economic development.

Government Initiatives and Infrastructure

The Okinawan Prefectural Government has undertaken significant initiatives to support and preserve its traditional martial arts, acknowledging their status as intangible cultural heritage. These efforts extend beyond mere recognition, encompassing tangible support through funding for cultural centers, dedicated research, and international exchange programs. A prime example of this commitment is the Okinawa Karate Kaikan, a magnificent facility opened in 2017. More than just a training hall, the Kaikan serves as a central hub for the global Karate community, featuring a traditional dojo, a museum dedicated to Karate's history, and facilities for international seminars and events. For local practitioners, it is a symbol of pride and a resource for advanced study and cultural connection. For foreign visitors, it represents a pilgrimage site, offering a direct link to the art's origins. The Kaikan, therefore, embodies the government's strategic vision: to provide a world-class facility that supports both local preservation and international outreach, acting as a beacon for the art's authenticity.

Growth and Growing Pains of Karate Tourism

The strategic promotion of "Karate Tourism" has become a significant initiative for the Okinawan government and local businesses, aiming to attract foreign practitioners and generate essential revenue for the island's economy. This initiative invites enthusiasts from around the world to train at the very source of these arts, stand on the hallowed ground where they were forged, learn directly from the living masters of Okinawan martial arts, and immerse themselves in the rich cultural tapestry from which these arts emerged. The economic benefits are evident: a noticeable increase in patronage at traditional dojos, a growth in shops specializing in martial arts gear, and a boost for local accommodations, restaurants, and transportation services.

However, as a practitioner observing this unfolding phenomenon, I am acutely aware of the inherent tension introduced by commercialization. Can authenticity truly thrive under such scrutiny?

The act of packaging and promoting something so deeply rooted for external consumption raises critical questions. Does the pursuit of economic viability, while necessary, risk subtly diluting the core principles of the art? It may nudge practitioners toward superficial displays rather than fostering profound internal cultivation. While the influx of foreign interest undeniably brings financial support and broadens global recognition, it also places a nuanced burden on traditional masters and their dojo: the weighty responsibility to maintain unwavering integrity amid growing commercial pressures. It is, indeed, a delicate balance between sharing a cherished heritage and safeguarding its essence.

On the other hand, this international exchange enables Okinawan masters to share their invaluable knowledge with a global audience, reaffirming the island's rightful position as the birthplace of Karate. These interactions foster not only cross-cultural understanding but also, crucially, ensure the continued vitality of these profound traditions by exposing them to new generations of dedicated students worldwide. While a detached observer might view external interest as a potential threat to the purity of the art, many Okinawan practitioners, grounded in their culture, embrace it as a testament to the art's universal appeal and a chance to ensure its accurate and unblemished transmission across the globe, reinforcing Okinawa's unique and enduring cultural contribution to humanity.

Business Engagement and Economic Integration

Beyond direct government initiatives, local businesses in Okinawa also play a crucial role in supporting the martial arts community. Numerous examples can be seen of local enterprises, ranging from small shops to larger corporations, sponsoring dojos, funding local martial arts events, or supporting individual martial artists. This collaboration reflects a deep cultural understanding that Karate and Kobudo are not merely hobbies but integral parts of Okinawan life, deserving of ongoing community investment.

Moreover, martial arts branding is often seamlessly integrated into local commerce and identity. You can find martial arts motifs on various local products, from traditional crafts featuring iconic Karate designs to modest eateries proudly showcasing photographs of esteemed masters. This widespread integration underscores how martial arts permeate daily life, commerce, and the collective identity of Okinawa.

Pride and Preservation: The Okinawan Spirit in Defense of the Do

Beyond the structured initiatives of government and the ebb and flow of economic engagement, there lies a more visceral, profound force that safeguards Okinawan Karate and Kobudo: the fierce pride of its people. This is not a pride born of arrogance, but one deeply rooted in identity, resilience, and a collective guardianship of a heritage forged in the crucible of history. It is a quiet defiance, a steadfast commitment to preserving the sacred flame of their island's unique martial spirit. This section, for me, is the very spine of this paper, the emotional and philosophical apex where the living tradition truly resonates.

Karate as a Cultural Identity

For many Okinawans, their martial arts are inextricably linked to their very identity, serving as a powerful distinction from mainland Japan. In a history marked by subjugation and cultural pressures, Karate and Kobudo emerged as symbols of survival and cultural defiance. They represent a unique Ryukyuan spirit, a testament to the ability to endure, adapt, and ultimately, to thrive even under the shadow of foreign rule. The historical narrative of resilience under occupation is not merely a bygone chapter; it is a living memory, woven into the fabric of every kata, every technique. The arts are a constant reminder of their ancestors' ingenuity and quiet strength, a source of profound local pride that transcends mere physical prowess. To practice Karate in Okinawa is not just to learn self-defense; it is to connect with a lineage of defiance, a spirit of perseverance that defines the island's soul. As the late Grand Master Shoshin Nagamine, founder of Matsubayashi-ryu, once stated, "Karate is the spirit of Okinawa. It is the spirit of overcoming adversity." This sentiment captures the essence of Uchina-damashii—the Okinawan spirit—a quiet, indomitable will to persevere, deeply embodied in their martial heritage.

Guardians of Integrity

This deep connection to identity fuels a powerful, almost sacred, desire among Okinawan practitioners to maintain the "true" Karate and Kobudo. This commitment often manifests as a resistance to what is perceived as the "sportification" or superficial interpretations of the art, particularly those that have gained widespread popularity outside Okinawa. The "Okinawan Spirit" in martial arts is not a vague concept; it is a non-negotiable core, emphasizing internal strength, practical application, and ethical conduct over competitive accolades or flashy demonstrations. There is a quiet, yet firm, critique of external influences that are seen as diluting the art's essence, turning a profound do into a mere game. I think Gichin Funakoshi put it best when he said, "They want the movements, but they do not want the heart. The heart is here, in Okinawa."

The preservation of Okinawan martial arts is not left to chance; it is a shared duty, a collective responsibility felt deeply by senior instructors and much of the broader community. There is an unwavering commitment to pass on accurate traditions, ensuring that the nuances of each technique, the historical context of each kata, and the philosophical underpinnings of the art are transmitted without compromise. This emphasis on lineage and continuous learning from local masters is paramount. Students are encouraged not just to mimic movements but to understand the "why" behind them, to internalize the principles that make the art effective and meaningful. This sense of shared stewardship creates a powerful, living link to the ancestors who forged these forms. When a practitioner performs a kata, they are not just executing techniques; they are embodying history, channeling the spirit of those who came before them. It is a profound act of remembrance and continuation, carrying the weight of years of shared dedication and the silent promise of continued effort.

Physical Testaments to Heritage

The fierce pride of Okinawa finds tangible expression in the physical landscape of the island. Statues of revered masters, monuments commemorating historical events in Karate's development, and plaques detailing significant dojo serve as constant, visible reminders of their heritage. The Okinawa Karate Kaikan, mentioned earlier, is perhaps the most prominent example, its very architecture echoing the traditional Okinawan castle gates. Beyond grand monuments, the pride is also found in more personal symbols: a meticulously preserved lineage certificate passed down through generations, or a worn black belt, once tied by a revered, now-departed teacher, carrying the weight of years of shared dedication and the silent promise of continued effort. These physical manifestations are more than mere decorations; they are sacred spaces, points of pilgrimage, and powerful symbols that reinforce the martial arts as an integral, celebrated part of Okinawan life. They stand as silent sentinels, embodying the island's enduring spirit and its unwavering commitment to its unique martial legacy.

The Legacy That Lives

The journey through the living landscape of Okinawan Karate and Kobudo reveals an art form far richer and more profound than its global popularity often suggests. We have seen how intergenerational practice, nurtured within the intimate confines of dojos and families, forms the very pulse of these traditions, instilling values of discipline and respect that extend far beyond physical technique. We have examined the strategic efforts of the Okinawan government and local businesses to safeguard this heritage, navigating the delicate balance between cultural preservation and the opportunities presented by global tourism. And most powerfully, we have felt the fierce pride of the Okinawan people, a deep-seated commitment to their martial arts as an inseparable part of their identity, a quiet defiance forged in centuries of resilience.

This is the ongoing challenge and the enduring beauty of Okinawan martial arts: to balance the demands of modernity and global reach with an unwavering commitment to authenticity. The tension is real, the path often complex, but the resolve to maintain the "true" do remains steadfast. What ensures the continued vitality of Okinawan martial arts in their homeland, despite the pressures of commercialization and the allure of sport? Perhaps it is precisely this deep-seated pride, this continuous local engagement, and the profound understanding that the heart of Karate beats not in grand arenas, but in the quiet dedication of each practitioner. It echoes in the whisper of the waves on a predawn beach, a timeless rhythm flowing from the past into the future. It is a legacy not merely preserved, but perpetually lived, a line of footprints in the dojo dust, each one a testament to an enduring spirit.

Glossary

A

- **Aji** (按司) – Regional lords of the Ryukyu Kingdom, often of noble lineage, responsible for governing local domains.
- **Ananku** (安南空 / アーナンクー) – See Chapter on Ananku Kata. A modern kata attributed to Chōtoku Kyan.
- **Atemi-waza** (当身技) – Striking techniques aimed at vital points.

B

- **Bō** (棒) – Six-foot staff, the most fundamental kobudō weapon.
- **Bojutsu** (棒術) – The art of staff fighting (bō = staff, jutsu = technique).
- **Budo** (武道) – "Martial Way." Japanese term referring to martial disciplines as paths of physical and moral cultivation.
- **Bunbu Ryōdō** (文武両道) – "The dual path of literary and martial arts"; the ideal of balancing scholarship with martial prowess.
- **Bunkai** (分解) – Analysis and application of kata movements in practical combat scenarios.
- **Bushi** (武士) – Warrior; in Okinawan context often applied to gentry-class martial practitioners.
- **Butokukai** (武徳会) – Japanese "Martial Virtue Society" that influenced standardization of martial arts in the early 20th century.

C

- **Chinkuchi** (チンクチ) – Okinawan concept of integrated power, combining skeletal structure, breath, and intent.
- **Chikudun Pechin** (筑登之親雲上) – Mid-ranking pechin class within Ryukyuan society; many martial arts instructors came from this level.
- **Confucianism** (儒教, Jukyō) – Chinese philosophical system deeply embedded in Ryukyuan governance and education, emphasizing hierarchy, morality, and order.

D

- **Do** (道) – "Way" or "path"; in martial arts, denotes a lifelong journey of discipline, practice, and moral cultivation (e.g., Karate-dō).
- **Dojo** (道場) – Training hall; literally "place of the way."

E

- **Eku** (エーク / 櫂) – Oar used as a weapon, originating from fishing communities.
- **Enbusen** (演武線) – Performance line or floor pattern of a kata.

G

- **Gedanh-barai** (下段払い) – Downward sweeping block.
- **Gojūshiho** (五十四歩) – See Chapter on Gojūshiho Kata.
- **Gusuku** (城) – Okinawan castles/fortresses, often linked to martial defense.

I

- **Ibuki** (息吹 / 息吹き) – Explosive, audible breathing method used in kata like Sanchin; comparable to qigong breathing methods.
- **Index** – See Zanshin.

J

- **Jitte** (十手) – See Chapter on Jitte Kata. Also refers to a Japanese truncheon-like weapon.
- **Jodan-uke** (上段受け) – Upper-level block.

K

- **Kakidī** (掛け手) – Hooking hands; tactile sensitivity training foundational to Okinawan grappling (tuite).
- **Kakedameshi** (掛け試し) – "Testing hands"; free-style sparring derived from kakidī.
- **Kama** (鎌) – Sickle weapon adapted from agriculture, often used in pairs.
- **Kamae** (構え) – Guard or ready posture.
- **Kanegawa** (金川) – Family name linked to kobudō kata involving specialized weapons like nichōgama and tinbē.
- **Kanshiwa** (観士和) – Kata blending influences of Kanryō Higaonna and Shōshin Nagamine. See Chapter on Kanshiwa Kata.
- **Karate** (空手) – "Empty hand." Okinawan martial art, developed from indigenous Te and Chinese influences, standardized during the late 19th–20th centuries.
- **Kata** (型 / 形) – Prescribed form; training pattern encoding principles of combat.

- **Kiai** (気合) – Spirit shout coordinating breath and intent.

- **Kiba-dachi** (騎馬立ち) – Horse-riding stance.

- **Kihon** (基本) – Basic techniques or fundamentals.

- **Kobudō** (古武道) – "Old martial ways"; in Okinawa, refers specifically to classical weapon arts.

- **Kokutsu-dachi** (後屈立ち) – Back stance.

- **Koryū** (古流) – "Old schools." Japanese term for pre-Meiji martial traditions; some influenced Okinawan practice via Satsuma.

- **Kumite** (組手) – Sparring or partnered fighting drill.

- **Kusanku** (公相君) – See Chapter on Kusanku Kata. Kata named after a Chinese envoy to Ryukyu.

M

- **Meiji Restoration** (明治維新): Japanese political and cultural reforms beginning in 1868 that heavily impacted Okinawa's martial and social systems.

- **Muchimi** (ムチミ) – "Sticky/heavy" movement quality; connected, rooted body motion.

- **Musubi-dachi** (結び立ち) – Heels together stance.

- **Mushin** (無心) – "No-mind," a state of non-attachment in combat.

N

- **Naihanchi-dachi** (ナイハンチ立ち) – Side-facing stance used in Naihanchi kata.

- **Nichōgama** (二丁鎌) – Pair of sickles used in kobudō.

- **Nunchaku** (ヌンチャク) – Two sticks connected by rope or chain; debated origins include flail, bridle, or indigenous tool.

O

- **Omoro Sōshi** (おもろさうし) – Oldest anthology of Ryukyuan songs/poems (16th–17th c.), preserving cultural and spiritual traditions.

P

- **Pechin** (親雲上) – Warrior-bureaucrat class of the Ryukyu Kingdom. See also: Chikudun Pechin, Yukatchu.
- **Pinan** (平安) – See Chapter on Pinan Kata. "Peaceful/Safe," series created by Itosu Ankō.

R

- **Rochin** (露鎮) – Short spear used in conjunction with the tinbē shield.
- **Rohai** (鷺牌) – See Chapter on Rohai Kata. "Vision of a heron," kata referencing crane imagery.
- **Ryūkyū Shobun** (琉球処分): The 1879 "Disposition of Ryukyu" —Japan's formal annexation of the Ryukyu Kingdom, abolishing its monarchy

S

- **Sai** (釵) – Three-pronged iron truncheon; defensive weapon used to trap, block, and strike.
- **Sakugawa** (佐久川) – See Chapter on Sakugawa Kata. Influential 18th-century master credited with early staff kata.
- **Sakoku** (鎖国) – Japan's "closed country" isolationist policy (1603–1868), indirectly shaping Okinawa's position.
- **Sanchin** (三戦) – See Chapter on Sanchin Kata. "Three Battles," emphasizing breath, tension, and rooted stance.

- **Sanseru** (三十六) – See Chapter on Sanseru Kata. "Thirty-six," kata reflecting Chinese numerological influence.

- **Satunushi Pechin** (里之子親雲上): Higher rank within the Pechin class, often held by prominent martial figures.

- **Satsuma** (薩摩藩): The southern Japanese domain that invaded Ryukyu in 1609, placing it under dual subordination to both Japan and China.

- **Satsuma Invasion** (薩摩侵攻) – 1609 conquest of Ryukyu by the Shimazu clan of Satsuma; led to centuries of vassalage under Japan.

- **Seipai** (十八) – See Chapter on Seipai Kata. "Eighteen," kata with Buddhist/Daoist numerological resonance.

- **Seisan** (十三) – See Chapter on Seisan Kata. "Thirteen," one of the oldest Okinawan kata.

- **Shisa** (シーサー) – Guardian lion-dog statues from Okinawan culture, placed on rooftops or gates for protection.

- **Shisochin** (四向鎮) – See Chapter on Shisochin Kata. "Four Directions Battle," kata emphasizing angular defense.

- **Shizoku** (士族): Japanese term for samurai-descended class, applied in Okinawa after annexation by Japan in 1879.

- **Stances** (立ち, -dachi) – Foundational postures in karate; include zenkutsu-dachi (front stance), kokutsu-dachi (back stance), naihanchi-dachi (side stance), kiba-dachi (horse stance), musubi-dachi (heels together), sanchin-dachi (hourglass), tsuru-ashi-dachi (crane stance).

- **Suparinpei** (壱百零八 / 百零八手) – See Chapter on Suparinpei Kata. "108," longest kata; ties to Buddhist symbolism.

T

- **Te** (手) – "Hand"; indigenous martial art of Okinawa, predecessor of karate.

- **Tekko** (鉄甲) – Iron knuckles or stirrups repurposed as striking weapons.

- **Tinbē** (ティンベー) – Shield (often turtle shell or vine); paired with a rochin spear in kobudō.

- **Tokumine** (徳嶺) – Noble Pechin associated with bo-jutsu kata. See Chapter on Tokumine Kata.

- **Tonfa** (トンファー) – Side-handled baton adapted from mill handles.

- **Tributary Missions** (冊封使 / 冊封体制): Formal envoys exchanged between Ryukyu and China as part of the tributary system, which strongly shaped Ryukyuan culture and martial practice

- **Tsuken** (津堅) – Small Okinawan island known for its contributions to bo and eku traditions.

- **Tsuru-ashi-dachi** (鶴足立ち) – Crane stance; balancing on one leg.

- **Tuidi / Tuite** (取手) – "Seizing hand"; Okinawan grappling emphasizing joint locks and manipulations.

U

- **Uchinaaguchi** (沖縄口) – Okinawan language.

- **Ueekata** (親方) – Senior rank in Ryukyuan government hierarchy; advisors and high officials.

- **Uke-waza** (受け技) – Blocking techniques.

- **Ukemi** (受身) – Falling techniques.

210

- **Unsu** (雲手) – See Chapter on Unsu Kata. "Cloud Hands," kata with dynamic jumping and spinning.
- **US Occupation of Okinawa** (1945–1972): American military governance following WWII that influenced the modernization and global spread of karate.

W

- **Wakizashi** (脇差) – Short sword carried by samurai alongside the katana; symbol of status.
- **Wankan** (王冠) – See Chapter on Wankan Kata. Sometimes translated as "King's Crown."
- **Wansu** (汪楫) – See Chapter on Wansu Kata. Linked to Chinese envoy Wang Ji.

Y

- **Yokogeri** (横蹴り) – Side kick.
- **Yukatchu** (良人 / 士族) – Warrior-scholar class of the Ryukyu Kingdom, embodying the scholar-warrior ideal.

Z

- **Zanshin** (残心) – Lingering awareness; continuing mental focus after a technique.
- **Zenkutsu-dachi** (前屈立ち) – Forward stance, long and rooted.

Biographies

This collection of biographies serves as a brief companion to the studies included in this volume. Each profile provides essential details about the individuals mentioned throughout the chapters; scholars, warriors, officials, and teachers whose lives and legacies have significantly influenced Okinawa's martial traditions.

These entries are not exhaustive accounts and do not aim to capture the full depth of each person's contributions. Instead, they offer readers a concise reference point, helping to contextualize the names encountered in the text within the broader historical and cultural landscape of the Ryukyu Kingdom and beyond.

Many of these individuals exist as much in oral tradition and folklore as they do in historical records. Reliable sources are acknowledged where they exist, and where accounts differ, these brief notes highlight the uncertainties while still recognizing the importance of each individual's role in Okinawa's martial narrative.

Together, these sketches create a gallery of the people whose decisions, practices, and teachings continue to resonate through kata and kobudō today. They are presented not as final portraits but as introductions; starting points for further study and reflection as readers explore the roots of Okinawa's martial heritage.

Peichin Takahara

Life Dates: 1683–1760 (approx.)

Trained With: Unknown, Yara of Chatan (according to oral traditions).

Notable Students: Sakugawa Kangi (according to oral traditions).

Biography: Peichin Takahara, a member of the warrior-scholar class known as Yukatchu, was an early and influential figure in Okinawan martial culture. Remembered primarily through oral tradition as a Buddhist priest or scholar, he profoundly shaped the philosophical bedrock for generations of martial artists. Takahara is widely credited in Okinawan martial arts lore with advocating a strong moral and philosophical foundation for martial study, championing character development, strict etiquette, and a clear sense of purpose within training. While concrete historical documentation of his life and teachings is minimal, his legacy is profound due to his pivotal impact on Sakugawa Kanga, who would go on to shape early Te. Takahara's emphasis on the ethical dimension of martial practice, including the importance of a virtuous spirit and respectful conduct, is believed to have permeated the nascent Okinawan martial systems. He represents a period when martial training was intrinsically linked to personal cultivation and societal responsibility, a precursor to the bunbu ryodo ideal of the warrior-scholar. His teachings, even if transmitted through oral accounts, underscore the early Okinawan understanding of martial arts as a path to holistic human development. He is believed to have trained with an unknown indigenous Okinawan tradition, and his most notable student was Sakugawa Kanga.

Chatan Yara

Life Dates: Late 1668–1756 (approx.)

Trained With: Reputedly, Chinese masters during his travels, such as Kusanku (according to oral traditions).

Notable Students: Unknown, Takahara Peichin (according to oral traditions)

Biography: Hailing from Chatan village in central Okinawa, Chatan Yara was likely of the Yukatchu class, indicating a learned background. He is a legendary figure in Okinawan martial arts, widely believed to have traveled to China and returned with a formidable array of advanced martial knowledge, playing a crucial role in the island's unique martial synthesis. His name is prominently associated with the preservation and transmission of significant kata, including the intricate Chatan Yara no Sai (a weapon form) and a version of Kushanku (an empty-hand form). Accounts describe him as a martial artist possessing a highly practical and combative approach, emphasizing realistic application over mere display. His expertise in both unarmed combat and kobudo (weapon arts) left a lasting and profound imprint on the burgeoning Okinawan martial traditions. Yara's legacy is particularly important in demonstrating the consistent flow of martial ideas from China to Okinawa, and how these foreign influences were adapted and integrated into the island's unique fighting systems, contributing to the rich diversity that defines Okinawan martial arts. He is reputed to have been trained by Chinese masters during his travels, and his influence is evident in the transmitted kata, as his students are largely unknown.

Wang Ji (Wanshū)

Life Dates: 1621–1689 (approx.)

Trained with: Unknown Chinese masters.

Notable Students: Early Okinawan Te practitioners, such as Matsuhiga (according to oral traditions)

Biography: Wang Ji, a Chinese envoy to the Ryukyu Kingdom, is believed to have been a scholar and a highly skilled martial artist from Fujian province, a region with deep cultural and historical ties to Okinawa. His presence in the Ryukyu Kingdom marked a significant milestone in both martial and cultural exchange. Wang Ji is renowned in Okinawan martial arts tradition as a Chinese master who led a diplomatic mission to Okinawa in 1683. During his stay, he is said to have shared elements of his unique martial arts knowledge with local practitioners. His most enduring legacy is his traditional credit for influencing Okinawan martial arts through the Wanshū kata (which later evolved into Empi in some Japanese styles). This form is notably characterized by its dynamic entries, use of evasive body movements, and effective throwing or off-balancing techniques, differentiating it from other forms prevalent in Okinawa at the time. Wang Ji's presence symbolizes a crucial period of direct martial and cultural exchange between the Fujian region of China and the Ryukyu Kingdom, where practical combat knowledge was shared and adapted, deeply enriching the burgeoning Okinawan Te. Though historical details of his life are scarce, his folkloric importance in shaping specific kata and techniques is undeniable. He trained with unknown Chinese masters, and his notable students were reputedly early Okinawan Te practitioners such as Matsuhiga.

Matsu Higa (Matsuhiga)

Life Dates: 1647-1721 (approx.)

Trained with: Indigenous Okinawan and early Chinese influences, such as Zhang Xue Li and Wang Ji.

Notable Students: Unknown; his influence is primarily seen through the kata attributed to him.

Biography: Matsu Higa was an 18th-century Okinawan martial artist, likely of Yukatchu status, implying a background in scholarship and official service. Traditionally associated with the coastal regions of Okinawa, he may have fostered a connection to practical, versatile fighting methods. Matsu Higa is remembered in Okinawan folklore and oral tradition as an influential and highly skilled martial artist, particularly renowned for his expertise with kobudo weapons, such as the bo, sai, and tonfa. He is specifically associated with the transmission and development of weapon kata, most notably Matsuhiga no Kon, which demonstrates a unique approach to staff techniques. While confirmed historical documentation about his life and specific teachings is limited, his prominent legend reflects the early, vital efforts to codify and systematize the use of weapons within Okinawan Kobudo. His stories highlight the practical application of everyday tools as formidable instruments of defense, a core theme in the analysis of the origins of Kobudo. Matsu Higa embodies the historical period when Okinawan weapon arts were evolving from necessity into formalized, yet still pragmatic, combative systems.

Tsuken Shitahaku

Life Dates: 18th century

Trained With: Unknown.

Notable Students: Unknown; his influence is primarily seen through the *kata* attributed to him.

Biography: Tsuken Shitahaku was an Okinawan martial artist, originating from Tsuken-jima, a small island east of Okinawa's main island. Oyakata Shitahaku, the Tsuken Island magistrate, and later (c. 1682 CE) the administrator of the Chinese embassy in Naha. Tsuken Shitahaku is a significant figure in Okinawan Kobudo, widely credited with developing Tsuken no Kon, a distinct bo kata (staff form) that reflects the unique fighting techniques and adaptations of Tsuken Island. His legacy is crucial for understanding the regional diversification of weapons practice within Okinawa, illustrating how isolated communities developed their own specialized methods based on local needs and available resources. The techniques embedded in Tsuken no Kon are often characterized by powerful strikes and practical applications, indicative of a system rooted in both the necessity of self-defense in daily life and the unique traditions that flourished away from the major urban centers of Shuri or Naha. Tsuken Shitahaku's story highlights the decentralized and organic development of Okinawan martial arts, where innovation frequently emerged from specific geographical and societal contexts, resulting in a rich tapestry of localized combative knowledge. He trained with unknown practitioners, likely through local practice and necessity. His influence is primarily seen through the kata attributed to him, as his students are largely unknown.

Soeishi Ryutoku

Life Dates: 1772-1825

Trained with: Unknown, likely within aristocratic circles.

Notable Students: Soeishi Ryoshu (son),

Biography: Soeishi Ryotoku was a high-ranking Yukatchu in the Ryukyu Kingdom, holding the distinguished title of Oyakata and serving as the king's secretary in Shuri's castle district. His prominent social standing meant he was steeped in both intellectual pursuits and the martial traditions cultivated by the Ryukyuan elite. Soeishi Ryotoku is primarily remembered for his significant, albeit obscure, contribution to Okinawan Kobudo, particularly through his mastery and development of bojutsu. He is widely credited with devising powerful methods of using the wooden staff, which came to bear his name in the kata known as Soeishi no Kon. This complex form is preserved in only select Kobudo systems, underscoring its rarity and the specialized nature of its transmission within closely guarded lineages. The sophistication, depth, and efficient applications embedded within Soeishi no Kon strongly suggest profound martial insight and elite-level practice.

Furthermore, it is believed that the kata "Choun" and "Shushi" also originated from his fundamental techniques. His legacy highlights the existence of highly refined, often privately transmitted, weapon techniques within the upper echelons of Ryukyuan society, distinct from the more widely disseminated methods. While his direct teachers are unknown, likely being part of aristocratic circles, his first son, Ryoshu (1787-1867), played a crucial role in further developing and passing down this unique cudgel tradition, thereby ensuring the survival of this important, yet elusive, lineage.

Kusanku (Kushanku)

Life Dates: 1670-1762 (approx.)

Trained with: Unknown Chinese masters in Fujian.

Notable Students: Sakugawa Kanga, among other early Okinawan Te practitioners.

Biography: Kushanku was a prominent Chinese diplomat or military attaché from Fujian province, believed to have resided in Okinawa during the 18th century. He represented a direct and significant link for the transmission of Chinese martial arts to the island. Kushanku is a seminal and revered figure in Okinawan martial arts history, widely reputed to have taught sophisticated Chinese chuan fa (fist law) to Okinawan students, most notably Sakugawa Kanga. His teachings profoundly influenced the development of early Te, providing a critical infusion of advanced Chinese fighting principles and techniques. The lasting impact of his instruction is most visibly seen in the Kushanku kata. This complex and highly dynamic form remains a foundational and essential element across numerous traditional Karate systems (including its variants like Kanku Dai in Shotokan). Kushanku's visit symbolizes the crucial role of cultural and martial exchange between China and Ryukyu, demonstrating how external expertise was absorbed and adapted into the unique Okinawan context. His legacy highlights the ongoing synthesis that defined Okinawan martial arts long before their modern systematization and global spread. He trained with unknown Chinese masters in Fujian, and his notable students included Sakugawa Kanga, among other early Okinawan Te practitioners.

Sakugawa Kangi

Life Dates: Circa 18th Century, specific dates unknown

Trained with: Indigenous Okinawans, such as Yara of Chatan and Takahara Peichin, and early Chinese influences, such as Kusanku.

Notable Students: Sakugawa Kanga and Makabe Choken.

Biography: Sakugawa Kangi is recognized as the father and initial teacher of the prominent Sakugawa Kanga, a key figure in Okinawan Te. Although historical documentation about Kangi's life and accomplishments is limited, his importance lies in being the originator of the Sakugawa martial lineage, passing down early martial knowledge to his son.

Kangi is believed to have laid the foundation for the formalized martial arts that Kanga would later develop. Oral traditions suggest that the teachings of the Sakugawa family emerged during a time when martial arts were closely linked to family practices. Kangi likely trained with indigenous Okinawan practitioners and may have been influenced by figures like Peichin Takahara and Chinese masters such as Kusanku.

His direct training of Kanga provided the essential groundwork for Kanga to integrate various influences and become a master in his own right. Thus, Kangi stands as a crucial link in the continuity of Okinawan martial traditions and serves as the elusive patriarch of a distinguished martial family.

Sakugawa Kanga (Tode Sakugawa)

Life Dates: 1733–1815

Trained With: Peichin Takahara, Kushanku.

Notable Students: Matsumura Sokon.

Biography: Born in Shuri's Akata village, Sakugawa Kanga was of Yukatchu (scholar-official) status, indicating a background of both intellectual and potentially martial training. He is widely considered one of the earliest and most pivotal figures in the direct lineage of Okinawan Te. Often referred to as the "father of Okinawan Karate," Sakugawa Kanga played an instrumental role in bridging the early, less formalized Te with the more structured martial arts that would eventually evolve into modern Karate. He is said to have studied under both the Okinawan priest Peichin Takahara and the Chinese envoy Kushanku, effectively integrating Chinese chuan fa techniques with native Okinawan methods. Sakugawa is credited not only with refining existing Te techniques but also with developing more systematic training methods and perhaps early versions of kata such as Sakugawa no Kon. His tireless dedication to instruction ensured the transmission of this evolving art to the next generation, most notably to Matsumura Sokon, whose own contributions would further solidify the foundations of Shuri-te. Sakugawa's legacy is central to understanding Karate's evolution from a collection of individual fighting methods into a more coherent and transmissible system. His most notable student was Matsumura Sokon.

Annan (Chinto)

Life Dates: Unknown

Trained with: Unknown Chinese masters.

Notable Students: Matsumora Kosaku, Oyadomari Kokan, Gusukuma, Kanagusuku, Yamasato, and Nakasato, with some even suggesting Matsumura Sokon.

Biography: Annan is a semi-legendary figure in Okinawan martial arts, traditionally depicted as a Chinese sailor, pirate, or martial artist who was shipwrecked on Okinawa or sought refuge there. His background is shrouded in folklore rather than historical documentation. Though largely a figure of folklore rather than verifiable history, Annan is linked to the creation and unique characteristics of the Chinto kata (known as Gankaku in some Japanese styles). Legend describes him as a master of evasion and agility, who, when pursued by local authorities, used his exceptional fighting prowess to evade capture through dynamic movements, leaps, and precise strikes. His tale embodies the romanticized view of mysterious Chinese martial influence arriving on Okinawan shores, often through dramatic circumstances. The Chinto kata itself reflects this legend, being characterized by its complex footwork, rapid changes in direction, and high-level balance requirements. Annan's story, regardless of its factual basis, serves as a powerful narrative element in Okinawan martial arts history, underscoring the profound respect for Chinese martial knowledge and making a significant contribution to the rich tapestry of the art's origins and lore. He trained with unknown Chinese masters, and his notable students were reputedly among the early practitioners of Okinawan Te.

Matsumura Sokon (Bushi Matsumura)

Life Dates: 1809–1899

Trained with: Sakugawa Kanga, Chinese masters, including Iwah and possibly Annan.

Notable Students: Itosu Anko, Azato Anko, Kentsu Yabu, Chomo Hanashiro, Matsumura Nabe (grandson).

Biography: Born in Shuri, the royal capital of the Ryukyu Kingdom, Matsumura Sokon was a high-ranking Yukatchu (scholar-official). His distinguished background led him to serve as a royal bodyguard to several Ryukyuan kings and engage in diplomatic missions, exposing him to various martial traditions. Matsumura Sokon stands as a pivotal and legendary figure in the development of Shuri-te, a precursor to modern Karate. As a chief martial arts instructor for the Ryukyu Kingdom's royal family, his influence was immense. He notably studied under Sakugawa Kanga and is believed to have also trained in China. Matsumura refined existing kata and is credited with developing new forms such as Passai (Bassai), Chinto (Gankaku), and Seisan, which became cornerstones of many later styles. His emphasis on practical application, combined with his understanding of both Okinawan and Chinese martial principles, made him a formidable martial artist and teacher. Matsumura's legacy is central to the foundations of Shorin-ryu traditions. It represents a critical stage in Karate's evolution from a collection of individual fighting methods (Te) into more systematized forms, firmly establishing its place as one of the most important martial arts in Okinawan history. His notable students included Itosu Anko, Azato Anko, Kentsu Yabu, Chomo Hanashiro, and Matsumura Nabe (his grandson).

Matsumura Nabe

Life Dates: 1850-1933

Trained with: Matsumura Sokon (his grandfather).

Notable Students: Soken Hohan.

Biography: Matsumura Nabe was the grandson of the legendary Matsumura Sokon. Growing up within such a prominent martial arts lineage, he inherited the deep traditions and rigorous training methods of the Matsumura family, dedicating his life to preserving them. Matsumura Nabe played a crucial, albeit often understated, role in protecting the orthodox "Matsumura Seito" teachings; the pure and traditional martial arts knowledge passed down directly from his grandfather, Matsumura Sokon, who was his teacher. Unlike some contemporaries who began to adapt Karate for wider public dissemination, Nabe Sensei maintained a private and highly traditional approach to his training and teaching. His efforts were primarily focused on ensuring the continuation of pre-modern Shuri-te traditions in their purest form, free from the pressures of modernization or systematization. He meticulously transmitted these techniques, principles, and kata to a select few students, most notably Hohan Soken, who would later bring this valuable, classical lineage to greater public awareness. Matsumura Nabe's dedication ensured that a direct link to the martial arts of the Ryukyu Kingdom period survived into the 20th century, making him an indispensable figure for understanding the less-publicized aspects of Shuri-te's development. His most notable student was Soken Hohan.

Itosu Anko

Life Dates: 1831–1915

Trained With: Matsumura Sokon, Nagahama.

Notable Students: Gichin Funakoshi, Choki Motobu, Kenwa Mabuni, Kentsu Yabu, Chomo Hanashiro, Chibana Choshin.

Biography: Itosu Anko was a Yukatchu (scholar-official) from Shuri. Beyond his martial arts prowess, he served as a government official for the Ryukyu Kingdom and later as a schoolteacher, placing him in a unique position to influence public education. Itosu Anko, a direct student of Matsumura Sokon and Nagahama, is widely regarded as the "Grandfather of Modern Karate" due to his pivotal role in transforming the art from a secretive, private practice into a more accessible form suitable for public instruction. His most significant contribution was the systematization of Karate for inclusion in the Okinawan public school system in 1901. To achieve this, he modified and simplified traditional kata, creating the Pinan series (also known as Heian in Japanese), making them easier to learn for large groups. He also wrote the influential "Ten Precepts of Karate," advocating for its benefits beyond self-defense. Itosu's reforms, while simplifying some aspects, were crucial for the art's survival and widespread adoption, shaping modern Karate curricula and laying the groundwork for its eventual introduction to mainland Japan and global spread. His vision ensured Karate's longevity, albeit with a shift from its strictly combative roots. His notable students included Gichin Funakoshi, Choki Motobu, Kenwa Mabuni, Kentsu Yabu, Chomo Hanashiro, and Chibana Choshin.

Motobu Choyu

Life Dates: 1857–1928

Trained With: Motobu family tradition (Udun-di), Itosu Anko (briefly).

Notable Students: Seikichi Uehara.

Biography: Born into the prestigious Motobu Udun (royal family) noble house, Motobu Choyu was steeped in the martial and cultural traditions reserved for Okinawa's elite. Unlike his younger brother Choki, Choyu remained primarily in Okinawa, preserving the secretive family art. Motobu Choyu was a master of the ancestral martial arts of the Motobu royal family, a unique system often referred to as Motobu Udun Di or Goten-te. This art specialized in palace-based grappling, joint manipulation, control techniques, and close-quarters combat, distinct from the striking-focused Te common to other noble families. Having trained within the Motobu family tradition (Udun-di) and briefly under Itosu Anko, Choyu dedicated himself to preserving these highly specialized aspects of Okinawan grappling traditions, which were typically not shared outside aristocratic circles and emphasized practical self-defense within a strict etiquette. His teachings provided a rare glimpse into a sophisticated, lesser-known aspect of Okinawan martial arts, contrasting sharply with the more widely disseminated styles of the time. Motobu Choyu represents a crucial link to Okinawa's feudal past, embodying the secretive and pragmatic martial skills developed for the highest echelons of Ryukyuan society, ensuring the survival of a unique and ancient lineage. His most notable student was Seikichi Uehara.

Higaonna Kanryo

Life Dates: 1853–1915

Trained With: Seisho Aragaki (in Okinawa), Ryu Ryuko (in Fuzhou, China).

Notable Students: Chojun Miyagi, Kenwa Mabuni, Kanki Izumikawa, Tsuyoshi Chitose.

Biography: Higaonna Kanryo hailed from Naha, a bustling port city with strong commercial ties to China. He came from a merchant-class background, and his early exposure to Chinese culture likely fueled his desire to seek martial arts instruction directly from its source. Higaonna Kanryo was a seminal figure in the development of Naha-te, the precursor to Goju-ryu Karate. Driven by a passion for martial arts, he embarked on a perilous journey to Fuzhou, Fujian province, China, where he studied for years under the renowned master Ryu Ryuko, following initial instruction from Seisho Aragaki in Okinawa. Upon his return to Okinawa, Higaonna established a highly effective and distinctive system that profoundly influenced later styles. His Naha-te emphasized internal power development, sophisticated breathing techniques, and the rigorous practice of Sanchin kata. He blended the complex, external techniques he learned with a focus on internal strength and health. Higaonna's teachings directly led to the formation of Goju-ryu by his student Chojun Miyagi, cementing his legacy as a master who successfully transplanted and adapted advanced Chinese martial arts principles into the Okinawan context, deeply enriching its combative heritage. His notable students included Chojun Miyagi, Kenwa Mabuni, Kanki Izumikawa, and Tsuyoshi Chitose.

Chomo Hanashiro

Life Dates: 1869–1945

Trained With: Matsumura Sokon, Itosu Anko.

Notable Students: Choshin Chibana, Anbun Tokuda, Higa Yuchoku.

Biography: Chomo Hanashiro was a Yukatchu (scholar-official) from Shuri. His background, which combined intellectual pursuits with rigorous martial arts training, made him a bridge between the traditional Ryukyuan elite and the emerging modern era. He also served as a schoolteacher, placing him in a position to influence the next generation. Chomo Hanashiro was an influential Okinawan martial artist who uniquely bridged the classical and modern styles of Karate. As a direct student of both Matsumura Sokon and Itosu Anko, he possessed a comprehensive understanding of both the older, combative Te traditions and Itosu's systematized approach for public education. Hanashiro is historically significant for being credited with one of the first known public uses of the modern spelling "Karate" (空手, meaning "empty hand") in place of "Tode" (唐手, meaning "China hand") in 1905, signifying a shift in the art's identity towards a more indigenous and philosophical interpretation. He advocated for both reform and preservation, recognizing the need for adaptation while striving to maintain the core principles of the art. His insights into kata and practical application continue to be studied, marking him as a pivotal figure in Karate's conceptual evolution and its transition into the 20th century. His notable students included Choshin Chibana, Anbun Tokuda, and Higa Yuchoku.

Gichin Funakoshi

Life Dates: 1868–1957

Trained With: Itosu Anko, Azato Anko.

Notable Students: Masatoshi Nakayama, Hironori Otsuka, Shigeru Egami, Yoshitaka Funakoshi (son).

Biography: Gichin Funakoshi hailed from Shuri, the historical capital of the Ryukyu Kingdom, and came from a scholarly background. His intellectual inclinations would later prove instrumental in his efforts to popularize and legitimize Karate in a new cultural context. Gichin Funakoshi is widely recognized as the individual primarily responsible for introducing Okinawan Karate to mainland Japan and subsequently initiating its globalization. Trained under influential masters Itosu Anko and Azato Anko, Funakoshi synthesized their teachings, adapted forms, and developed the foundation of what would become Shotokan Karate. In 1922, he performed a landmark demonstration in Tokyo, captivating the Japanese public. He tirelessly promoted Karate throughout Japan, advocating for its benefits beyond self-defense, emphasizing character development and physical discipline. Funakoshi published numerous influential books, including "Karate-Do Kyohan: The Master Text," which became foundational for countless practitioners. His meticulous efforts to align Karate with Japanese budo ideals, including the adoption of kyu/dan ranking and uniform (gi), were crucial to its acceptance and rapid spread, forever transforming it from a regional Okinawan art into a global phenomenon. His notable students included Masatoshi Nakayama, Hironori Otsuka, Shigeru Egami, and Yoshitaka Funakoshi (his son).

Motobu Choki

Life Dates: 1870–1944

Trained With: Itosu Anko, Sokon Matsumura, Kosaku Matsumora.

Notable Students: Shoshin Nagamine, Tatsuo Shimabuku, Jigen (Hidenobu) Yagi, Sennen Tamagusuku.

Biography: Motobu Choki was the second son of the prestigious Motobu Udun (a noble family of royal descent), the same lineage as his elder brother, Choyu. Despite his aristocratic background, Choki was renowned for his rugged, street-tested approach to martial arts and his more informal training methods, which differed from those of some of his contemporaries. Motobu Choki was a formidable and controversial figure in Okinawan Karate, renowned for his emphasis on practical self-defense and live application over formalized training. Trained by masters such as Itosu Anko, Sokon Matsumura, and Kosaku Matsumora, Motobu vigorously opposed what he saw as the dilution of the art into mere sport or physical exercise. He spent considerable time testing his techniques in real-world situations, earning a formidable reputation. His analysis of kata bunkai (the application of forms) was profound and pragmatic, emphasizing efficiency and directness in combat. Motobu Choki's teachings, though sometimes unconventional, significantly influenced a generation of practitioners who sought the deeper, combative essence of Karate. His unwavering commitment to the realistic aspects of self-defense provided a critical counter-narrative to the prevailing trends of modernization, solidifying his legacy as a vital proponent of traditional Okinawan fighting principles. His notable students included Shoshin Nagamine, Tatsuo Shimabuku, Jigen (Hidenobu) Yagi, and Sennen Tamagusuku.

Uechi Kanbun

Life Dates: 1877–1948

Trained With: Shushiwa (Zhou Zihe) in Fujian, China.

Notable Students: Uechi Kanei (son), Ryuko Tomoyori, Seiyu Shinjo, Seiko Itokazu.

Biography: Uechi Kanbun was born into a farming family in Iejima, Okinawa. At the age of 20, he emigrated to Fuzhou, Fujian province, China, a pivotal decision driven by his intense desire to study authentic Chinese martial arts, particularly after avoiding military conscription in Japan. Uechi Kanbun is regarded as the founder of Uechi-ryu, a distinctive style of Okinawan Karate that retains many strong elements from southern China. In Fuzhou, he underwent rigorous training under the Chinese master Shushiwa (Zhou Zihe), dedicating 13 years to mastering his Pangainoon (a blend of half-hard and half-soft) chuan fa. Upon his return to Okinawa in 1910 and later in mainland Japan, Uechi began teaching, establishing a system characterized by circular blocks, powerful body conditioning, finger-tip strikes, and intense Sanchin training. His teachings prominently highlight the depth of Sino-Okinawan martial exchange, demonstrating how foreign systems could be adopted and preserved with remarkable fidelity within the Okinawan context. Uechi-ryu offers a powerful counterpoint to the predominantly Shuri-te derived styles, showcasing the rich diversity that flourished from Okinawa's historical connections with China and solidifying Kanbun's legacy as a preserver of unique combative traditions. His notable students included Uechi Kanei (his son), Ryuko Tomoyori, Seiyu Shinjo, and Seiko Itokazu.

Yabiku Moden

Life Dates: 1882–1941

Trained With: Itosu Anko (Karate), Chinen Sanda (Kobudo).

Notable Students: Shinken Taira.

Biography: Yabiku Moden was a dedicated Okinawan martial artist and researcher from Shuri, deeply concerned about the potential loss of traditional Kobudo knowledge during the early 20th century—a period of rapid modernization and cultural shifts. Yabiku Moden played a crucial pioneering role in the systematic collection and documentation of Kobudo (Okinawan weapon arts) kata. Recognizing that many traditional weapon forms were endangered due to declining practice and lack of formal instruction, Yabiku devoted himself to their preservation. He trained with Itosu Anko (Karate) and Chinen Sanda (Kobudo). He traveled extensively, seeking out remaining masters and diligently recording their techniques. In 1911, he established the Ryukyu Kobujutsu Kenkyukai (Ryukyu Kobujutsu Research Association) to promote and teach Kobudo. Yabiku collaborated closely with other prominent figures, most notably Taira Shinken, to ensure that endangered traditions such as the bo, sai, nunchaku, and tonfa were not lost to time. His tireless efforts laid the groundwork for the modern systematization and popularization of Kobudo, ensuring its continued practice and demonstrating its vital connection to Okinawa's combative heritage. His most notable student was Shinken Taira.

Matayoshi Shinko

Life Dates: 1888–1947

Trained With: Chotoku Kyan (Karate), Gushikawa (bo), Yamani (sai), Kingai (kama), Ryukyu Kobudo Masters.

Notable Students: Matayoshi Shinpo (son).

Biography: Born in Naha, Okinawa, Matayoshi Shinko was a prodigious martial artist who cultivated a truly unique and comprehensive Kobudo tradition, laying the foundational pillars for what would become known as Matayoshi Kobudo. His deep martial lineage began with a vast inheritance of weapon arts from his family, a heritage that instilled in him an early and profound understanding of Ryukyuan weaponry. To further refine and expand his skills, Shinko embarked on extensive travels, most notably to China, where he immersed himself in martial studies in both Shanghai and Fuzhou. These travels were pivotal, exposing him to diverse Chinese martial traditions and contributing significantly to the eclectic nature of his Kobudo. He trained with a variety of masters, including Chotoku Kyan for Karate, Gushikawa for bo, Yamani for sai, and Kingai for kama, alongside numerous other Ryukyu Kobudo masters. This broad training enabled him to master an extensive repertoire of weapon kata, including rare and sophisticated forms that utilized the timbe (shield and spear) and suruchin (rope with weights). Matayoshi Shinko's meticulous dedication to the preservation and development of these forms ensured that his knowledge laid the bedrock for one of the most respected and comprehensive Kobudo traditions in Okinawa. His work was not merely about technique but also about systematizing the vast array of Okinawan weaponry, ensuring its continued practice and future transmission.

Matayoshi Shinpo

Life Dates: 1921–1997

Trained With: Matayoshi Shinko (his father), Choshin Chibana (Karate).

Notable Students: Yoshiaki Gakiya, Takashi Kinjo, and his many international students.

Biography: As the son of revered Kobudo master, Matayoshi Shinko, Shinp was born into a distinguished martial arts lineage, inheriting an unparalleled wealth of knowledge in traditional Okinawan Kobudo and dedicated his entire life to its preservation and global promotion. Shinpo Sensei's primary instruction came from his father, Matayoshi Shinko, ensuring an authentic transmission of the intricate Matayoshi Kobudo style, though he broadened his understanding of martial arts by training in karate with Choshin Chibana.

Building upon his father's immense groundwork, Shinpo Sensei tirelessly continued the monumental task of systematizing the Matayoshi Kobudo curriculum. His efforts transformed a rich collection of family traditions into a more formalized and accessible system without sacrificing its depth or traditional integrity.

In 1972, demonstrating his commitment to the art, he founded the Zen Okinawa Kobudo Renmei (All Okinawa Kobudo Federation); an organization that has served as a crucial vehicle for preserving and propagating the classical teachings passed down through his lineage.

Matayoshi Shinpo's tireless seminars, demonstrations, and the establishment of international organizations were instrumental in bringing Matayoshi Kobudo to global audiences, making him a living bridge between Okinawa's rich martial past and its global future.

Soken Hohan

Life Dates: 1889–1982

Trained with: Matsumura Nabe (his grandfather).

Notable Students: Fusei Kise, Choyu Handa, Yuichi Kadekaru, Seizen Kinjo.

Biography: Born in Shuri, Soken Hohan was the grandson of Matsumura Nabe, placing him in a direct and highly traditional lineage stemming from the legendary Matsumura Sokon. He spent a significant portion of his life in Argentina before returning to Okinawa. Soken Hohan was a pivotal figure in reintroducing and popularizing the orthodox "Matsumura Seito" lineage of Shuri-te publicly after World War II. Having received the deeply traditional teachings directly from his grandfather, Matsumura Nabe, Soken dedicated his life to preserving what he considered the pure, pre-modern essence of Karate. After living in Argentina for many years, he returned to Okinawa and began performing demonstrations and teaching, bringing much-needed visibility to this classical branch of Shuri-te. Soken emphasized the practical and combative applications of kata, eschewing the sport-oriented trends of the time. His efforts ensured that the rigorous, unadulterated techniques and principles of Matsumura's direct line were passed on to a new generation of practitioners across Okinawa and abroad, establishing him as a crucial link to Karate's feudal past and a champion of its traditional spirit. His notable students included Fusei Kise, Choyu Handa, Yuichi Kadekaru, and Seizen Kinjo.

Shinken Taira

Life Dates: 1897–1970

Trained With: Gichin Funakoshi (Karate), Yabiku Moden (Kobudo).

Notable Students: Motokatsu Inoue, Ryusho Sakagami, Konishi Yasuhiro, and many others through his organization.

Biography: Shinken Taira hailed from Nakazato, Kumejima Island, Okinawa. He served as a veteran of the Japanese army, an experience that likely influenced his disciplined approach to martial arts. He later moved to mainland Japan, where he dedicated his life to the study and preservation of Kobudo. Shinken Taira stands as one of the most important figures in the modern history of Okinawan Kobudo (weapon arts). A dedicated student of Gichin Funakoshi (Karate) and Yabiku Moden (Kobudo), Taira tirelessly collected, researched, and systematized dozens of Kobudo kata from various Okinawan lineages and regions. He traveled extensively throughout Okinawa, interviewing elder masters and meticulously documenting their unique weapon forms. In 1955, he founded the Ryukyu Kobudo Hozon Shinkokai (Ryukyu Kobudo Preservation Society) in Tokyo, a pioneering initiative dedicated solely to the preservation and promotion of traditional Okinawan martial arts. Taira's meticulous documentation and formalization efforts were instrumental in organizing and ensuring the continued practice of many endangered Kobudo traditions, transforming them from fragmented local practices into a more cohesive and accessible system for future generations worldwide. His notable students included Motokatsu Inoue, Ryusho Sakagami, and Konishi Yasuhiro, among many others, through his organization.

Shushiwa (Zhou Zihe)

Life Dates: Late 1800s–early 1900s

Trained with: Unknown Chinese masters in Fujian.

Notable Students: Uechi Kanbun.

Biography: Shushiwa was a Chinese martial arts master from Fujian province, China, renowned for his expertise in Southern Chinese fighting systems, including Tiger and Crane forms. His presence in Fuzhou made him a key figure for Okinawans seeking authentic Chinese instruction. Shushiwa is a pivotal figure in the history of Okinawan Karate, most notably as the primary teacher of Uechi Kanbun, the founder of Uechi-ryu. Shushiwa taught a distinctive style of Southern Chinese martial arts, often referred to as Pangainoon (a blend of hard and soft), which emphasized rigorous body conditioning, circular movements, and specialized breathing techniques. His instruction provided Uechi Kanbun with a comprehensive understanding of Chinese chuan fa, a knowledge that Uechi Sensei faithfully brought back to Okinawa. Shushiwa's legacy extends beyond his direct instruction to Uechi, as he became a symbolic figure representing the legitimate and profound Chinese lineage that influenced certain Okinawan systems. His teachings highlight the enduring and tangible impact of direct cross-cultural martial arts exchange, demonstrating how specific Chinese methods were not just absorbed but meticulously preserved within the Okinawan martial arts tradition. He trained with unknown Chinese masters in Fujian, and his most notable student was Uechi Kanbun.

Kise Fusei

Life Dates: 1935–present

Trained With: Soken Hohan, Nobutake Shingake, Nakamura Shigeru, Zenryo Shimabukuro, Akamine Seiyu, Makabe Chosaburo, Arakaki Seiki.

Notable students include Kise Isao (son), as well as many international students and instructors within the OSMKKF.

Biography: Kise Fusei is a contemporary Okinawan martial artist, born in Kumejima, Okinawa. He dedicated his life to martial arts from a young age, embarking on a career that would see him become a prominent figure in the preservation and global dissemination of traditional Okinawan Karate and Kobudo. Kise Fusei is a highly respected modern master and a direct student of Soken Hohan, Higa Yuchoku, and Shinzato Shima, making him a crucial inheritor of the orthodox "Matsumura Seito" lineage. Kise Sensei received comprehensive training in both empty-hand Karate and Kobudo, dedicating his life to maintaining the combative integrity and traditional principles of the Matsumura line. In 1972, he founded the Okinawa Seito Karate and Kobudo Federation (OSMKKF), with the explicit mission of preserving and propagating the classical teachings passed down through his lineage. His efforts have been instrumental in bringing the unique characteristics of Matsumura Seito Karate and Kobudo to global audiences through seminars, demonstrations, and international organizations. Kise Fusei's unwavering commitment ensures the survival of this profound art into the 21st century, making him a living bridge between Okinawa's rich martial past and its global future. His notable students include Kise Isao (his son), along with many international students and instructors within the OSMKKF.

Kōsaku Matsumora (1829–1898)

Teachers: Karyu Uku, Kojo-ryu practitioners, and possibly Tomari-based instructors.

Notable Students: Chōtoku Kyan, Choki Motobu, and others.

Kōsaku Matsumora was a vital link in the evolution of Tomari-te, the martial tradition of the Tomari village in Okinawa. Revered as one of the most colorful and rebellious figures of 19th-century Ryukyuan martial arts, Matsumora's legacy combines technical mastery, community leadership, and patriotic spirit. He was known for his skill in both unarmed and armed combat, particularly bōjutsu and sai. A popular tale recounts his courageous act of disarming a Japanese samurai officer with a fan—a symbol of both technical ingenuity and resistance to foreign domination.

Matsumora's teachings emphasized evasion, speed, and the use of angles, setting Tomari-te apart from the Naha and Shuri-based systems. His students, such as Choki Motobu and Chotoku Kyan, would go on to become highly influential figures in the propagation of Karate. Though less is known about Matsumora's formal training compared to his peers, his role in preserving and transmitting the Tomari tradition is undisputed. His legacy reflects the fusion of personal defiance and communal responsibility—hallmarks of Ryukyuan martial ethos. Today, Matsumora is remembered as a folk hero and master whose contributions helped define the character of Okinawan martial arts.

Motobu Chōyū (1857–1927)

Teachers: Matsumura Sōkon, Anko Itosu, and Sakuma Pechin.

Notable Students: Primarily influenced his brother Motobu Chōki and family lineage.

Motobu Chōyū was the eldest son of the Motobu Udun, a noble branch of the Ryukyuan royal family, and a prominent figure in the transmission of Shuri-based Karate. Unlike his younger brother, Motobu Chōki—who gained fame for his street-fighting prowess—Chōyū was known for his scholarly and refined approach to martial arts. Having studied under Matsumura Sōkon, Sakiyama, and Anko Itosu, Chōyū developed a deep understanding of internal principles, grappling techniques (Tegumi/Tuite), and the preservation of traditional kata.

He is believed to have been a custodian of older, more formal teachings reserved for the nobility, including secret applications and inner training methods. While much of his legacy has been overshadowed by his more flamboyant brother, Motobu Chōyū played a critical role in quietly preserving the intellectual and internal aspects of Okinawan martial arts, particularly in his instruction of key figures like Uehara Seikichi of Motobu-ryū.

Today, he is honored as a martial artist who upheld the classical warrior-scholar ideal of the Ryukyu Kingdom. His disciplined and private nature, combined with a deep technical foundation, makes Chōyū a representative of a more hidden but equally essential lineage in Okinawan martial history.

Aragaki Seishō (1840–1920?)

Teachers: Chinese martial artists (possibly Wai Xinxian), Kojo-ryu influences.

Notable Students: Higaonna Kanryō, Kyan Chōtoku, Chōjun Miyagi (indirect influence).

Aragaki Seishō was a master of both Karate and Kobudō, and an important figure in bridging Okinawan martial traditions with Chinese martial influences. Fluent in Chinese and well-versed in the Chinese classics, Aragaki served as an interpreter and official during Ryukyuan diplomatic missions to Fujian. These journeys not only affirmed his scholarly credentials but also allowed him to absorb Chuan Fa techniques and internal training methods, which he later infused into his own teachings.

He was particularly known for his mastery of kata such as Unshu, Niseishi, and Sochin, many of which carry evident Chinese influence. Aragaki was also a noted weapons practitioner, skilled with the sai and bō. His student, Higaonna Kanryō, would become a pivotal figure in the formation of Naha-te and the foundation of modern Goju-ryū. Aragaki also taught Kyan Chōtoku, passing on his refined kata and deep understanding of body mechanics.

Aragaki's role as a cultural bridge between China and Okinawa cannot be overstated. His integration of Chinese forms and philosophy into the Okinawan context helped set the stage for future generations of Karateka. His name endures as a symbol of technical excellence and cosmopolitan martial learning within Ryukyuan history.

Kyan Chōtoku (1870–1945)

Teachers: Matsumora Kōsaku, Itosu Ankō, Yatsune Itarashiki, and Tokumine Pechin.

Notable Students: Shimabukuro Zenryō, Nakamura Shigeru, Chotoku Omine, and Tatsuo Shimabuku.

Kyan Chōtoku, often referred to as "Chan Miigwaa" (Kyan the Light), was a charismatic and influential master of the Shuri-Tomari-te tradition. Born into an aristocratic family, Kyan had access to some of the greatest teachers of his time, including Matsumora Kōsaku and Itosu Ankō. Small in stature but formidable in technique, Kyan developed a style that emphasized evasion, speed, and deceptive power—attributes that later influenced the creation of systems like Shōrin-ryū.

Known for his generosity and openness in teaching, Kyan helped shift martial training from the aristocratic elite to the general public. He preserved and transmitted classic kata such as Chintō, Wanshū, Passai, and Ananku, each bearing his unique interpretations. Kyan taught many future founders of prominent Karate styles, ensuring his influence across Okinawa and beyond.

Despite suffering hardships later in life—including injury and poverty—Kyan continued to teach and demonstrate an unwavering commitment to the art. He reportedly died during the Battle of Okinawa, refusing to abandon his students or homeland. Today, Kyan is remembered not only for his technical prowess and dynamic teaching style but also for embodying the resilient, unbreakable spirit of Okinawan martial culture.

Gōkenki (1886–1940)

Teachers: Chinese Fujian White Crane lineage (exact names uncertain).

Notable Students: Mabuni Kenwa, Miyagi Chōjun (collaborative influence).

Gokenki was a Chinese tea merchant from Fuzhou who settled in Okinawa in the early 20th century. More than just a trader, he was a skilled practitioner of Baihequan (White Crane Fist), a Chinese martial system that had a profound and lasting influence on Okinawan Karate. Though not a formal teacher in the Ryukyuan tradition, Gokenki was highly respected by local masters for his knowledge of Chinese fighting arts and internal methods.

He is most famously associated with his collaboration and friendship with Kenwa Mabuni and Chōjun Miyagi, both of whom incorporated elements of White Crane into their respective styles of Shitō-ryū and Gōjū-ryū. Through shared practice and technical exchanges, Gokenki helped introduce essential breathing methods, the tension-release dynamics of Sanchin kata, and the internal movement principles characteristic of Chinese martial systems.

His presence in Okinawa represents a key moment in the cultural and technical synthesis that defined modern Karate's evolution. While he left behind no formal Okinawan lineage, Gokenki's influence ripples through nearly every system of Naha-te lineage today. He remains a vital, if sometimes overlooked, figure in the story of Okinawan martial arts as a living crossroads between Chinese and Ryukyuan combat traditions.

Nabe Matsumura (c. 1860–1930s)

Teachers: Matsumura Sōkon (grandfather).

Notable Students: Hohan Sōken.

Nabe Matsumura, also known as Nabe Tanmei, was the nephew and direct student of the legendary Matsumura Sōkon, founder of Shuri-te and senior martial figure in the Ryukyu Kingdom. Though lesser known in popular accounts, Nabe Matsumura was a critical link in the preservation of the original Matsumura family kata, bunkai (applications), and Tuite-jutsu (grappling techniques). He is best remembered as the primary teacher of Hohan Sōken, to whom he transmitted the classical system now often referred to as "Matsumura Seito."

A traditionalist at heart, Nabe Tanmei upheld the austere and internalized aspects of Okinawan martial arts, focusing on combative realism, subtle control of body mechanics, and moral discipline. He is believed to have preserved older versions of kata such as Passai, Seisan, and Kusanku, unaltered by modern sport influences. He taught primarily within the family or to a trusted few, shunning public recognition and emphasizing personal transformation over rank or fame.

Today, he is revered by serious students of classical Okinawan Karate as a quiet guardian of the old ways; a man who carried the legacy of his uncle and the Ryukyuan warrior-scholar ethos into the turbulent modern era.

Seiki Arakaki (1924–2014)

Teachers: Chotoku Kyan and others within the Shuri-te lineage.

Notable Students: Yuichi Kuda, Chokei Kishaba.

Seiki Arakaki was a senior student of Hohan Sōken and a crucial figure in the postwar preservation and transmission of Matsumura Seito Karate. Known for his precision, humility, and depth of internal understanding, Arakaki Sensei was instrumental in maintaining the integrity of the system as it transitioned from the secluded instruction of Nabe Matsumura to a more publicly accessible form through Sōken.

Training under Sōken during the post-war years, Arakaki not only inherited advanced kata and Tuite principles but also absorbed the philosophical and ethical teachings central to the Matsumura tradition. Though not as widely known as some of his peers, Arakaki played an essential role in mentoring key figures like Kise Isao and Yuichi Kuda, both of whom would go on to become influential masters and spread the art internationally.

Arakaki's teaching emphasized quiet intensity, internal development, and the importance of bunkai (application) in every movement. He held a deep reverence for tradition, insisting on preserving the art's functional roots and avoiding unnecessary modernization. His legacy endures through his students, who credit him with embodying the quiet dignity and combative integrity of true Okinawan Bujutsu.

Yuichi Kuda (b. 1935–)

Teachers: Seiki Arakaki, Chokei Kishaba.

Notable Students: Multiple students across the Americas and Okinawa

Yuichi Kuda is a senior exponent of Matsumura Seito Shōrin-ryū, renowned for his deep technical knowledge, humility, and cross-cultural teaching. A direct student of both Seiki Arakaki and Hohan Sōken, Kuda Sensei was instrumental in transmitting the classical methods of the Matsumura lineage to new generations, particularly in North and South America. His dedication to both preserving and responsibly expanding the tradition has made him a central figure in the global Okinawan Karate community.

Kuda is especially known for his detailed understanding of kata application, Tuite-jutsu, and the internal mechanics of traditional Karate. He emphasized not only correct form but the intent behind each movement, balancing combative realism with cultural preservation. His ability to articulate subtle principles across linguistic and cultural lines earned him respect from students worldwide.

Having taught in numerous international seminars and supported the development of many dojos outside Okinawa, Kuda became a quiet but steady bridge between the old guard of Okinawan masters and the global community seeking authentic instruction. He is widely credited with ensuring that the deeper nuances of Matsumura Seito, particularly those passed through Arakaki and Sōken, remain alive, accessible, and deeply rooted.

Chokei Kishaba (1929–2000)

Teachers: Seiki Arakaki, Shoshin Nagamine.

Notable Students: Katsuhiko Shinzato, Yuichi Kuda.

Chokei Kishaba was a dedicated Okinawan Karateka and one of the most respected students of Hohan Sōken. Also trained by Shinyei Kyan, Kishaba became known for his extraordinary sensitivity to body mechanics and movement efficiency, traits that would define the unique character of the Kishaba Juku—a branch of Shōrin-ryū Karate that he helped establish and guide.

Kishaba's approach emphasized soft power, joint alignment, and subtle adjustments, often taught through unique training tools such as the makiwara, heavy bo, and mirror work. He was particularly known for unlocking the internal mechanisms of kata, demonstrating how even minor variations in timing or posture could dramatically alter the effect of a technique.

Although not widely known in the Western mainstream during his life, Kishaba Sensei's legacy continues through the Kishaba Juku, now led by his senior students, most notably Katsuhiko Shinzato. The system continues to attract serious martial artists interested in traditional Okinawan Karate as both a combative art and a lifelong discipline of internal refinement.

Chokei Kishaba remains a symbol of Okinawan martial depth—an innovator grounded in tradition who helped shape the conversation around "inner Karate" for generations to come.

Nishihira Kosei (1942–2007)

Teachers: Soken Hohan (private student for over 30 years).

Notable Students: Tamaki Tsuyoshi, Jorge Monteiro, Patrick McCarthy (collaborator) Nishihira Kosei was a senior student of Hohan Sōken and Seiki Arakaki, and one of the most influential yet enigmatic transmitters of Matsumura Seito Karate in the 20th century. Known for his unassuming demeanor and intense focus on combative function, Nishihira was chosen by Sōken to preserve and carry forward the old family methods with exacting detail.

He was particularly renowned for his expertise in Tuite-jutsu (joint manipulation and grappling), kyusho (vital point striking), and kata application. Nishihira shunned commercialism and trained in relative obscurity, maintaining a private dojo and teaching a close-knit group of serious students. His approach to Karate was uncompromisingly pragmatic, emphasizing efficiency, power generation, and devastating application, while preserving the ethics and cultural heart of the Ryukyuan warrior tradition.

After Sōken's passing, Nishihira became one of the few sources for the unaltered Matsumura family system. His transmission to students like Tamaki Tsuyoshi and Jorge Monteiro helped preserve the tradition in its classical form. Collaborations with researchers like Patrick McCarthy brought further recognition to his teachings posthumously.

To many, Nishihira remains a symbol of the true Okinawan warrior spirit—deeply skilled, quietly devoted, and unswayed by fame or recognition.

Roy Suenaka (1940–2023)

Teachers: Morihei Ueshiba (Aikido), Hohan Soken (Karate), Koichi Tohei.

Notable Students: Students of Wadokai Aikido and Suenaka-ha Shorin-ryu.

Roy Suenaka was a highly accomplished martial artist, blending deep training in both Okinawan Karate and Japanese Aikidō. Born in Hawaii, Suenaka began his martial journey early and, during his time in Japan with the U.S. Air Force, became a direct student of Aikidō founder Morihei Ueshiba. He was also deeply influenced by Koichi Tohei, Ueshiba's top disciple at the time. Parallel to his Aikidō training, Suenaka studied Okinawan martial arts under Seiyu Oyata and Hohan Sōken, gaining expertise in both empty-hand and weapons systems.

Suenaka founded Wadokai Aikidō, a system that integrated his Aikidō training with the pragmatic techniques of Okinawan Karate and Tuite-jutsu. He emphasized what he called "Complete Aikidō"—a blend of spiritual development and realistic self-defense. His understanding of internal power, balance disruption, and vital point control made his teachings uniquely broad and practical.

With an open mind and a deep reverence for his teachers, Suenaka became a bridge between cultures and systems. His books and seminars reached thousands, helping to contextualize both Aikidō and Okinawan Karate in a global, modern setting. He is remembered as a thoughtful and powerful teacher who honored tradition while fostering innovation and cross-disciplinary growth.

Kyoda Jūhatsu (1887–1968)

Teachers: Higaonna Kanryō.

Notable Students: Meitoku Yagi, Eiichi Miyazato (indirect influence).

Kyoda Jūhatsu was the founder of Tōon-ryū Karate and one of the most dedicated disciples of Higaonna Kanryō, the famed Naha-te master. Born into a prominent Okinawan family, Kyoda was introduced to the internal disciplines of Okinawan martial arts from a young age. He studied under Higaonna for 15 years and remained loyal to the tradition, choosing to preserve its original spirit after the master's death.

In 1958, Kyoda officially established Tōon-ryū (named in honor of "Tō-on," the Okinawan pronunciation of Higaonna), creating a system to preserve his teacher's original methods, particularly the breathing techniques, rooted stances, and dynamic tension that characterized early Naha-te. He emphasized a well-rounded development of body and character, integrating Sanchin kata with deep internal cultivation.

Unlike many of his contemporaries, Kyoda resisted modernization for its own sake, seeking instead to honor the original teachings without excessive alteration. His few but deeply trained students, such as Uehara Seikichi and Nakaima Kenko, became vital in passing along the art with integrity. Though less commercially visible than other founders, Kyoda remains a quiet giant in the history of Okinawan Karate—an exemplar of loyalty, discipline, and uncompromising preservation of lineage.

Gima Shinkin (1896–1989)

Teachers: Itosu Ankō, Gichin Funakoshi.

Notable Students: Japanese Shotokan and Shito-ryu circles.

Gima Shinkin, also known as Makoto Gima, was an influential figure who served as a vital link between Okinawan Karate and its Japanese evolution. Born in Shuri, Okinawa, he trained under Itosu Ankō and Yabu Kentsū before attending university in Tokyo, where he assisted Gichin Funakoshi in introducing Karate to mainland Japan in the early 1920s. He is perhaps best known for standing beside Funakoshi during the first public Karate demonstration in Japan at Keio University in 1922.

Though often overshadowed by Funakoshi's fame, Gima was a technical powerhouse in his own right, holding dan ranks in both Karate and Judo. He continued to practice and teach throughout his life, quietly influencing the early development of Shotokan and helping ensure Okinawan methods were not entirely lost in translation during Karate's Japanization.

Gima emphasized both kihon and kata, along with an understanding of the historical context behind movements. In later years, he spoke out about the importance of returning to Karate's Okinawan roots and preserving its philosophical and combative depth. His humility and technical fluency made him a respected figure across both Okinawan and Japanese Karate communities.

Kanken Tōyama (1888–1966)

Teachers: Itosu Ankō, Kanryō Higaonna, Chibana Chōshin.

Notable Students: Tetsuhiro Hokama and others in Shudokan.

Kanken Tōyama was a pioneering Okinawan Karate master and the founder of the Shūdōkan school in Japan. Born in Shuri, he studied under prominent figures like Itosu Ankō, Yabu Kentsū, and Higaonna Kanryō, bridging the traditions of both Shuri-te and Naha-te. Tōyama also briefly studied Pangai-noon (later Uechi-ryū) in southern China under Kanbun Uechi, enriching his understanding of Chinese internal principles.

After moving to Tokyo in 1930, he established the Shūdōkan dojo, which would become one of the earliest Japanese-based Karate schools. Tōyama held an academic background and emphasized the cultural, historical, and ethical dimensions of Karate alongside rigorous physical training. He taught many students who went on to become influential instructors in both Japan and abroad, helping shape post-war Japanese Karate's development.

Unlike some contemporaries, Tōyama rejected the notion of rigid style boundaries and advocated for a unified understanding of Karate rooted in Okinawan tradition. He worked tirelessly to preserve Okinawan kata and transmit them to future generations, even while operating in a rapidly modernizing Japanese martial arts environment. His writings, leadership, and cross-training philosophy have left a lasting mark on both the Okinawan and Japanese martial arts communities.

Tsuru Yonamine (19th c., active date unknown)

Teacher: Oral tradition suggests tutelage under a noted martial artist of her time (name unknown)

Notable Students: None formally documented

Tsuru Yonamine is a legendary figure in Okinawan martial folklore, remembered for her strength, skill, and defiance of gender norms during a time when female martial artists were virtually unrecognized. Her name surfaces primarily through the writings of Gichin Funakoshi and the oral traditions of Okinawa, where she is remembered as a fearsome practitioner of tegumi, the indigenous Okinawan grappling art.

Unlike many martial legends built around formal rank and lineage, Yonamine's story is one of raw physicality and instinctual talent. It is said that her power surpassed that of many men, earning her not just local fame but respect from martial figures of her era. Her acceptance as an understudy to a prominent martial artist (whose name remains lost to time) marked a major break from prevailing gender customs, particularly in a culture that formally excluded women from martial training.

Though her techniques and teachings were not codified or transmitted through a formal school, her story has endured as a symbol of the unacknowledged yet powerful role women have played in the survival and application of Okinawan martial principles. Tsuru Yonamine stands as a quiet rebel in history—an embodiment of hidden strength and historical possibility.

Nobuko Oshiro (1947– present)

Teachers: Masami Chinen, Chozo Nakama.

Notable Students: Multiple international students; operates her own dojo.

Nobuko Oshiro is a pioneering female martial artist whose life and work have carved out vital space for women in the traditionally male-dominated world of Okinawan Karate and Tuite-jutsu. Born in postwar Okinawa, Oshiro began training at a time when it was highly unusual for women to enter the dojo. Undeterred, she studied under legendary masters such as Hohan Sōken and Seiyu Oyata, both of whom recognized her talent and dedication despite prevailing cultural norms.

Throughout her training, Oshiro faced intense resistance—from peers, instructors, and society at large. Yet her perseverance, technical excellence, and inner strength allowed her not only to master the art but to redefine the possibilities for future generations. In 1994, she established her own dojo, becoming one of the first women in Okinawa to open and lead a martial arts school. Her teaching blends traditional Okinawan Karate with an emphasis on internal development and practical self-defense, particularly through the lens of Tuite.

Oshiro has become a beacon of empowerment for women in martial arts, mentoring countless students and championing inclusivity without compromising the rigor and depth of the art. She stands as a living testament to quiet defiance, cultural continuity, and evolving tradition.

Kikuyo Ishikawa (1984–present)

Teachers: Okinawan Karate and Mixed Martial Arts (names not widely published)

Notable Students: Still actively teaching; known more for public influence than lineage

Kikuyo Ishikawa is a prominent contemporary martial artist from Okinawa whose career has helped redefine the role of Okinawan women in the international martial arts community. With roots in traditional Okinawan Karate, Ishikawa transitioned into the global arena of Mixed Martial Arts (MMA), where she gained recognition for integrating classical Okinawan techniques with modern combat strategies.

Her rise in MMA represents more than individual achievement, it signals Okinawa's living martial legacy adapting to and thriving within modern contexts. Ishikawa's performances, often marked by sharp striking, strategic grappling, and mental resilience, reflect the enduring value of Okinawan training principles such as economy of motion, leverage, and internal discipline. Her career showcases how traditional martial foundations can be fluid and functional in full-contact competition.

As a female martial artist competing in high-stakes global venues, Ishikawa has become a symbol of strength, adaptability, and cultural pride. She inspires a new generation of martial artists—particularly women—both in Okinawa and internationally. While not formally tied to a single style or lineage, her impact lies in her ability to make Okinawan martial heritage visible and viable in contemporary combat sports, reminding the world that these island arts still evolve, adapt, and endure.

Chōmo Hanashiro (1869–1945)

Teachers: Matsumura Sōkon, Itosu Ankō.

Notable Students: Chibana Chōshin, Gima Shinkin.

Chōmo Hanashiro was a key figure in the modernization and formalization of Shuri-te and one of the most influential martial artists in Okinawan history. A direct student of both Matsumura Sōkon and Itosu Ankō, Hanashiro helped bridge the classical methods of old Ryukyu with the emerging needs of early 20th-century education and culture. He was a contemporary of Gichin Funakoshi and part of the intellectual movement to preserve and adapt Karate for future generations.

Perhaps most notably, Hanashiro was the first to write the term "Karate" (空手) using the characters meaning "empty hand" rather than the older "China hand" (唐手), in a 1905 publication. This symbolic change marked a philosophical and cultural shift in how Okinawan martial arts were viewed, aligning the art more with self-cultivation and less with Chinese origin, though the debt to Chinese systems remained.

Hanashiro worked within the public school system and advocated for Karate's inclusion in physical education curricula, emphasizing its value for moral development and physical fitness. His efforts laid essential groundwork for Karate's spread to mainland Japan and the world. A tireless teacher and reformer, Hanashiro remains a central figure in the transformation of Karate from secret art to national treasure.

Yoshimura Chōgi (1866–1945)

Teachers: Matsumura Sōkon, Itosu Anko

Notable Students: Possibly Hanashiro Chomo, Motobu Chōki.

Yoshimura Chōgi was a member of the Ryukyuan aristocracy and a martial artist who played a unique role in preserving and recording the culture of classical Okinawan martial arts during a period of significant political and cultural transition. Born into the Yoshimura Udun royal family, he had access to elite education and trained with the most respected martial figures of his time, including Matsumura Sōkon and Itosu Ankō.

Unlike many martial practitioners who focused primarily on transmission through teaching, Yoshimura contributed as a cultural historian, artist, and preserver of Ryukyuan traditions. His writings, drawings, and personal accounts provide valuable glimpses into the martial culture of the late Ryukyu Kingdom and early Meiji-era Okinawa. As a nobleman with deep roots in the Yukatchu class, he viewed martial arts as an extension of cultural refinement and personal development, echoing the Confucian values of his upbringing.

Though not remembered for founding a specific style or training a known lineage of students, his intellectual and historical contributions have earned him a place of reverence among martial historians. His life exemplifies how the cultural elite of Ryukyu helped document and dignify the martial traditions during their transition from private art to public discipline.

Yabu Kentsū (1866–1937)

Teachers: Matsumura Sōkon, Itosu Ankō.

Notable Students: Chibana Chōshin, Shōshin Nagamine.

Yabu Kentsū was one of the earliest Okinawan martial artists to actively promote Karate in both military and educational settings, earning him the nickname "Kenpō no Hi" ("Fire of the Martial Way"). A disciplined and charismatic figure, Yabu was both a student of Matsumura Sōkon and Itosu Ankō, and he served as a crucial bridge between the private training of the old Ryukyu and the emerging public-school-based Karate of the Meiji era.

Yabu's experience as a military officer in the Imperial Japanese Army gave him a commanding presence and a belief in the role of Karate as both physical discipline and character development. He was among the first to formally demonstrate Karate on mainland Japan (Kyoto, 1921), helping to legitimize and spread the art outside Okinawa. His role in the school system made him an early standardizer of Karate training for youth and an advocate for structured physical education.

Though not a system founder in the modern sense, Yabu's emphasis on etiquette, conditioning, and moral strength had lasting influence, particularly on students like Chōshin Chibana, founder of Shōrin-ryū. He remains a symbol of the martial scholar-soldier ideal and a central figure in Karate's modernization.

Hohan Sōken (1889–1982)

Teachers: Nabe Matsumura (uncle).

Notable Students: Nishihira Kosei, Roy Suenaka, Fusei Kise.

Hohan Sōken is one of the most influential figures in 20th-century Okinawan martial arts, credited with preserving and systematizing the Matsumura Seito Shōrin-ryū lineage. Born into a family with direct martial ties, Sōken studied under his uncle Nabe Matsumura, grandson of the legendary Matsumura Sōkon. This direct family lineage gave Sōken unparalleled access to the internal methods of Shuri-based Karate, including kata, tuite (grappling), and kyusho (vital point) techniques.

After spending time abroad in Argentina teaching and working, Sōken returned to Okinawa in the 1950s and began openly sharing his family's previously guarded methods. He was known for his deep understanding of kata bunkai (application), subtle body mechanics, and a powerful sense of martial realism. His teaching style combined the traditional warrior ethos with a pragmatic approach to self-defense.

Sōken's decision to begin teaching publicly marked a turning point for the Matsumura Seito tradition, which had long been kept private within aristocratic circles. Through students like Fusei Kise and Roy Suenaka, Sōken's methods spread internationally. He is revered not only for preserving classical technique but for revitalizing interest in the roots of Okinawan Karate, emphasizing its grappling, striking, and internal dimensions in equal measure.

Kise Isao (1957–2025)

Teachers: Hohan Sōken, Kise Fusei, Yoshio Kuba (Goju ryu)

Notable Students: Kise Chofu (son), global OSMKKF practitioners.

Kise Isao was the heir to the Okinawa Shōrin-ryū Matsumura Seitō Karate and Kobudō Federation (OSMKKF), continuing the legacy built by his father, Hanshi Kise Fusei. Born into a family of martial excellence, he began training from an early age under his father and was also influenced by Yushio Kuba, a respected practitioner of Okinawan Karate. His upbringing immersed him in the classical traditions of Matsumura Seito, as well as his family's own Kenshinkan system, including its striking methods, tuite-jutsu, and weaponry.

As a second-generation master, Kise Isao took on the responsibility of preserving the system's integrity while supporting its global growth. Though more reserved than his father, he played a pivotal role in grading, instructor oversight, and high-level training seminars for OSMKKF members worldwide. His leadership emphasized authenticity, discipline, and respect for the historical and spiritual foundations of Okinawan martial arts.

Isao Sensei passed away in February 2025, leaving behind a deeply respected legacy as both a practitioner and steward of one of Okinawa's oldest living Karate lineages. His dedication ensured the continued vitality of the Matsumura tradition, and he is remembered as a quiet but powerful force who upheld his family's martial heritage with humility, depth, and unwavering commitment.

References & Suggested Reading

Foundational Histories & General Studies

•Bishop, Mark. *Okinawan Karate: Teachers, Styles and Secret Techniques.* London: A & C Black, 1989; reprinted Boston: Tuttle Publishing, 1999.

•Bishop, Mark D. *Okinawan Weaponry: Hidden Methods, Ancient Myths of Kobudo & Te.* Lulu Press, 2017.

•Clarke, Christopher M. *Okinawan Karate: A History of Styles and Masters, Vol. 2: Fujian Antecedents, Naha-te, Goju-ryu, and Other Styles.* Independently published, 2012.

•Clarke, Christopher M. *Okinawan Kobudo: A History of Weaponry Styles and Masters.* Independently published, 2013.

•Cramer, Mark I. *The History of Karate and the Masters Who Made It: Development, Lineages, and Philosophies of Traditional Okinawan and Japanese Karate-do.* Independently published, 2018.

•Hokama, Tetsuhiro. *100 Masters of Okinawan Karate.* Okinawa Godo Shuppan, 1999 (later reprints include Naha: Okinawa Prefectural Government, 2002; Ozata Print, 2005).

•Hokama, Tetsuhiro. *Okinawa Karate-do: Its Roots, History, and Evolution.* Dragon Books, 2005.

•Hokama, Tetsuhiro. *Okinawa Karate-do History and Masters.* Independent, 2012.

•Kerr, George H. *Okinawa: The History of an Island People.* Rutland, VT: Charles E. Tuttle, 1958; reprint Tokyo: Tuttle Publishing, 2000.

•Nagamine, Shōshin. *The Essence of Okinawan Karate-Do.* Rutland, VT: Charles E. Tuttle, 1976.

•Nagamine, Shōshin. *Tales of Okinawa's Great Masters.* Boston: Tuttle Publishing, 2000.

•Quast, Andreas. *Karate 1.0: Parameters of an Ancient Martial Art.* Germany: KarateResearch, 2013.

•Quast, Andreas. *Matsumura Sōkon: The Seven Virtues of Martial Arts.* Amazon Digital Services, 2020.

•Quast, Thomas. *The History of Karate: From Okinawa to the World.* London: Routledge, 2021.

•Tokashiki, Iken. *History of Karate in Okinawa.* Okinawa, 1970 (reprinted).

Primary Sources & Early Masters

•Funakoshi, Gichin. *Karate-dō Kyōhan: The Master Text.* Tokyo: Kodansha International, 1973 (original Japanese edition 1935).

•Funakoshi, Gichin. *Karate-dō: My Way of Life.* Tokyo: Kodansha International, 1975.

•Funakoshi, Gichin. *Karate-dō Nyūmon: The Master Introductory Text.* Tokyo: Kodansha International, 1994.

•Higaonna, Morio. *The History of Karate: Okinawan Goju-ryu.* Tokyo: Dōshinsha, 1995.

•Itosu, Ankō. "Ten Precepts (Tōde Jukun)." 1908. Translated in various martial arts historical anthologies.

•Motobu, Chōki. *My Art of Karate.* Various translations.

•Motobu, Naoki. *Meoto-de (Husband and Wife Hand).* Various translations.

•Uehara, Seikichi. *The Essence of Okinawan Karate-Do.* Translated by Okinawa Prefectural Karate Museum. Naha, 1999.

•Yoshimura, Jinsai. "Jiden Budoki" (Autobiography of Martial Arts). *Monthly Okinawa,* Vol. 2, No. 8, September 1941.

Specialized Works on Kobudō

•Akamine, Eisuke. *Ryukyu Kobudo: The Classical Weapon Arts of Okinawa.* Okinawa: Ryukyu Kobudo Hozon Shinkokai, 2005.

•Inoue, Motokatsu. *Ryukyu Kobudo: Ancient Weaponry of Okinawa.* Tokyo: Japan Publications, 1972.

•Kim, Richard. *Kobudo: Okinawan Weapons of Matsu Higa.* Richard Kim, 1985.

•Kim, Richard. *Kobudo: Okinawan Weapons of Chatan Yara.* Richard Kim, 1986.

•Kim, Richard. *Kobudo Vol. 1–3: Okinawan Weapons of Matsu Higa, Hama Higa, and Chatan Yara.* Independently published, 2006.

•Taira, Shinken. *Ryukyu Kobudo Taikan* (1964) and *Ryukyu Kobudo Taikei* (Encyclopedia of Kobudo Kata). Self-published, later reprints in multiple editions.

Patrick McCarthy's Translations & Research

- McCarthy, Patrick. *Bubishi: The Classic Manual of Combat.* Boston: Tuttle Publishing, 1995; revised editions 2008.

- McCarthy, Patrick. *The Bible of Karate: Bubishi.* Tokyo: Tuttle Publishing, 1995 (variant title).

- McCarthy, Patrick. *Ancient Okinawan Martial Arts: Koryu Uchinadi,* Vols. 1 & 2. Boston: Tuttle Publishing, 1999.

- McCarthy, Patrick. *Classical Kata of Okinawan Karate.* Boston: Tuttle Publishing, 1999.

Comparative & Academic Studies

- Clarke, Christopher M. *Okinawan Karate: A History of Styles and Masters.* Independently published, 2012.

- Cook, Harry. *Shotokan Karate: A Precise History.* UK: Cook Communications, 2001.

- De Lange, William. *The Katana: The Samurai Sword.* Floating World Editions, 2011.

- Draeger, Donn F. *Classical Budo.* Tokyo: Weatherhill, 1973.

- Draeger, Donn F. *Classical Bujutsu and Classical Budo.* Tokyo: Weatherhill, 1973.

- Farrer, D. S., and John Whalen-Bridge, eds. *Martial Arts as Embodied Knowledge: Asian Traditions in a Transnational World.* Albany: State University of New York Press, 2011.

- Friday, Karl. *Samurai, Warfare and the State in Early Medieval Japan.* London: Routledge, 2004.

•Green, Thomas A., and Joseph R. Svinth, eds. *Martial Arts in the Modern World.* Westport: Praeger, 2003.

•Hassell, Randall. *Conversations with the Master: Masatoshi Nakayama.* Missouri: Focus Publications, 1982.

•Keegan, Simon. *Karate Jutsu: History and Evolution of the Okinawan Martial Art.* New Haven: New Haven Publishing, 2018.

•Nair, Sreedharan Chirakkal T. *Kalarippayattu: The Complete Guide to Kerala's Ancient Martial Art.* Westland Publications, 2023.

•Sakihara, Mitsugu. *A Brief History of Early Okinawa Based on the Omoro Sōshi.* Tokyo: Honpōsha, 1987.

•Skoss, Diane, ed. *Koryu Bujutsu: Classical Warrior Traditions of Japan.* Koryu Books, 1997.

•Smits, Gregory. *Visions of Ryukyu: Identity and Ideology in Early-Modern Thought and Politics.* Honolulu: University of Hawai'i Press, 1999.

•Pearson, Richard J. *Ancient Ryukyu: An Archaeological Study of Okinawa before the Contact.* Honolulu: University of Hawai'i Press, 2013.

•Zarrilli, Phillip B. *When the Body Becomes All Eyes: Paradigms, Discourses and Practices.* Oxford: Oxford University Press, 2000.

Articles, Essays, & Digital Sources

- Abernethy, Iain. "An Interesting Essay on the Japanization of Karate." IainAbernethy.com.
- Noble, Graham. "Karate's Grappling Roots: Tuite and Tegumi in Okinawan Martial Culture." *Martial Arts Studies Journal,* 2017.
- Oyata, Seiyu. *Life Protection: The Art of Tuite.* Oyata Enterprises (unpublished training materials, ca. 1980s–1990s).
- Swift, Joe. "Karate-dō and Its Grappling Roots." *FightingArts.com,* 2003.
- Wikipedia contributors. "Ankō Itosu." https://en.wikipedia.org/wiki/Ank%C5%B3_Itosu
- Wikipedia contributors. "Kentsū Yabu." https://en.wikipedia.org/wiki/Kents%C5%AB_Yabu
- Okinawa Kenpo Karate Association Archives: https://okinawa-kenpo.com
- Hakuakai Karate History Resources: https://hakuakaikarate.org/history

About the Author

Nathan Batson has dedicated nearly forty years to exploring and teaching the martial traditions of Okinawa. As both a lifelong practitioner and researcher, he combines hands-on training with historical study, making karate, kobudō, and tuite accessible to practitioners and curious readers alike.

He is the founder of the Tyler Karate Academy, where he has taught thousands of students and led seminars across the United States and abroad. His training includes senior ranks in karate, kobudō, and tuite, with additional study in Musō Jikiden Eishin-ryū iaidō, Filipino martial arts, judo, and jiu-jitsu.

Nathan is the author of the *Okinawa Kata Encyclopedia: Exploring Ryukyu's Hidden Secrets*, a comprehensive reference work documenting the history, lineage, and practice of Okinawan karate and kobudō kata. His forthcoming work, *Foundations of Okinawan Tuite: Building a Path to Mastery*, explores the often-overlooked principles of Okinawa's grappling arts. Inspired by his students and shaped by research trips to Okinawa, he writes to preserve and share the enduring spirit of Uchinā Damashī, the Okinawan spirit that defines both culture and martial soul.

www.ingramcontent.com/pod-product-compliance
Lightning Source LLC
Chambersburg PA
CBHW060127130626
46556CB00006B/2262